4

# THE MODELING OF MIND

CONTRIBUTORS

Anatol Rapoport    Norman Sutherland

Lejaren Hiller    Aron Gurwitsch

Leonard Isaacson    Michael Polanyi

Allen Newell    Donald MacKay

Gilbert Ryle    Hao Wang    Michael Scriven

Ludwig Wittgenstein    John Lucas

Kenneth Sayre    Frederick Crosson

# THE
# MODELING
# OF MIND

COMPUTERS AND INTELLIGENCE

EDITED BY

*Kenneth M. Sayre and Frederick J. Crosson*

UNIVERSITY OF NOTRE DAME PRESS

# Acknowledgments

"Technological Models of the Nervous System," by A. Rapoport, reprinted by permission of the author and of the editor of *Methodos.*

"Experimental Music," by L. Hiller and L. Isaacson, reprinted by permission of the author and publisher from *Experimental Music,* by L. Hiller and L. Isaacson; copyright 1959, McGraw-Hill Book Company, Inc.

"The Chess Machine," by A. Newell, appearing originally as "The Chess Machine: An Example of Dealing with a Complex Task by Adaption," reprinted by permission of the author and of the editor of the *Proceedings of the Western Joint Computer Conference.*

"Towards Mechanical Mathematics," by H. Wang, reprinted by permission of the author and of the manager of Corporate Technical Publications of International Business Machines Corporation.

"Remarks on Mechanical Mathematics," by L. Wittgenstein, reprinted with permission of the publishers from *Remarks on the Foundations of Mathematics* by Ludwig Wittgenstein; first published in the United States in 1956 by the MacMillan Company.

"Sensation and Observation," by G. Ryle, reprinted from *The Concept of Mind* by permission of the author and of Barnes and Noble, Inc.

"Human and Mechanical Recognition," by K. Sayre, reprinted by permission of the author and the editor of *Methodos.*

"Stimulus Analysing Mechanisms," by N. Sutherland, reprinted by permission of the author and of the director of the National Physical Laboratory, Teddington, England.

"On the Conceptual Consciousness," by Aron Gurwitsch, reprinted by permission of the author, of the editor of *Edmund Husserl 1859-1959* and of Martinus Nijhoff, The Hague, and of the editor of *Studies in Phenomenology and Psychology* and of Northwestern University Press.

"Experience and the Perception of Pattern," by M. Polanyi, appearing originally as "The Unaccountable Element in Science," reprinted by permission of the author and of the editor of *Philosophy*.

"Mindlike Behaviour in Artefacts," by D. MacKay, reprinted by permission of the author and of the editor of *The British Journal for the Philosophy of Science* and of Thomas Nelson and Sons, Ltd.

"The Mechanical Concept of Mind," by M. Scriven, reprinted by permission of the author and of the editor of *Mind*.

"Minds, Machines and Gödel," by J. Lucas, reprinted by permission of the author and of the editor of *Philosophy*.

This book is designed to open a channel of communication between two groups of persons concerned with the impact of computer technology upon our conception of the human mind. As such, it should prove useful to students in either group. The two fields to which we refer may be described as (a) the philosophy of mental acts, and (b) the computer-oriented technology of the simulation of mental behavior. For convenience of reference, we will dub these two fields simply (a) "philosophy" and (b) "technology." While we have attempted to keep the needs of the classroom in mind while preparing this book, we have been equally interested in serving the person who is also an active contributor in one of these areas, and who feels that his understanding of his own particular problems might be increased by learning something of similar problems which researchers in other areas have encountered.

High-speed calculating machinery first came into the news shortly after World War II. By the end of the decade which followed, computers had proved their ability to relieve scientists and engineers of countless hours of drudgery in routine calculations. Applications were found for high-speed computers as well in the operations of government, business, industry, administration, and the military, and a brand-new technology began to take shape, self-consciously and soberly, under the title "Operations Research." Our concern in this volume is not with Operations Research, for which a number of introductions already exist, but with another use of computers which is more provocative and considerably more speculative.

By the middle of the last decade, several research groups in the United States of America and in Europe had begun to experiment with computer systems which were intended to imitate behavior which a few years before generally would have been considered uniquely human. Computers were designed to play chess, compose music, write poetry, recognize letter-patterns in print and in script, and to do rather sophisticated problems in logic and mathematics. Success in these applications at first was quite modest. But as more and more time was spent in puzzling over the problems posed by these applications, and as more effective computers were brought into use, improved chess-playing, pattern-recognizing, and theorem-proving machines began to appear. Thousands of articles and reports were published about ways of doing these things just a little better, and hundreds of persons soon were occupied with reading and writing this literature and with performing expensive experiments on computers to add their own contribution to "the state of the art."

With the establishment of a distinct class of computer simulation experts, confidence in the machine's ability to take over many or most of man's mental functions hardened from merely a working hypothesis to an explicit article of faith. Appropriating the language of philosophical and experimental psychology, technologists began to speak of building machines which can recognize universals, of constructing machines which learn by organizing themselves in selective response to their environment, and of reproducing important functions of the human brain by networks composed of electronic rather than neurological elements. Reflecting this confidence on the layman's level, a rash of articles began to appear in the popular press which intimated that the day is not far off when almost anything we can do can be done better and faster by machines. It is not unusual today to encounter the presentment that humanity may soon have to face the choice between becoming mere servants within a society of mechanical brains, or of becoming extinct save perhaps for a few specimens of *homo sapiens* preserved in a museum to be studied by scholarly robots interested in natural history.

Apart from the question of the desirability of having such machines, it is not in fact established that these goals are capable of being realized. Centuries of philosophic debate on the problem of universals, on the operations of the intellect, and on the mind-body problem, testify forcefully that these problems are not so simple as to be solvable within a few years by investigators whose only advantage over their unsuccessful predecessors is to have available machines which operate more swiftly and efficiently than conventional engines of the past. Technologists cannot be justly censored for being ignorant of the problems encountered within traditional philosophical analyses of our mental behavior. But it is only professional prudence on the part of the technologist that he be concerned to find out what philosophers have said or might be able to say to clarify the task he has cut out for himself.

It is commonly conceded, indeed, that no pattern-recognition system yet devised performs nearly as well as its designers might desire, that existing chess-playing machines are not really very clever, and that mechanical compositions of music and poetry are far from being imaginative. What is not realized sufficiently often is that the reason for these relative failures may not be simply that the right combination of components and instruction has not been found, but rather that the very functions which the technologist is attempting to simulate are not themselves well understood. One principle of methodology, upon which philosophers and technologists should agree, is that a person does not have a very good chance of simulating behavior which he does not understand. And the fact of the matter is that no one, regardless of professional training, has an especially clear conception of what is involved in the function of pattern recognition, in artistic creation, or in the insightful decision-making exemplified in the behavior of even an amateur chess player. The attempt to understand behavior of this sort has been the occupation of philosophers for many centuries now, and contrary to the general opinion that there is no progress in philosophy, some of the more helpful analyses of behavior of this sort are found among recent philosophic publications. Since no one's conception of these functions is decisive, what insight the philosopher is able to offer to the simulation specialist, if it is offered humbly, might well be humbly received.

Our conception of the role to be played by philosophic analysis in this matter is that the criticism it offers ought to be primarily constructive. It does not help to inform a technologist that, according to one's own philosophic orientation, what he is trying to do with machines cannot be done. As competent philosophers know, there is no consensus on any of the several philosophic problems regarding the nature of mental events upon which they may presume for purposes of "instructing" a technologist, or anyone else. It *would* be helpful, on the other hand, if the philosopher were able to help the technologist conceptualize more clearly the structure of the behavior he is trying to simulate, to understand better the nature of the difficulties encountered in the process of doing this, and to formulate new approaches for overcoming such of those difficulties as arise from an inadequate conception of the function to be simulated. This, at least, is the role which we hope some of the present essays will play, and the hope which governed our selection of those essays which are primarily philosophic in orientation.

It must be admitted at once that philosophers suffer no less than technologists from the lack of effective channels of intercommunication. Philosophers number among laymen, by and large, in respect to this exciting new phase of technology, despite the fact that there is an increasing overlap between the fields of philosophy of mind and of computer simulation. Lines of communication already have been opened between technologists and social scientists involved in a study of mental behavior and brain functioning. But there has been very little interchange between technologists and philosophers actively concerned with the analysis of mental capacities. Perhaps the main reason for this is the relative inaccessibility of many of the better technical discussions of simulation problems, and the formidable task of distinguishing between what is worth reading in this area and what is not. Philosophers generally have no guide lines for seeking out, and often have inadequate preparation for understanding, technological literature relevant to their interests.

While there is no nostrum to make philosophers out of technologists, or to impart technical competence to philosophers, there is at least some hope for bridging the informational gap which exists between these two groups of researchers committed to furthering our understanding of the human mind. The present volume is intended to serve as a plank in this bridge. We believe that the philosophic essays included in this volume are relevant to the interests of the technologist and might well prove helpful as he seeks to understand the nature of his own problems. The technological essays, on the other hand, are among the best available, and are both pertinent to philosophic problems of mind and understandable by most persons with philosophic competence. The selected bibliography at the end of each section will assist the reader in searching out further publications of importance in the areas treated in that section. A more extensive, but non-selective, bibliography has been compiled by M. Minsky for the *Institute of Radio Engineers Transactions of Human Factors* (1961), pp. 39-55, and has been revised for reproduction in *Computers and Thought,* J. Feldman and E. Feigenbaum (eds.), forthcoming.

The first section of this volume contains an introductory essay by the editors and a general survey from a technological viewpoint of the recent history of attempts to devise mechanical models of the human mind. The second section includes what are perhaps the most comprehensive discussions available of the use of machines to compose music, play chess, and prove mathematical theorems, and is terminated by some critical remarks on mechanical mathematics by one of the most influential philosophers of our century. Under the third heading are two essays concerning observation and recognition, and a group of three essays on the organization of the perceptual field as it relates to recognition. In the final section, two philosophers and a technologist contribute appraisals of present achievements and future possibilities in the effort to learn about the human mind by constructing models which simulate its behavior.

All essays save the first have appeared previously either in scholarly or professional journals, or as parts of books. The date and place of previous publication of each is noted below. Essays 12, 13, and 14 have been slightly revised for the present reprinting.

Grateful acknowledgment is due the National Science Foundation, the support of which was instrumental in our being able to prepare this volume, and to Dr. Milton Fisk of Yale for his encouragement and critical advice.

2. A. Rapoport, "Technological Models of the Nervous System," *Methodos* (1955), pp. 131-46.

3. L. Hiller and L. Isaacson, *Experimental Music*. New York: McGraw-Hill, (1959), pp. 1-2, 16-35, 165-177.

4. A. Newell, "The Chess Machine" (originally "The Chess Machine: An Example of Dealing with a Complex Task by Adaption"), *Proceedings of the Western Joint Computer Conference* (1955), pp. 101-108.

5. H. Wang, "Towards Mechanical Mathematics," *IBM Journal of Research and Development* (1960), pp. 2-22 (reprinted with omissions). Also reprinted in *A Survey of Mathematical Logic* by the author, distributed through the North-Holland Publishing Company.

6. L. Wittgenstein, "Remarks on Mechanical Mathematics," selected from *Remarks on the Foundations of Mathematics,* trans. G.E.M. Anscombe. New York: MacMillan, 1956.

7. G. Ryle, "Sensation and Observation," from *The Concept of Mind*. New York: Barnes and Noble, 1949, pp. 222-34.

8. K. Sayre, "Human and Mechanical Recognition," *Methodos* (forthcoming).

9. N. Sutherland, "Stimulus Analysing Mechanisms," *Mechanisation of Thought Processes*. London: Her Majesty's Stationery Office, 1959, Vol. II, pp. 577-601.

10. A. Gurwitsch, "On the Conceptual Consciousness," trans. F. Crosson, from *Edmund Husserl 1859-1959*. La Haye: Martinus Nijhoff, 1959, pp. 275-82.

11. M. Polanyi, "Experience and the Perception of Pattern," (originally "The Unaccountable Element in Science"), *Philosophy* (1962), pp. 1-14.

12. D. MacKay, "Mindlike Behaviour in Artefacts," *The British Journal for the Philosophy of Science* (1951-52), pp. 105-21.

13. M. Scriven, "The Mechanical Concept of Mind," *Mind* (1953), pp. 230-40.

14. J. Lucas, "Minds, Machines and Gödel," *Philosophy* (1961), pp. 112-26.

*Contents*

*Part I*

*Introduction*

# CHAPTER 1

# Modeling: Simulation and Replication*

FREDERICK CROSSON AND
KENNETH SAYRE

## INTRODUCTION

It is commonplace to predict that attempts now underway to duplicate human behavior in machines are destined to bring about a revolution in our way of living. Discussions of the various forms this
process is likely to take are seldom without emotion. No segment of
our society, in fact, will be able to escape the effects of this change,
and many have begun to feel the effects already. On one hand is the
fear of laboring people that their jobs will continue to be usurped
by automation. With this is the concern of specialists in social relations that the problems of personal and group adjustment accompanying this social revolution will become increasingly difficult. These
are serious concerns, but not within the scope of this essay.

On the other hand is the apprehension typified by the feeling of
the person who fears that "thinking machines" soon will render man
obsolete in achievements which traditionally have been the glory of
the human intellect. If machines are constructed to compose beautiful music, win chess championships, and make a routine matter out
of proving difficult mathematical theorems, it might be asked, what
reason is left for attaching unique value to the abilities of the human
mind?

One factor which accounts in part for the feeling that computer
technology poses a threat to our intellectual and spiritual values is
that too few people have a fair conception of what is involved in the
mechanical "duplication" of a human ability. If technologists were
able to synthesize intelligent creatures of flesh and blood, by some
magic of the laboratory having nothing to do with the fertilization

---

*Mr. Crosson is primarily responsible for the final section and for the criticism
there expressed; Mr. Sayre is primarily responsible for the remainder of the essay.

by human sperm of a human egg, then indeed we would have cause to re-examine our conception of the uniqueness of the human intellect. Technologists, however, are not about to do this, and there seems to be no sober reason at the moment for thinking that they ever will. What technology does promise for the near future are machines which are considerably more efficient than present devices at performing tasks similar in many respects to those performed typically by the human intellect. "Mechanical composers" might perhaps be constructed which produce music of aesthetic worth. But it is not clear that this should pose for us a matter of apprehension. "Mechanical potters" and "mechanical cobblers" on the whole seem to have increased rather than decreased the value of the hand-made pot or shoe, and it seems reasonable to anticipate that the production of mechanical music will not have a radically different effect upon our appreciation of Bach and Beethoven. "Mechanical mathematicians" of considerable proficiency may indeed produce proofs which human mathematicians have overlooked, or could not find. But should this possibility call for a diminution in our esteem for living mathematicians? Why should the possibility of mechanical chess-players or mechanical decision-makers, even if these appeared imminent, influence our evaluation of the human being who is proficient in these matters?

These are not intended as rhetorical questions. But they are questions for the answering of which one must have a better conception of the sense in which a machine can model human behavior than can be obtained from the popular press, or even from most technical discussions. It would be one thing to have a machine capable of doing what people do in a different ("mechanical") way, but quite a different thing to have a machine which could do what people do in the same ("non-mechanical") way. The latter possibility, if it were realized, would add new and perhaps conclusive evidence to the old controversy around the question whether minds aren't after all just complex machines. The authors do not believe that any outcome of contemporary technology now foreseeable will have such a decisive effect upon this controversy. A more likely outcome of current research with "giant brains" is that machines will be developed which can do more and more òf the tasks we have up to now considered a human prerogative, but that the way in which these tasks are accomplished mechanically will differ radically from the way in which humans do them. Rather than pose a threat to the value status of the human intellect, the development of these machines should heighten our estimation of the human mind which is capable of constructing them. The actuality of these machines will indicate, not that the mind is radically different than we had always believed, but rather that we have come to understand the functions of the mind well enough to construct models of its behaviour.

The purpose of this essay is to distinguish various senses in which mechanical models of the mind might possibly be provided. This in itself will not answer the question whether machines "can do everything" that people can do, nor will it completely allay our apprehensions about the future of a society in which both human and mechanical "intelligences" operate. We hope, however, that some degree of clarity can be added to these issues by a calm examination of these distinctions and of some of the questions which appear in the making of them.

TYPES OF MODEL

It will be helpful to consider several ways in which an object might be modeled, under the general headings: (a) Replication, (b) Formalization, and (c) Simulation.

(a) The first heading is intended to be broad enough to accommodate reproductions, facsimiles, test models, duplications, and dummies. Included under this heading, therefore, would be statues, reproductions of statues, toy animals, and voodoo dolls. The purpose of such objects generally is one of play, enjoyment, or ceremony. Different from these in function, but replications nonetheless, are what have been called "mock-ups" or scale-models". The motor-coach designer's models are not toy cars, but research instruments, as are the airfoils of the aerodynamical engineer, and the various earth-bound panels and chambers used in designing space enclosures for astronauts. Yet another type of replica designed for research is the war exercise, used for experimenting in peace time with new battle tactics and weapons. The purpose of such research instruments is to aid in the study of behavior and design characteristics of objects or processes either which are not available for direct study, or the variables of which do not admit convenient control and measurement.

The common characteristic of these examples is that each reproduces at least some of the physical characteristics of the original object or process which is replicated. Both the model and the "real" airfoil are constructed out of materials which, if not identical, at least are semi-rigid and toolable. Both war games and actual combat involve the employment of soldiers and battle equipment, and the mock-up spaceship capsule is adequate for its purposes only insofar as its controls look, feel, and act like their counterparts in an actual space vehicle. A mere photograph of an airplane, however, is not a replication; whereas the airplane is an object in three dimensions constructed out of metal, the picture is two-dimensional and, in the relevant sense, not constructed out of anything. A plaster-of-Paris reproduction of Mestrovic's *Moses* would be considered a replication, while a drawing of the statue, whether by the artist or another, would be called a study or a sketch, but not a replication. A copy of one of the artist's studies in a similar medium, however, would probably count as a replication.

Although there are limitations of this sort upon the degree of dissimilarity between a replication and its original, there seems to be no limitation of the degree of similarity. If there were a reproduction of the *Mona Lisa* which is like the original in every respect, save in having been painted with another's brush and paints, it would be a replication nonetheless. (A second painting on a theme by the same artist would seem not to be a copy, but rather a work as original in its own right as the first. When one views the two paintings of St. Martin and the Beggar by El Greco, it does not seem natural to question which came first.) Every flag today with thirteen stars and thirteen stripes, for another example, is likely to be counted as a reproduction of the first flag of that description.

This description, while neither exhaustive nor rigorous, is adequate for the comparison of replications with formal models, a typical feature of which is that none of the physical characteristics of the original are present in the model.

(b) In a formal model, both the components of the system modeled and the interconnections among these components are represented by symbols which can be manipulated according to the provisions of a well-defined formal discipline, typically a branch of logic or mathematics. We will consider only those models which represent systems of operations or modes of behavior, in distinction from "merely static" characteristics of objects.

For example, the behavior of a system of interconnected switches, each capable of exactly two positions, can be studied by a model provided by a two-valued logic which permits operations of conjunction and negation. The switches may be represented within the model by logical variables, and the interaction between any two switches or sets of switches can be represented by an appropriate grouping of logical operators. Since logical operators and variables can be "controlled" more readily than interactions among systems of actual switching devices, it is advantageous for some purposes to study these interactions within the formal structure provided by the logical model. A typical use of a formal model, indeed, is to study interactions among components or behavioral aspects of systems which themselves cannot be conveniently controlled within the sanctions of natural or civil law.

There are at least two respects, however, in which a logical model of a switching circuit is not typical of formal models generally. First, each working component of the system can be identified and represented individually by a distinct variable within the model. Second, to every change in the circuit from one distinct set of switch positions to another there corresponds within the model a change from one distinct set of values of logical variables to another. In this rather intuitive sense, the behavior of the model seems to be structurally isomorphic to the behavior of the circuit itself. An example of a formal model which has neither of these characteristics is provided by an equation known, within a discipline currently called "Operations Research", as "Lanchester's N-square Law". This equation illustrates both the strength and the weakness of the formal model.

According to Lanchester's N-square Law, the "fighting strength" of a combat force "may be broadly defined as proportional to the square of its numerical strength multiplied by the fighting value of its individual units."[1] If the individual units of two armies are of equal effectiveness, their relative strength is measured by the proportion of the squares of the numbers of fighting units in actual combat. Thus, for example, by sundering the enemy's forces and concentrating total fire power upon first one and then the other segment, an army can meet with equal fighting strength an enemy greater in numbers by as much as the square root of two.[2]

This law applies in the ideal to a situation in which each combat unit is able to engage each unit of the opposing force, an ideal more closely approached in combat with long-range weapons than in hand-to-hand combat. The major shortcoming of this law, as a means for studying the dynamics of actual military combat, is the fact that application of the law to particular circumstances must involve the assumption that all factors other than manpower which influence the tides of battle are constant. As Lanchester himself remarked, "superior morale or better tactics or a hundred and one other extraneous causes may intervene in practice to modify the issue," although this is claimed not to "invalidate the mathematical statement"

[1] *Aircraft in Warfare,* quoted in *The World of Mathematics,* ed. James R. Newman, p. 2145.
[2] Consider that force $A$ and force $B$ number respectively $n$ and $n\sqrt{2}$ units. If $A$ encounters separately one half and then the other half of $B$'s forces, the total fighting strengths of $A$ and $B$ are equal, since

$$n^2 = \left( \frac{n\sqrt{2}}{2} \right)^2 + \left( \frac{n\sqrt{2}}{2} \right)^2$$

of the law.[3] Because of its very simplicity, Lanchester's model of combat by itself is of little use as a research tool for studying the dynamics of actual combat.

The strength of a model of the type illustrated by this example, on the other hand, lies in the fact that it can be solved by known formal techniques. The behavior of the variables within the model can be studied under a variety of conditions by strictly formal manipulations, without regard for problems of feasibility involved in bringing the actual system represented by the model into corresponding physical circumstances.

Indeed, the techniques of replication and of formalization complement each other in regard to their relative strengths and weaknesses. Compare a full-scale military war game, for example, with Lanchester's equation as research implements for studying interactions among armed forces in combat. While the N-square Law, or any other formal model comparable to it in generality, involves necessarily some simplification regarding a number of factors pertinent to the study, it seems that the only limitations upon the realism of a war game are imposed by moral and humane considerations. The strength of the formal model, on the other hand, is in the precision of control which it allows over the interrelations among its variables, while with the war game it is practically impossible to maintain adequate control over even the more accessible of the variables which it may be intended to study.

The feature of formal models which distinguishes them most sharply from replicas is the fact that the representation they afford of the original system is entirely symbolic. This feature is generally characteristic of simulations also, as we shall see shortly. The essential distinction between formal models and simulations, in turn, is a matter of whether the symbolic functions which constitute the model are capable of analytic solution. We will say that the set of symbolic expressions is analytic, and hence that it provides a formal model of a system to be studied, if all equations within the set which symbolize operations of the system can be solved by known and practicable techniques of formal manipulation. These techniques might be provided by set theory, game theory, theory of equations, theory of probability, Boolean algebra, the theory of propositions, or other systems of formal relationships which admit mechanical solutions. A set of expressions which cannot be solved analytically, on the other hand, either in theory or in practice, is the mark of a simulation model.

(c) The distinction between formal modeling and simulation comes into sharp focus when one turns to consider the practical re-

[3] *Ibid.*, p. 2146.

quirements of these two methods of modeling. Useful results should be obtainable from a formal model by paper-and-pencil operations on the part of a skilled applied mathematician. A computer might be employed to relieve the tedium of routine calculations, or to speed the result. But the result in any case is an analytic solution to a set of general equations which might be hoped to illuminate some general aspect of the workings of the system under study. It is often essential for the application of a simulation model, on the other hand, to have available the services either of an electronic computer or of a battery of clerks with hand-computers and a great deal of time. The equations with which the computing facility works, although not capable of analytic solutions in a general form, must admit solution in terms of specific numerical values of their dependent variables for all admissible combinations of numerical values given to their independent variables. Although these equations cannot be solved in general terms, the behavior of the equations in general can be determined by obtaining particular solutions over a sufficiently wide range of numerical values for its more important variables. A statistical description of a large number of particular solutions under typical conditions might be every bit as useful in the application of the model as would be a general solution if one were available.

A very simple illustration will indicate the flexibility of the simulation method. Suppose a set of two equations gives a unique value for $x$ under each admissible combination of values of $w$, $y$ and $z$. Since there are four unknowns, but only two equations, it is not possible to solve the equations in a way which exhibits a direct relationship between $x$ and $y$ alone. Thus, if one's motivation in forming the model is to study the interactions between two aspects of a working system which have been symbolized by these two variables, no strictly formal technique is available for that purpose. But one's purpose might be served adequately if he were able to determine the relationship between $x$ and $y$ under a representative sampling of the values which might be admitted by the other variables. This could be accomplished by allowing $w$ and $z$ to vary through a range of typical values, selected according to the particular purpose of the study, and computing $x$ as a function of $y$ for all combinations of these values of $w$ and $z$. It might be possible to represent $x$ as a probabilistic function of $y$, within these particular ranges of values for $w$ and $z$, or even to approximate the relationship between $x$ and $y$ under these conditions which he considers particularly important for his study. His estimation of which conditions in regard to $z$ and $w$ are important, of course, may change as his study progresses. The researcher's first application of the model may well be for purposes of experimentation, to determine what value ranges of the variables with which he must deal are likely to be most sensitive for his study.

A model of this sort might be called, perhaps not ineptly, a "function simulator." Any system which accomplishes a describable transformation under known conditions, from a given input $\alpha$ to a specific and predictable output $\beta$ conceivably could be simulated in this fashion.[4] The function of a system which under given conditions produces $\beta$ as output when presented with $\alpha$ as input is to transform $\alpha$ to $\beta$ under those conditions. This function is simulated by a set of expressions which establish between variables $x$ and $y$, a relationship such that for every value of $x$ which is interpreted as representing an instance of $\alpha$, there is associated a value of $y$ which may be correctly interpreted as representing the corresponding instance of $\beta$, under values of contributing variables which may be interpreted as representing the conditions under which the function transforms $\alpha$ into $\beta$. The strength of this approach to modeling is that the researcher may vary the relationships which he sets up among $x$ and $y$ and the contributing variables $z$ and $w$, as demanded by the observed behavior of the system to be modeled, without being concerned with limiting himself to equations which are analytically solvable. The simulation technique thus combines the precision in expression and measurement of variables which is characteristic of a purely formal model with the ability to represent a wide range of functional interrelationships which is characteristic of some forms of replication.

It should be clear from the discussion above that the problem of modeling the function of a system is independent from the problem of reproducing the operations by which the system performs its function. The former is a matter of simulation, the latter a matter of replication. This distinction may be illustrated by the difference in purpose between a standard pattern-recognition program[5] and the well-known Perceptron by Rosenblatt and his collaborators. The purpose of a pattern-recognition program is usually conceived to be that of discriminating between inscriptions which are instances of a certain pattern and inscriptions which are not, with reference to a set of features which are taken to be essential to the pattern which is to be recognized. The mark of success of a simulation system designed primarily for this purpose is that it be able to respond affirmatively when presented with an inscription which displays all these features and to respond negatively upon presentation of an inscription which

[4] As MacKay puts it (pp. 228-229 below), "any pattern of observable behaviour which can be specified in terms of unique and precisely-definable reactions to precisely-definable situations can in principle be imitated mechanically."

[5] As described, for instance, on pp. 167-169 below.

lacks any of these features. The successful pattern-recognition system thus is one which transforms one specific set of input data into an affirmative response, and which transforms all other input data into a negative response. In a word, the successful simulation of a human's pattern-recognition capability is a system which performs the same function, given a particular pattern as input, as is performed by the human recognizer. The Perceptron, on the other hand, is constructed according to the purpose of reproducing in simplified form the very behavior exhibited by the neural networks of percipient organisms.[6] This behavior has been developed to a stage where recognition of some patterns can be performed, along with other functions similar to those performed by a sentient organism, but this is incidental to the main purpose of the experiments being carried on with this system. In the terminology proposed above, the Perceptron experiments may be described as a series of attempts to replicate the structure and the behavior of the brain. A mechanical pattern-recognition system, by contrast, is primarily an attempt towards the simulation of a function characteristic of the human nervous system.

### WHAT CAN BE MODELED?

It is not adventuresome to suggest that all material systems can be replicated. The statement that this is so is nearer to being a tautology than an empirical generalization. Replicability is a mark of being a material object or system of material objects. Molecules are replicated for purposes of classroom lectures, and the solar system is replicated for the illustration of talks on astronomy. We need not have detailed or highly accurate knowledge of a system in order to replicate it. Although a replication based on inadequate knowledge is likely to be defective, we would probably say in criticism of it that it is not a good replication rather than that it is no replication at all. Plato presumably had access to an armillary sphere while composing the *Timeaus* which, despite our increased knowledge of the solar system, we would still consider a replication.[7]

A replication of a dynamic material system may or may not constitute at the same time a simulation of the function of that system. If a model airplane flies, for example, it is both replication and simulation of a full-scale airplane. Yet model ships often do not float, and toy fire engines seldom are useful for putting out fires. On the

[6] A concise description of the purpose of the Perceptron experiments is contained in "Analysis of Perceptrons", by H. D. Block, in *Proceedings of the Western Joint Computer Conference* (1961), pp. 281-89.

[7] See F. M. Cornford, *Plato's Cosmology* (New York: Harcourt, Brace, 1937), p. 74.

other hand, a simulation of the function of a system may or may not constitute a replication of that system. Tires are sometimes tested by machines which simulate the action of an actual automobile on an actual road, but which could scarcely be said to replicate an automobile, and the rivet-gun performs the function without duplicating the operations of the manual riveter. Although replication and simulation are distinct procedures, there seems to be no good reason for disbelieving that any dynamic system which can be replicated can be simulated. The only limitation on what can be simulated is imposed by our understanding of the function. Molecules which are understood well enough to be replicated might not be understood well enough to allow the chemist to simulate their combining action. Indeed, our inability to simulate a material function would normally be taken as an indication that we do not understand that function fully. The nature of the limitation imposed by degree of understanding becomes even more crucial with the question of simulating mental functions, to which we may now turn.

We frequently speak of modeling systems which would not be called "material" in any ordinary sense of the word. The legal system or constitution of a country may be modeled after that of another country. The curriculum of a university might be modeled after that of another university. A son might more or less deliberately imitate the mannerisms of his father. But when the question arises of constructing mechanical models of those aspects of human behavior which would normally be considered mental rather than strictly physiological (i.e., material), the question becomes involved with emotionally-charged convictions that there are some talents which are the unique privilege of the human mind and which cannot be duplicated by an unconscious, non-mental system. It is not within the scope of this essay to undertake the worthwhile project of removing the emotion from this question. It might be a step in the right direction, however, to point out afresh that the problem of *replicating* mental behavior is quite different from the problem of *simulating* mental behavior. Crude replications of brain operations already exist, as in the case, for example, of Rosenblatt's Perceptron mechanisms. But despite imaginative extrapolations from the present state of technology by popularizers of science, it seems unlikely on a technical basis alone that sufficiently authentic *replications* of the human mind will be constructed which will change the traditional mind-body controversy from a speculative to an empirical question.

It is more pertinent, if we are to understand the remarkable achievements of current technology in this field, to restrict our attention to the *simulation* of mental behavior. The question whether certain aspects of human mental behavior can be simulated is not speculative, and in fact is no longer open. Behavior which most persons would be willing to consider typical of the human mind has already been simulated by essentially mechanical systems. Let us attempt to clarify what it means to speak of the simulation of mental behavior.

Since the introduction of calculating machinery into the world of business, it is a standard concession that mere calculation is not a human prerogative. "But the discovery of mathematical proofs and theorems," it might be said, "is quite another matter, one involving the exercise of a function of which man alone is capable. Machines will never be capable of this activity, any more than they will be capable of writing great music, understanding the subtleties of inspired poetry, or discovering a basic scientific principle." This claim suggests something which is probably true, but something which is false as well. It probably is the case, as suggested above, that man will never confront a machine which reproduces the operations by which he proves theorems, writes music, or understands meanings. But it is the case as well that machines *can* be constructed which prove theorems, produce music, and extract intelligible data from language. They do not accomplish these things in the same way that humans accomplish them. But they accomplish them nonetheless; and this is what is involved in the simulation of these human accomplishments.

Let us consider in more detail the example of proving a mathematical theorem. Grasping axioms and reasoning from these to a theorem, distinct from the axioms but related to them by a series of steps according to distinct rules of inference, is behavior of a type characteristic of a sophisticated human mind. In performing this function, the mind provides a transformation from the axioms to the theorems. The effect of the transformation is determined by the rules of inference. When a theorem is proposed which follows from the axioms according to the rules of inference, the mind's function has been discharged correctly. Now the operations which are involved in the performance of this function by the mind are not understood. But the function itself is understood, and has already been simulated on several separate occasions.[8] The function is to arrive at a theorem (the output) from axioms (the input) according to specific rules of inference, which when considered in this fashion, are the rules of transformation. Since it is a fortunate characteristic of mathematicians to insist upon precise articulation of their rules of inference, the task of constructing a machine to perform transformations of this sort generally is more or less routine, depending upon the complexity

[8] See, for example, Professor Wang's essay in this volume.

of the axioms and the rules of inference, and upon the "novelty" desired for the theorems to be proved.

Any mental function which is such that (1) its input and output can be specified with precision, and (2) the transformation it performs can be approximated by equations which express a determinate relationship between input and output, can for these reasons alone be simulated with some degree of adequacy. If, on the other hand, we do not have a clear understanding of either the input, the output, or the transformation, we will be unable to achieve an adequate simulation of that function. Our inability in such a case, however, is a discredit to the human mind, and not a symptom of any "transcendence" of mental functions. Let us consider in detail the ways in which lack of understanding of a function can block its successful simulation.

## CONCEPTUAL FACTORS IN SIMULATION

Let 'F' represent the mental function of perceiving, 'x' an object of perception, and 'y' the behavior and behavior traits characteristic specifically of a person who has perceived x. Typical of such behavior traits might be a preference to avoid contact with x if such contact would be expected to be unpleasant, a tendency to respond affirmatively when asked if x is now visible, and an ability to focus one's attention on x when so directed. Consider the task of simulating the function F. When x and y are clearly defined, finding a transformation which will yield y when x is present is an experimental problem, towards the solution of which contributions might be expected from behavioral science. But if attempts to find a satisfactory transformation are unsuccessful, or if attempts to improve upon a partially adequate transformation persistently fail, the fault is not necessarily to be charged to the experimentalist. The reason for failure might be instead an inadequate conception of x. There might be unclarity about what features of x are relevant to the transformation between x and y, about how to characterize these features for purposes of formalizing the transformation, or about the very structure of x itself insofar as it stands as an object of perception. There might be confusion as well regarding the type of function performed in perceptual behavior. Each of these would furnish an example of conceptual inadequacy, and any one of them could block a simulation attempt which might otherwise stand a chance of success.

An hypothetical example will illustrate how a faulty conception of x might preclude a successful simulation. If an experimentalist thinks of x, the object of perception, as a set of sensations localizable simultaneously with reference to the sense organs of a percipient, he will conceive the problem of simulating $F$ as one of constructing a transformation which will require as an input a set of impulses corresponding to these sensations. Apart from the sheer technical difficulties of making a mechanical system responsive to sensations, or to impulses sufficiently similar to sensations to warrant identifying them with $x$, the fact is that an object of perception is different from a set of simultaneous sensations in several respects which seem relevant to the perception of the object. First, some awareness of the structure of an object is usually part of our perception of it, and this structure is at least partially lost by analysis of an object into sensations associated with it when it is perceived. Second, objects of perception have histories, some awareness of which often enters into our perception of them, and which cannot be identified with any set of simultaneous sensations. A third respect, related to this, is noted by Sluckin in his *Minds and Machines*: "A psychological examination of perception indicates that what is perceived depends not only upon the impact of stimuli from the outside world but also, most emphatically, upon the past experience of the perceiver," a factor which clearly cannot be represented by sensations associated with an object of present perception.[9] The experimenter may have his own reasons for representing $x$ as a set of sensations. But while he does, he should not expect to achieve a satisfactory simulation of $F$. Even if he were wholly successful in simulating a function which responds as he wishes with a particular set of sensations as input, he will not with this alone have achieved a simulation of our perception of ordinary physical objects, insofar as its input does not consist entirely of sensations.

Let us consider the importance of having a clear conception of $F$. There are at least two respects in which a confused or inarticulate conception of a function can hinder its successful simulation. (a) It could lead one to construct a transformation which could never bear more than a gross resemblance to the function to be simulated; or (b) it could encourage the application of inappropriate criteria of successful performance of the simulation system which, when failure is encountered, could result in our inability to isolate the factors which contribute most to the failure. These possibilities may be illustrated.

(a) Suppose that the human capacity which is exercised when a physical object $x$ is perceived is thought of as a function which results merely in an *identification* of $x$ when $x$ is presented as input. In this case, the task of simulating the human function of perception would

[9] W. Sluckin, *Minds and Machines* (Baltimore: Penguin Books, 1960), p. 142.

be to construct a system which issues an affirmative response when $x$ is present, and which issues a negative response or no response at all when $x$ is not present to the system. But a system which performs only this function is a poor simulation of human perception, for it is characteristic that humans are capable of perceiving things which in fact they cannot identify. Moreover, humans sometimes simply fail to perceive objects which are "in full view" before them. Thus a human perceiver might respond in any of three ways when an object is presented for its perception: he may perceive and identify, he may perceive but not identify, or he may neither perceive nor identify. This function of human perception thus cannot be adequately simulated by a system which responds in only *one* way ("affirmatively") when an object $x$ is presented to it as input.

(b) It is not unusual to find, in current literature on mechanical pattern recognition, descriptions of attempts to simulate recognition of letter-inscriptions by systems which classify inscriptions according to their configurational or topological characteristics.[10] For an example, a system might classify any configuration with two vertically ordered closed loops as a $B$. Success of a classification system of this sort is judged according to percentage of "correct" classifications achieved during a series of tests with a prepared group of inscriptions. One recent attempt to classify inscriptions according to the way typical line-segments of cursive script fit into their configurations was reported to be 87 per cent successful, a good percentage as attempts of this sort have gone.[11]

Reports like this leave the impression that an adequate simulation of human recognition will be at hand when a classification system which is 100 per cent successful is finally achieved. This criterion of success is unsatisfactory for at least two reasons. For one, it is not clear what would be meant by talking about a 100 per cent correct classification of letter-inscriptions. What is and what is not a $B$, to continue the example above, is what a person who knows the alphabet calls a $B$. But for many inscriptions there is likely to be disagreement among people who know the alphabet as to whether they are or are not inscriptions of a certain letter. The notion of a classification of inscriptions which is 100 per cent correct does not in itself *provide* a criterion. Rather, if it is to be meaningful, it *calls for* a criterion of what it is to be or not to be an inscription of a given letter. The second difficulty is a reflection of the fact that, however humans

[10] This is discussed more fully in essay 8, of this volume.
[11] See "Machine Reading of Cursive Script", by L. Frishkopf and L. Harmon, in *Information Theory*, ed. Colin Cherry (1960), p. 313. A commercial group, advertising in the *Scientific American* of March, 1963, reports 98.5 per cent success for a similar endeavor.

recognize specific letters of the alphabet, they do not do so with reference to configurational properties of letter-inscriptions alone. Whether a particular cursive inscription of the word 'boat' begins with a 'b' depends, not merely upon the shape of the first few line-segments in the word, but upon whether the word conveys to a reader (*some* reader) the sense of the word 'boat'. This in turn depends upon a number of features of the written context and the reader's expectation, many of which at best could not be analyzed in terms of the mere configuration of the inscription.

Perfect performance of a classification system is not a satisfactory criterion of success in the simulation of human pattern-recognition, and the fact that this criterion has been used belies a confusion between the concepts of classification and recognition. Although these concepts are related, they are distinct in essential respects. They are related in that a person who recognizes an object will be able to classify it as being an object of a certain sort. Part of being able to recognize an apple is being able to classify such an object both as a fruit and as an apple instead of a peach or a pear. Now people can' classify objects which, in an ordinary sense of the term, they would not be said to recognize. In this sense of the term 'recognize', when a person recognizes an object he is able to answer correctly the question "What is it?" But it is commonplace, for example in secret manufacturing work during time of war, that people handle mechanisms or papers which they are unable to identify. It may be the very point of maintaining secrecy in such an operation that the workers not learn *what* they are working with, even if their occupation for eight hours a day is "to put the red ones in this box and the blue ones in that."

At the same time, we would want to say that a worker must at least recognize an object as a *red* thing if he is to classify it correctly as being red. But even on such a level of recognition, at which one perhaps would *not* be able to say what a thing is, the function of recognition is distinct from that of classification. Classification is a *process,* something which takes up one's time, which one might do reluctantly, unwillingly, or enthusiastically, which can be done with more or less success, done very well or very poorly. Recognition, in sharp contrast, is not time-consuming. A person may spend a long while looking before recognition occurs, but when it occurs it is "instantaneous." When recognition occurs, it is not an act which would be said to be performed either reluctantly or enthusiastically, compliantly or under protest. Moreover, the notion of recognition being unsuccessful, or having been done very poorly, seems to make no sense at all. *Whether* one has classified an object correctly is a matter of whether a certain procedure has been followed and of whether certain criteria have been applied. But whether one has recognized an object is not a matter of having followed any specific procedure. Nor, it would seem, is it a matter of having applied any clearly specifiable criteria.[12] Perhaps it is not too much a paradox to say that whether an object has been recognized depends less upon what specific features the object has been found to *have* than upon what can be *done* with the object in specific circumstances. What is required of an inscription that it be an instance of the letter *n*, for example, depends upon the context in which the inscription occurs. In one context it might be necessary that it be capable of combining with inscriptions of *c* and *a* to form the first word of an intelligible question "Can you drive?" In another context, an inscription of exactly the same configuration might serve as an *r*, according to requirements imposed by the context, as with the last letter in the last word of "I came by car."

It is generally agreed that human recognition of letter-inscriptions often involves reference to context—to the word, sentence, or even the "subject matter" in the recording of which the inscription occurs. While one thinks of recognition as a type of classification, this suggests that to achieve a better recognition system one should develop a complex classification scheme involving features not only of the inscriptions to be recognized themselves but also of the words or sentences in which they occur. If the remarks above are reliable, however, increasing the *complexity* of a classification scheme will not necessarily make of it a more suitable instrument for recognition. What is needed is not a better *classification* of various letter-inscriptions, but rather better understanding of how recognition differs from classification, and how the type of behavior typical uniquely of recognition can be simulated mechanically. Understanding these things would appear to require emphasis upon the use of various inscriptions, rather than upon configurational features of inscriptions considered independently of the use to which they may be put by virtue of being recognized.

## MIND AND MACHINES

It has been suggested that the attempt to simulate letter-recognition has succeeded only in offering a substitute function, namely the *process* of classification. This reduction of attainment to process has been characteristic of efforts thus far to imitate human behavior. As we have seen, a function may be simulated without replicating the

---

[12] This is argued in essay 8, section 2, below.

operations which accompany that function in the simulated proto-type. The relation between these two kinds of functions (attain-ments and processes) needs to be further clarified. The example of recognition is not a unique instance of such imitation of attainment by process. Consider for example the case of memory. Like recogni-tion, remembering is not a process: it does not admit of degrees of success, or take up time, nor is it done better by one person than another. One either remembers or not. There is indeed a process associated with remembering, which we refer to in saying "He's try-ing to remember." This process lends itself to the model of retrieval from storage, and it is this image which has dominated the attempts to simulate memory.[13] But if one reflects on many activities which are spoken of as remembering, this model does not always fit. Con-sider: "He remembered his friend after many year's absence"; "He remembered that it was his turn to play"; "He showed that he re-membered the poem by reciting it"; "The way he ended the sentence showed that he remembered how he began it"; "He remembered to pull the door in as he turned the key."

The model suggests that remembering proceeds by comparing in some way an input $S_1$ (at some stage of transformation) with a pre-vious input $S_2$ (which may be a programmed configuration of states.) The question here is whether any such process is a part of the at-tainment which we call remembering. There seems to be little doubt that some process can always be associated with the attainment. That is, we can always analyze the attainment in the sense of finding a process which more or less successfully effects a similar transforma-tion of the input data. If this is done consistently, so that the same transformation is always performed on the same input (i.e., the same output is achieved), then we would say that the attainment function had been successfully simulated. (For practical purposes, of course, 100 per cent agreement might not be necessary.) More precisely then, the question to be discussed now is whether this criterion of success-ful simulation entails some duplication of the function.

It has already been suggested that the functions are not equivalent, on the basis of certain fundamental differences between attainments and processes: the former do not take time, do not admit of partial success, etc. But it might be supposed that (as the word suggests) the attainment presupposes the process as its necessary condition.

---

[13] The relevance of memory to the problem of recognition has been pointed out above, p. 15. See also E. Straus, "On Memory Traces" in *Tjdschrift Voor Philosophie* (Maart 1962), pp. 91-122, and G. Ryle, *Concept of Mind* (New York, 1949), pp. 272-79. Recent essays by technologists have noted the deficiencies of this model, and suggested ameliorations of it by considering memory as a function of the state of the system as a whole.

It seems possible, however, to cite instances of recognition which do not involve any classification process. For example, I can easily distinguish the typeface of the *New York Times* from that of the *Chicago Tribune,* although I could not begin to enumerate the criteria by which I perform that act of discrimination. Not only am I not aware of them in performing the act, but I cannot even enumerate them by reflecting on my memory of the two newspapers.

Or take the case of depth perception. We can indeed find "clues" in the visual field (such as relative size, gradient density, linear perspective, etc.), the noting of which can motivate a judgment of relative depth. But as Wittgenstein remarked, "If we have a picture of two men, we do not say first that the one appears smaller than the other, and *then* that he seems to be further away. It is, one can say, perfectly possible that the one figure's being shorter should not strike us at all, but only its being behind."[14]

The argument here is not that these attainments are magical functions which proceed in utter disregard of the elements which are disengaged by process-analysis of the function, but merely that they do not involve a step-by-step observation and confirmation of those elements. Rather, the latter are present (in an ambiguous sense of 'present') as the *ground* or field of marginal awareness, in distinction from the *figure* or area of explicit focal awareness. This is, of course, the language of Gestalt psychology. The functionalist conception of figure and ground, of part and whole, which the gestaltists developed, suggests that "when a 'whole' is destroyed, really or mentally, the products of the decomposition, the resulting 'elements' must not be confused with the 'parts' which were contained in the whole before its decomposition."[15]

In other words, the unnoted elements in the perceptual field, in spite of being unnoted, have a functional meaning, i.e., have a function in the constitution of the meaning of the figure or area of focal awareness, and this functional meaning changes when those elements are brought to specification, i.e., explicitly noted. Hence in a real sense the analysis which effects this explication is introducing new elements rather than merely resolving a complex into its parts. (This is the reason why *Gestalten* resist topological analysis, namely that in such formal analysis the relations of the parts are assumed to be invariant under transformation.)

[14] L. Wittgenstein, *Remarks on the Foundations of Mathematics,* trans. G.E.M. Anscombe (New York: Macmillan, 1956), II, 40, pp. 81-82. He adds, "This seems to me to be connected with the question of the 'geometrical' conception of proof."

[15] A. Gurwitsch, *Théorie du champ de la conscience* Desclée de Brouwer (Paris, 1957), p. 125.

To recapitulate, it has been suggested that some human functions are at times performed by utilizing information or clues which are not explicitly or focally attended to, and that this seems to mark a fundamental difference between such functions and the processes by which they are simulated by automata. The reason for this difference is that the operations of the digital computers which are employed as models are binary in nature. Consequently, the function which the machine can perform (and by which it can simulate an attainment) must be, at each stage, all-or-none, i.e., sufficiently specific and explicit so as to be answered 'yes' or 'no'.

It is true that "at each stage" does not necessarily mean the individual element of the machine (vacuum tube, electro-mechanical relay, etc.), since the excitation of an individual element can be made to depend on the (simultaneous or serial) excitation of other elements or groups of elements by a system of linkages. The threshold (amount of input required for excitation) of an individual element or a linkage of elements can also be varied, either randomly, or as a function of some other elements, so that the probability of excitation is not constant for a given input. (This could be the operational counterpart of including the context of a letter in the process of classifying it.)

The possibility of variable adjustment of thresholds suggests an objection to the above statements about "unspecified clues." One might contend that the information about the background of a figure *is* unambiguously specified as part of the input, but that while being above the threshold of individual elements, it is not sufficient to excite the *set* of neurons whose combined stimulation would bring the information into awareness. In a computer model, therefore, we could simulate the role of unspecified clues by treating them as equivalent to the stimulation of a number of elements in such a set, but not of the whole set.

This objection could be made stronger by noting the distinction between the threshold which we have been discussing, and the psychological threshold. Neurons, like computer elements, either fire or they do not: they are binary in character.[16] But for the psychologist, the threshold is not so determinate: the sensory neurons respond to stimulation before the perception of the stimulation occurs. For the psychologist, therefore, 'threshold' designates a *zone* in which the physical stimuli pass from having no perceptual effect, to having

[16]It is true that the neuron is not exactly a digital organ, but then, neither is the vacuum tube. Von Neumann has discussed this objection in his Hixon Symposium paper, reprinted as "The General and Logical Theory of Automata", in *The World of Mathematics,* ed. J. R. Newman (New York, 1956), IV, 2078-2079.

some effect, to having full and determinate effect. The threshold is therefore defined by the psychologist in a consciously arbitrary way as that point at which the stimulus is perceived *half the time*.

We can thus restate the objection in the following way: suppose that the implicit information utilized in recognition is sub-threshold stimulation, i.e., above the neurological threshold but below the perceptual threshold. Then it would seem possible to define as functionally equivalent such stimulation, and the threshold stimulation of a set of elements in a computer the number of which is below a certain parameter. We could then simulate what to conscious experience are unspecified clues by specific input to such a subset of elements, and thereby reduce the clues to formal contextual specification. If we can do this, then the function will be susceptible of simulation by the model.

In the case of translation machines (involving letter and word recognition), such resolution has thus far not succeeded. Some persons who have worked in the field (e.g., Bar-Hillel) believe that the "subconscious" background knowledge of human translators cannot be completely specified or articulated. The same reservation has been raised on the most general theoretical level by J. Von Neumann.[17]

If total simulation of human behavior is possible, then replication ceases to be philosophically interesting. As noted earlier, with a few exceptions (such as the Perceptron), simulators of human behavior today do not involve replication, but operate in a decidely non-human manner in solving problems. But the difference in the operations and processes between human and automaton is not itself philosophically significant. The fact that the same function might be differently performed by the simulator model and the simulated prototype provides no ground for supposing a fundamental difference in nature without other evidence. On the contrary. It is conceivable that mediums have spiritual powers, but so long as we can duplicate the phenomena they produce by natural means—mechanical, hypnotic, etc.—we are satisfied that the phenomena are not essentially preternatural. It would be logically incorrect to close off the possibility, but it could not be seriously entertained on grounds of evidence.

What other evidence could there be? The only alternative would appear to be an examination of the mechanism, of the interior of the "black box". It might be argued, for example, that man knows by direct apprehension (by self-consciousness) that his mind is immaterial in its operations. This was the thesis of Rene Descartes.[18]

[17] *Art. cit.*, p. 2091.
[18] *Meditations on First Philosophy.*

However, one thing that seems conclusively shown by both the philosophies and the psychologies of this century is that man has no such direct access to his "black box". To say the least, introspection, even if it were subject to verification by other observers, does not yield any observations of the mechanism of intelligent behavior. This is precisely why there are so many different theories of knowledge, theories of learning, etc. It is not a novel idea, but a classical theme, that man must understand himself in terms of what he does—his behavior—and as an image of what he encounters. He must decipher himself in the same way that he deciphers and analyzes other men and other beings. This implies that the philosophical problem of the difference between minds and automata is not to be resolved or even ameliorated by the distinction between simulation and replication.

The issue thus appears to be thrown back on the possibility of complete simulation, a possibility which seems real enough to many in the field though certainly still an open question. There is however, at least one gap in the previous argument, namely in the analysis of self-awareness or self-consciousness. It is true, as Hume first pointed out,[19] that the self is not a datum, i.e., not a specific object of awareness. But does the acceptance of this involve the rejection of consciousness, à la William James?[20]

Consciousness comes from the Latin *con-scire*, to know with. What does "withknowing" mean? Consider the following possibility (and note that this analysis is not of a process nor of a function, but rather of a quality of [at least] all characteristically human functions.) Suppose that when we speak of being conscious, we refer not to a specific object of awareness but to an indirect or oblique *awareness of being aware* of, e.g., a visual object. Conceive of consciousness then as parasitic, as incapable of being self-consciousness if this means awareness of itself as a specific object. Now if this is what we mean by 'conscious' and what we experience ourselves (a question to be decided by phenomenological and linguistic analysis), then it cannot be simulated (as it has been suggested that consciousness could be simulated) by a machine which is capable of scanning its own internal states. For such a machine would embark on an infinite regress of precisely the sort which Ryle has criticized in Descartes' argument: the scanner could never be, at the same moment, scanned.[21] Nor could the "scanner" in the above suggested concep-

---

19 David Hume, *A Treatise of Human Nature* (London, 1890), I, p. 533.
20 William James, *Psychology* (Cleveland, 1948), p. 215.
21 Ryle, *op. cit.*, pp. 195-98.

tion of consciousness. But the latter could *never,* in principle, be scanned: while this is not the case for the machine.

It is not accidental that there is a close analogy between this conception of consciousness and the previous analysis of human letter-recognition. In both cases, the object of focal awareness has an increment of meaning due to essentially implicit or marginal awareness. In both cases, the key to the problem of simulation would seem to lie beyond the capacities of digital process, unless the functional equivalence discussed above between unspecified and specific information can be achieved.

# CHAPTER 2

# Technological Models of the Nervous System

ANATOL RAPOPORT

It is not often that a book written in another age suddenly acquires an astonishing up-to-date-ness. This does happen when some prophecy suddenly passes from the realm of the fantastic to the realm of the imminent. Such a prophecy was contained in the book *Erewhon* by Samuel Butler, written in 1872. The prophecy has to do with the evolution of machines, particularly machines endowed with a property which has seldom been attributed to machines—intelligence. As stated by Butler in rather poetic terms, the prophecy envisages a world in which the machine becomes the dominant system of organization (in the way living things are systems of organization). Like living things, the machines of the future metabolize, reproduce, maintain themselves, and in general seem to have an aim in life. The one frightening thing about the *genus machina* is its parasitic dependence on the *genus homo*. The mechanism of natural selection is supposed to function in such a way on that form of "life" as to select those variations which are especially capable of catering to the compulsions of human beings—namely, their compulsions of caring for machines. Gradually, what had started as a symbiosis between man and machine passes into parasitism, so that finally man becomes domesticated by the machine.

Almost the same prophecy is stated in more realistic terms by N. Wiener in his *Cybernetics* (New York, 1949). Wiener envisages the Second Industrial Revolution ushered in by machines able to perform tasks requiring an average intelligence with the resulting dislocations and crises similar to those which followed the First Industrial Revolution, when the "stupid" machines first appeared on the scene of history.

Our purpose here is not to discuss the merits or the limitations of these prophecies, but rather to point out that the sudden dramatic revival of the "intelligent machine" idea (be it a metaphor or a myth or a profound insight) is indicative of a really significant historical event—a major intellectual revolution.

Like the second Industrial Revolution, of which Wiener writes, this intellectual revolution is also the second in recent times. The first one occurred in the seventeenth century with the creation of mathematical physics. Perhaps I should make clear what I mean by an intellectual revolution. I think of such revolutions metaphorically as crystallizations of thinking around new, powerful concepts. In the seventeenth century these central concepts were those of mechanics—force, momentum, particularly energy. They became the central concepts of classical physics and of technology which came into being during the First Industrial Revolution.

The second intellectual revolution, now occurring, brought forward another powerful new concept, that of "quantity of organization," a concept of high degree of sophistication and bearing within it the seeds of extremely far-reaching consequences. It is this concept, also called negative entropy and "amount of information," which makes the anthropomorphic conception of the machine especially intriguing, particularly because through it the common features of "intelligent" or "purposeful" behavior of the higher animals and "automatic" behavior of "higher machines" are made apparent.

Now the personification of machines and "mechanization" of organism are not new. The former has mythological roots in the medieval legends of the Golem and the Homunculus. The latter appears, for example, in the writings of Descartes.

The question "Are living beings machines?" has long been treated as a metaphysical question, presumably answerable on metaphysical grounds. Since metaphysics is more or less a lost art, we must learn to look at that question somewhat more critically, that is, with semantic awareness. We must translate it into other questions, such as, "To what shall the name 'living thing' be applied?" and "To what shall the name 'machine' be applied?" "Is there an overlap among the referents of the two terms?"

Putting the question this way, we see that the answers to the first are relatively clear, while the answers to the second are not nearly so clear. Barring certain borderline cases (viruses, etc.) we have no difficulty recognizing the class of objects to which the name "living thing" can be unambiguously applied. Not so with machines. This is so because living things are "given." They have remained about the same for as long as we can remember. But machines have evolved rapidly within the span of human history. We realize keenly that there are machines today which our grandfathers could not have dreamed of, and, by extrapolation, we feel that we can't really say what the limits of the world of machines may be. If we think about the matter a little more, we realize that machines in their evolution undergo "mutations" of tremendous magnitudes. Where it takes eons for a new biological species to develop, a new technological "phylum" has on occasion come into being within a generation.

By a technological phylum I mean something similar to a biological phylum. If the latter is defined by a very general plan of organization in a wide class of living things, the latter is defined in terms of a *principle of operation*. We can, if we wish, distinguish four technological "phyla," which came into being successively.

The first phylum we could call *Tools*. Tools appear functionally as extensions of our limbs and they serve primarily for transmitting forces which originate in our own muscles. In the transmission of force, sometimes a mechanical advantage is gained, as in the crowbar, a screw, or a pulley. However, the work done by a machine of this sort is actually work done by our own muscles. Therefore a machine of this kind, a tool, does not give the impression of "independent" action, and so it did not occur to anyone to compare tools to living things.[1]

With the second phylum it is a somewhat different story. This second phylum of machines we could call *Clockworks*. In a clockwork a new principle of operation is at work, namely, the *storing* of mechanical energy. A typical clockwork is wound up, that is, potential mechanical energy is stored in it, which may be released at an arbitrary later time and/or over a prolonged period of time. A clockwork does give the impression of autonomous activity, and doubtless this crude resemblance of a clockwork to a living thing (residing in its quasi-autonomous activity) gave the craftsmen of the late Middle Ages and of the Renaissance ideas of constructing mechanical dolls and animals. Perhaps the first ideas of automata sprang from the same sources. Characteristically, Descartes speculated on the possibility that animals were elaborate clockworks and, equally characteristically of his age, excluded humans from this class, as possessors of "souls."

We may observe in passing that the bow and the catapult are also clockworks by our definition, since mechanical energy is stored in these machines to be released later (in the case of the crossbow, it may be released much later). However, the "autonomous" action

[1] However, personification of weapons does occur. Note also the legend of the Sorcerer's Apprentice.

of these machines is so brief that they do not give even the appearance of being "alive."

The first comparison of living things to machines, therefore, was made with regard to clockworks. It is not surprising that this metaphor was not particularly fruitful for the understanding of the living process. We know now, of course, that *energy* is stored in living things, but this energy is not stored in the form in which it is stored in clockworks (mechanical stress) and so was not recognized as such. Living things are not wound up to keep going, and this absence of the most essential characteristics of a clockwork in living things made the early mechanical intepretation of life a sterile one.

This comparison got a new lease on life with the appearance of the third phylum of machines. This phylum includes primarily the *Heat Engines*. Again an entirely new principle enters into their operation. As with tools and clockworks, the output of the heat engine is an output of energy which had been put into it. But whereas the energy put into the earlier classes of machines was in the form of mechanical stress, which is obviously associated with our own muscular effort, the energy put into a heat engine is contained in a *fuel*.

Consider the vital difference between the two situations. It is obvious even to a child that the tool is not autonomous, because the tool is geared at all times to muscular effort. A child or a very primitive person may believe that a clockwork is autonomous, but it is still easy to convince him that it is not, because the winding up is still a result of someone else's muscular effort. No such effort is apparent in the fuel. Fuel is "fed" to the heat engine. The analogy to living things (which also need to be fed in order to operate) becomes ever stronger.

The comparison between heat engines and organism passed beyond the metaphorical stage and bore real scientific fruits. It became apparent that fuel is in a very real sense the food of the engine and equally apparent that food eaten by organisms likewise functions as "fuel." The principle of energy conservation was shown to hold in living things—a serious blow to the contentions of the vitalists, which sent them on their long and torturous retreat. Biochemistry was born. More and more processes characteristic of life were shown to be instances of processes reproducible in a chemical laboratory. An analogous revolution was occurring in technology. In fact, it would be not inaccurate to say that the First Industrial Revolution occurred when it became apparent that machines could be constructed which did not need to be "pushed" but only "fed" in order to do the work.

Driven out of physiology, the vitalists took refuge in psychology. Here, in the realm of thought and purpose, of emotion and insight they felt they would remain safe from the onslaught of the mechanists, materialists, determinists, and reductionists. The label "nothing-but-ism" was derisively pinned on the philosophical outlook of those who believed that even the most complex manifestations of the living process, including the intricacies of men's psyche, could somehow be described in terms of analyzable behavioral components which, in turn, could be related to observable events in space and time.

And so the focus of the battle between the vitalists and the physicalists shifted to psychology, where it remains at this time. The line between the two camps is, of course, not sharply drawn. Like the political spectrum ranging from extreme left to extreme right, the range of convictions concerning the nature of mental processes stretches from extreme behaviorism to vitalism or mysticism. The gestaltists can, perhaps, be assigned intermediate positions.

I am sure you all know the main outlines of the controversy. The opening offensive was undertaken by the behaviorists, the champions of what in some circles bears the unattractive name of S—R psychology. The method has a strong physiological bias. Technological analogies are frequently invoked. The earliest of these was the "telephone switchboard" model of the central nervous system. The environment was supposed to act on the organism by a series of stimulus configurations, which activated combinations of receptors, which initiated impulses, which traveled along nerve fibers, passed through the central nervous system to other nerve fibers and into the effectors, whose activity accounted for the overt behavior of the organism, which was proclaimed to be a sole legitimate object of study in psychology. Behavior was viewed as a grand collection of units called reflexes.

The model was seen to be inadequate from the start. If to every configuration of stimuli there corresponded a definite set of responses, how was learning (the acquisition of new responses to the same stimuli) possible? However, this seemingly embarrassing question proved a blessing in disguise, for the discovery of the conditioned stimulus by physiological means strengthened the reflex theory of behavior. It was shown that the paths of the impulses could be *systematically* changed. The switchboard model was shown to be still useful. Learning was accounted for by the "switchings" of the connections.

Hot on the heels of the behaviorists' successes, however, came a more serious critique called *gestaltism*. Gestaltism deserves serious attention, because its ideas were the direct precursors of a new approach to the theory of the nervous system, which is the subject of the present discussion. The gestaltist critique was not simply a reiteration of the vitalist faith and did not confine itself to derisive labels like "nothing-but-ism" directed against behaviorism. It was much more specific and constructive and was based on at least two clearly identifiable characteristics of behavior, which did not seem to fit into the behaviorist scheme, namely, the recognition of "universals" and the equi-finality of response.

The recognition of universals means the following. Suppose an organism learns to respond to the sight of a particular square in a certain way and to a particular circle in a different way (say open a box marked with a square but not with a circle). The phenomenon is clearly an instance of conditioning. A strict behaviorist (telephone switchboard) explanation would have to rest on the assumption that the stimuli originating from the receptors activated by the sight of the square are "switched" by the conditioning process to paths leading to the proper effectors for opening the box. However, it is known that the conditioned stimulus can be varied considerably *after* the conditioning has been established and still elicit the response. For example, if the original conditioning was to a white square on a black background, it can be subsequently changed to a black square on a white background, which, at least in the retina, excites the *complementary* receptors, i.e., precisely those which were *not* involved in the conditioning process. Roughly speaking, the organism responds to the square as a "square," regardless of the receptors involved. Hence the emphasis on the term *gestalt* (the configuration perceived as a whole, rather than a complex of elementary stimuli). The gestaltists maintained that the behaviorists' emphasis on the stimulus response pathways detracted from the importance of "universals" or abstractions in the act of perception.

(If a counter-argument is offered to the effect that in the perception of a geometric figure only the receptors affected by the edges of the figure are involved, it can be countered by other interesting evidence, such as the well-known phenomenon where familiar maps are not recognized if the continents appear in blue and oceans in yellow, or the still more baffling phenomenon that the shapes of objects can be recognized regardless of position, size, or orientation.)

The equi-finality of response argument is even more powerful. It has been observed that once an animal has learned to perform a task (say to run a maze to a reward) it will perform that task with whatever means are available to it. If its legs are amputated, it will roll through the maze. Clearly, such behavior cannot be explained in terms of a series of reflexes, each setting off the next, since the performance may involve totally different effectors each time.

This equi-finality of response naturally leads one to talk of *purposeful* behavior, in which only the *goal* is relevant and not the particular configuration of neural events which come into play. This seeming inevitability of invoking teleological notions opens the door to more vitalist arguments. The notion of "purpose" seems to resurrect the ancient classification of causes into "efficient" and "final" and to give new life to the ailing idea that the behavior of living and non-living things could not possibly be governed by the same set of laws.

It is at this point that concepts associated with the fourth phylum of machines become exceedingly important. We recall that the first phylum (tools) operated primarily as force transmitters; the second phylum (clockworks) as storages of energy resulting from mechanical stress; the third phylum (heat engines) as transformers of different forms of energy into mechanical energy. Now the fourth phylum of machines operates on the principle of storing and transmitting something called *information*.

Already the telephone switchboard model of the nervous system employs a technological analogy with a communication device rather than a conventional engine. The primary concern of psychology is not so much with "what makes the organism active?" as "how does it know what to do?" Not the source, the transformation, or the utilization of energy by the organism is of prime significance but its *organized* disposition. What the psychologist actually studies is not how much activity has been performed but the sequence of specifically directed acts, which when organized one way may give one set of results and organized in another way (or randomly performed) may give an entirely different set, even though the amount of energy expended remains the same. To give a homely example, consider the difference between closing the door and then turning the key and turning the key and then closing the door. The machines of our fourth phylum are primarily concerned with *systematizing* operations in which utilization of energy is involved. The amount of energy used is not important. The "power" of these machines is not "muscular" power but "mental." The giants among them are capable of receiving, transmitting, and storing complex sets of directions, i.e., large amounts of "information." This is why technological analogies with these machines are of particular interest in psychology. These machines simulate not muscular effort (like their ancestors did) but human intelligence.

Just as the concept of energy and its transformations was able to explain the "activeness" of organisms, which could not be explained on the basis of externally applied stress (as tools are activated) or by internally applied stress (as clockworks are activated), so the concept of "information" promises to do the same for a much larger area of the living process, namely, the "intelligent" and "purposeful" aspects of living behavior.

What is this thing called information? There is now a wealth of literature on the subject and it is not within the scope of this presentation to develop the ideas of this literature. I think, however, that a reasonably good idea of the nature of "information" can be given by a few examples. I will not attempt to make these ideas precise. I will try to appeal to intuitive understanding, even at the risk of being vague.

Information bears a similar relation to energy as organization to effort. One can best see this in an example where the inadequacy of a theory based on energetic considerations alone is obvious. Consider the automobile traffic in a large city. Suppose the proverbial man from Mars decided to study this traffic. He might measure the rate of flow of cars along the city's arteries. He would correctly relate that flow to the speed with which the cars traveled and, being a good physicist, he would relate the speed to the power of the engines. And so he would be satisfied, perhaps, in explaining the rate of flow by energetic considerations.

Next suppose that all the traffic lights failed. Certainly the speed of the cars and thus the rate of flow of traffic would be reduced. Suppose our Martian stuck to his conceptualization in terms of energetics. He would then have to ascribe the reduced flow (or speed) to some failure of the automobile engines, and he would be wrong. The failure is not of the engines but of the traffic lights. True, it takes energy to activate the traffic lights, but it is negligible compared with the energy it takes to move the cars. Energy has therefore little to do with the traffic problem under consideration. The key concept is not that of energy but of *directions for the utilization of energy* (commands "stop" and "go" properly patterned), i.e., a matter of *information*. If the traffic lights are not functioning, the driver of a car does not know what to expect at each intersection and, playing safe, he slows down. The accumulated slow-downs of all cars at all intersections turn out to have a greater effect on the over-all slowing of traffic than the occasional full stops at the red lights. In the case of regulated traffic lights, set for certain speeds, the flow of traffic is most efficient. The cars are, in effect, "organized" or bunched up along the roads in such a way that the bunches on one system mesh with the empty spaces on the system perpendicular to it, and the flow is continuous without stops.

Examples can be multiplied at will. Children well-trained in fire drills leave a burning building in a surprisingly short time, while a disorganized mob may never leave it. The success of a military action depends both on fire power and on proper coordination of the units. Fire power is measurable in terms of energy units, but coordination is measurable in terms of something else: the rate of flow of information and the precision of timing in carrying out the sequence of necessary steps. Productivity of an industry depends on the amount of power available (energetics) but to no less extent on the skill of the workers (coordination of activity within the individual) and the skill of management (coordination of activity of the several workers). While it was traditionally assumed that these coordinating functions must be performed by "reasoning beings," i.e., men, it became gradually apparent that a great many of them could be performed automatically (by traffic lights instead of policemen, IBM machines instead of filing clerks, automatic steering mechanisms instead of helmsmen, electronic computers instead of human calculators). There arose then the intriguing idea that there may be a general "psychology" applicable both to the behavior of these devices and at least to certain aspects of human behavior.

Now let us pause for a moment and take stock of what we have said. Historically the technological analogies purporting to explain the behavior of living things have been geared to prevailing technological concepts. As technology became more involved, the analogies could be extended to more facets of behavior. We are now entering a new technological era—the era of "intelligent machines," called automata and servo-mechanisms. The understanding of the principles on which these machines are constructed and operate promises to extend our understanding of the living process still further.

We must, however, if we are to say something significant, indicate more specifically where that promise lies. We have two pieces of evidence in support of our rather optimistic view. The first is the tremendous stride forward in the understanding of the living process, which resulted from the previous discovery of just one far-reaching principle—that of transformation of energy. The second is the progress being currently made in the analysis of the vague teleological and vitalistic notions of "purpose" and "intelligence."

Let us recall, at the risk of becoming repetitious, why the understanding of the living process presents difficulties. Living things seem to differ from nonliving in three fundamental respects (immediately apparent to the naive observer).

1. They seem to be "autonomously" active (i.e., the motive power seems to come from the inside rather than be impressed from the outside as in the case of moving inanimate objects).

2. They seem to be guided by purpose and intelligence.

3. They maintain their integrity, grow, and reproduce.

The first technological analogy (with the clockwork) attempted to explain only the first of these characteristics and it did so very poorly. A clockwork is, to be sure, activated from the "inside" for a while, but there is no question about what the source of this activation is. The clockwork simply gives a *delayed* response to a stress (a push) impressed on it.

It is different with a heat engine. There is no obvious push there. The engine is *fed* in a very real sense and is activated by the food it "eats." The analogy to a living organism is in the case of a heat engine far from superficial. But the "muscular effort" of the engine is still externally directed. The locomotive is guided by the rails; the boat by the rudder. A simple engine is "told what to do" at every step of the process. Here the analogy with the living organism fails.

Now it is clear why the development of automata and servos naturally extends the analogy. The mechanisms of *control* are now built into the machine. We now want machines to behave "purposefully" and intelligently, and since we have to design the machines, we have to analyze the notions of purposefulness and intelligence into component parts.

Really no sharp distinction can be drawn between intelligence and purposefulness. Any definition of one is sure to involve the other. Let me therefore describe very roughly the present status of "intelligence" and/or "purposefulness" in our machines which will then naturally lead me to the concluding remarks on the modern ideas of the nervous system. I view "intelligent" machines as consisting of two kinds, automata and servo-mechanisms. The only distinction I make between them is that the automaton is guided by a program of discrete steps or directions fed into it, while the servo-mechanism is guided by observing the effects of its action on the outside world. Thus a juke box which plays a number of selections in the order selected by the customer (in response to the buttons pushed) is an automaton, and so is an electronic computer. A target-seeking torpedo, on the other hand, or a gyroscope, I would call a servo-mechanism. Both exhibit "purposefulness" and "intelligience," although if we adhere to the intuitive popular meanings of these terms, the servo-mechanism seems to specialize in purposefulness and the automaton in intelligence. This seems so, because the automaton seems to be able to follow *explicit* directions, "When so and so, then so, unless so or so, in which case so . . ." (the program), while the servo seems to be guided by a goal. This difference is only apparent. To an outsider, the automaton may well seem to be guided by a "goal" ("Find the solution of this equation") while some one intimately familiar with the operation of a servo can describe its operation in terms of a program.

This equivalence of "program" and "goal" is the principal idea of the modern theories of the nervous system. One point must be kept in mind, however. Program and goal may be logically equivalent, but it does not by any means mean that a description of an operation of an organism or a machine is equally convenient in terms of one or the other.

Let us take a trivial example. We wish a ball in a cup to "seek" to come to rest at a particular point. Here the desired behavior of the ball is described in terms of a "goal," and nothing is simpler than to design a device which will exhibit just such behavior. Take a cup of any convex shape and place it so that the desired point is the lowest. To describe the same kind of behavior in terms of a "program" would necessitate an infinite number of statements, each of which tells which way the ball is supposed to move if it finds itself in a particular position. Such a description in terms of discrete statements (an explicit program) is, of course, out of the question. A description of "intermediate complexity," however, can be given, namely, as a set of differential equations of motion which imply a stable equilibrium at the desired point.

Of the three descriptions clearly the first, "stating the goal" of the ball, is the simplest. What enables us to realize this "goal" by a mechanical device is our ability to see the problem as a whole. Similar considerations apply, I believe, to the theory of the nervous system.

The first attempt to account for gestalt phenomena in strictly behaviorist terms was made by McCulloch and Pitts in 1943. They showed that any pattern of behavior which could be described by a *program* was realizable in an automaton of a specified construction and (herein lies the importance of their idea) they gave an "algorithm" for the construction of the automaton based on the program. Automata, of course, operate on the same principle. The limitations of this approach, however, are immediately evident. The *whole difficulty* is to describe the action of the nervous system in terms of a program of discrete elementary steps.

The task looks more hopeful if "goal-seeking" steps are allowed in the description of the program. If, for example, the construction of a mechanism for keeping a certain muscle-tone constant is known, one of the directions in the program may read, "Plug in that mechanism." Thus with one stroke an immense number of elementary steps is "described."

The value of information-theory in this approach to the nervous system is now apparent. The McCulloch-Pitts picture represents behavior in terms of firing patterns of individual neurons. With $10^{10}$ neurons in the human body, there are $2^{10^{10}}$ such possible patterns at each instant of quantized time. This number is utterly unthinkable. Nothing whatsoever can be said of a system with that many distinguishable states where nothing is known about how the states are to be classified.

To put it in another way, the amount of information per unit-time needed to describe such a system is $10^{10}$ bits (the amount of information coming over an ordinary telegraph wire is considerably less than 30 bits per unit-time).[2] It is quite another matter, however, when sub-systems are "organized" to work in prescribed ways, when touched off by proper signals. The *amount of organization* of such subassemblies *reduces* the amount of information necessary to transmit over the channels.

This consideration leads to two complementary conclusions. Rigidity of behavior in organisms requires smaller capacities of channels over which information flows. Contrariwise, greater channel capacities allow for greater flexibility of behavior.

We are thus led to ideas of the nervous system which involve not minute blueprint structures (a hopeless approach because of the tremendous complexity of the nervous system) but which involve overall statistical concepts such as channel capacity, storage capacity and other parameters familiar to the modern communication engineer, such as redundancy, signal-to-noise ratios, etc.

They are concepts analogous to the over-all concepts in terms of which the operation of the "muscle engines" is understood: power, efficiency, compression ratios, etc.

It is the development of the corresponding *over-all* concepts of communication and complexity which made intelligent machines possible and which gives us promise of future understanding of living behavior, particularly of the functions of the nervous system.

I need not, I hope, emphasize that none of these considerations are relevant to the question of whether thinking machines "really think." I admit I do not understand the question. The really pertinent question is whether similar *abstractions* can be utilized in both the theory of intelligent machines and in the theory of living behavior, particularly that governed by the nervous system.

We know that both organisms and machines receive, transmit, store, and utilize information. The question of how information is "utilized" is particularly interesting. We now know what food is used

---

[2] (Editor's note: in information theory, the unit measure of conveyed information is the "bit" (binary digit). If transmission of either of two symbols is equally probable the actual transmission of either would convey one "bit" of information).

for: three things, namely, as a source of heat, a source of locomotive and chemical energy, and a source of materials for growth and restoring worn-out tissues. All these elements are being constantly dissipated by the organism: heat by conduction and radiation, energy by motion, materials through breakdown and excretion.

Can it be that besides energy in the form of food and sunlight, organisms also feed on something called "information," which serves to *restore the order,* which is constantly being dissipated in accordance with the Second Law of Thermodynamics?

The formal mathematical equivalence between entropy (the measure of disorder in a physical system) and information (as defined mathematically) was commented on by Shannon, Wiener, MacKay, and others. Can it be that this is no mere formal mathematical equivalence, such as obtains between an oscillating mechanical system and the analogous electrical one, but a more fundamental equivalence such as that between heat and energy or between energy and matter? Can it be that 1.98 calories per degree mole (the difference in entropy between two moles of two separated perfect gases and two moles of their mixture in equilibrium) is actually equivalent to $6.06 \times 10^{23}$ bits of information—the amount it would take to separate the mixture into the constituent parts in terms of yes-no decisions?

If there is such a conversion factor, how do the information receiving, information transmitting, and information storing organs operate to convert information into negative entropy or its concomitant "free energy" and, perhaps, vice versa?

The intriguing nature of these questions has stimulated some of us to undertake the study of communication nets from the information-theoretical point of view. This approach necessitates the description of such nets not in terms of detailed structure but rather in terms of gross statistical parameters. The flexibility and far-reaching adaptability of the behavior of higher organisms almost demands this sort of approach. Perhaps the most fundamental characteristic of living behavior as distinguished from that of man-designed machines is in the *sacrifice of precision* for safety. It is not important that a response be precise but rather that an equivalent response be given under a great variety of conditions or handicaps. It is more important to be "roughly" correct in practically every case than be "precisely" correct in every case but one and altogether wrong in that one. It is necessary to relate totally new situations *approximately* to situations already experienced, and it is necessary to leave certain portions of the nervous system "uncommitted," so that new behavior patterns to meet new situations can be organized. When machines are built possessing these characteristics, we may expect an even closer analogy to the workings of actual nervous systems. That the day is not far off can be inferred from the fact that mathematicians like von Neumann already do not shirk from theoretical investigations aimed at throwing light on the most typical of life processes—reproduction. I am referring to his recent calculations on the number of elements required in an automaton which can not only perform specific tasks assigned to it but also is able to reproduce itself, given a mixed-up aggregate of its elementary constituents. An actual materialization of such a machine would, of course, give startling reality to the prophecy in Butler's *Erewhon*.

Such is the state of the present studies, which are extensions of the technological analogies of the living process, particularly of the integrating functions of the nervous system. It is hoped that these studies are now approaching a level sufficiently sophisticated to yield enlightening and lasting results.

# Selected Bibliography for Part I

1. Ashby, W. R., *Design for a Brain* (2nd Edition). New York: John Wiley and Sons, Inc., 1960.
2. Ashby, W. R., "The Nervous System as a Physical Machine: with Special Reference to the Origin of Adaptive Behaviour," *Mind,* Vol. 56 (1947), pp. 44-59.
3. Bowden, B. V. (ed.), *Faster Than Thought.* London: Sir Isaac Pitman and Sons, Ltd., 1953.
4. Brain, R., *Mind, Perception and Science.* Oxford: Blackwell, 1951.
5. Coburn, H. E., "The Brain Analogy," *Psychological Review,* Vol. 58 (1951), pp. 155-178.
6. de Latil, P., *Thinking by Machine* (trans., Y. M. Golla). Boston: Houghton-Mifflin Company, 1956.
7. Eccles, J. C., *The Neurophysiological Basis of the Mind.* Oxford: The Clarendon Press, 1953.
8. Feldman, J., and Feigenbaum, E. A. (eds.), *Computers and Thought.* New York: John Wiley and Sons, Inc., forthcoming 1963.
9. Green, B. F., "Computer Models of Cognitive Processes," *Psychometrika,* Vol. 26 (1961), pp. 85-91.
10. Harling, J., "Simulation Techniques in Operations Research—A Review," *Operations Research,* Vol. 6 (1958), pp. 307-319.
11. Hunt, E. B., and Hovland, C. I., "Programming a Model of Human Concept Formulation," *Proceedings of the Western Joint Computer Conference,* Vol. 19 (1961), pp. 145-155. Reprinted in *Computers and Thought,* Feldman and Feigenbaum (eds.).
12. Jeffress, L. A. (ed.), *Cerebral Mechanisms in Behavior: The Hixon Symposium.* New York: John Wiley and Sons, Inc., 1951.
13. Laslett, P. (ed.), *The Physical Basis of Mind.* Oxford: Blackwell, 1950.
14. Licklider, J. C. R., "Man-computer Symbiosis," *Institute of Radio Engineers Transactions on Human Factors in Electronics,* Vol. 1 (March 1960), pp. 4-11.
15. MacKay, D. M., "On Comparing the Brain with Machines," *The American Scientist,* Vol. 42 (1954), pp. 261-268.
16. McCulloch, W. S., "The Brain as a Computing Machine," *Electrical Engineering,* Vol. 68 (1949), pp. 492-497.
17. Precker, J. A., "Towards a Theoretical Brain-Model," *Journal of Personality,* Vol. 22 (1954), pp. 310-325.
18. Shannon, C. E., "A Chess-Playing Machine," *Scientific American,* Vol. 182 (February 1950), pp. 48-51.
19. Simon, H. A., and Newell, A., "Models: Their Uses and Limitations," *The State of the Social Sciences,* L. D. White (ed.). Chicago: University of Chicago Press, 1956, pp. 66-83.
20. Sluckin, W., *Minds and Machines.* Baltimore: Penguin Books, Pelican edition, 1960.
21. Thomson, R., and Sluckin, W., "Cybernetics and Mental Functioning," *The British Journal for the Philosophy of Science,* Vol. 3 (1953), pp. 130-146.
22. von Neumann, J., *The Computer and the Brain.* New Haven: Yale University Press, 1958.
23. Wisdom, J. O., "The Hypothesis of Cybernetics," *The British Journal for the Philosophy of Science,* Vol. 2 (1951-52), pp. 1-24.
24. Yovits, M., and Cameron, S. (eds.), *Self-Organizing Systems.* New York: Pergamon Press, 1960.

## Part II

Mental  Skills

# CHAPTER 3

# Experimental Music

LEJAREN HILLER AND
LEONARD ISAACSON

## THE AESTHETIC PROBLEM

### INTRODUCTION

Upon first hearing of the idea of computer music, a person might ask: "Why program a digital computer to generate music?" The answer to this question is not simple, since such an undertaking immediately raises fundamental questions concerning the nature of musical communication and its relation to formal musical structures. Moreover, it also raises the question of how far it is possible to express musical and aesthetic principles in forms suitable for computer processing. Lastly, it also brings up the problem of what role automation of the type exemplified by high-speed digital computers can be expected to fulfill in the creative arts.

We shall point out below that the process of musical composition can be characterized as involving a series of choices of musical elements from an essentially limitless variety of musical raw materials. Therefore, because the act of composing can be thought of as the extraction of order out of a chaotic multitude of available possibilities, it can be studied at least semiquantitatively by applying certain mathematical operations deriving from probability theory and certain general principles of analysis incorporated in a new theory of communication called *information theory*. It becomes possible, as a consequence, to apply computers to the study of those aspects of the process of composition which can be formalized in these terms.

## THE LOGIC OF MUSICAL COMPOSITION

There are five basic principles involved in musical composition which we shall consider in the present context to be of primary significance. The first principle is that the formation of a piece of music is an ordering process in which specified musical elements are selected and arranged from an infinite variety of possibilities, i.e., from *chaos*. The second principle recognizes the contribution to a musical structure not only of *order*, but also the relative lack thereof, and even, in certain extreme cases, of the absence of order, namely, *chaos*; that is to say, the degree of imposed order is itself a significant variable. The third principle is that the two most important dimensions of music upon which a greater or lesser degree of order can be imposed are pitch and time.[1] There are, of course, other necessary elements of music as ordinarily considered by the composer such as dynamic level and timbre, which also require ordering, but these will, for purposes of simplification, be considered less significant. Next, because music exists in time, the fourth principle is that memory, as well as instantaneous perception, is required in the understanding of musical structures. Lastly, as a fifth principle, it is proposed that *tonality*, a significant ordering concept, be considered the result of establishing pitch order in terms of memory recall.

The first principle, namely, that the process of musical composition involves the choice of musical elements from an essentially limitless variety of musical raw materials, has long received widespread recognition. In fact, the very name composition suggests an act of arranging, of an imposition of order, while the use of the word composer to characterize the writer of music suggests a person who assembles and builds forms. Indeed, the basic idea of composition as the extraction of *order* from *chaos* was formulated as long ago as the fourth century B.C. by Aristoxenus,[2] who remarked that: "The voice follows a natural law in its motion and does not place the intervals at random." Aristoxenus also recognized the necessity of the ordering process in both music and language when he stated that: "The order that distinguishes the melodious from the unmelodious resembles that which we find in the collocation of letters in language. For it is not every collocation but only certain collocations of any given letters that will produce a syllable."

This concept of opposing order and design to chaos has been a critical issue in musical aesthetics ever since. If we limit ourselves to current writers, we may note that Igor Stravinsky, in particular, has been most explicit in his defense of this principle. It is, in fact, the central theme of his *Poetics of Music*. Several representative passages from this book can be quoted to illustrate this point. For ex-

[1] A more generalized picture of musical structure is that of wave-form amplitude versus time. This concept lies at the root of experiments to synthesize musical structures directly on film, for example.

[2] Aristoxenus, *The Harmonics* (ed. and trans. by H. S. Macran) (New York: Oxford University Press, 1902).

ample, he remarks that: ". . . we feel [the necessity] to bring order out of chaos, to extricate the straight line of our operation from the tangle of possibilities"[3]; that: ". . . we have recourse to what we call *order* . . . order and discipline."[4] Stravinsky also defines art as the ". . . contrary of chaos. It never gives itself up to chaos without immediately finding its living works, its very existence threatened."[5] Stravinsky stresses the point that: "Tonal elements become music only by virtue of their being organized . . . so that to the gifts of nature are added the benefits of artifice."[6] Finally, he says that: ". . . to proceed by elimination—to know how to *discard* . . . that is the great technique of selection."[7]

Given, therefore, that order is imposed during musical composition, the second question immediately arises of *how much* order is imposed. Once we recognize that all composition involves the selection of certain materials out of a random environment toward order of one sort or another, we can then ask the question of how much selection is involved in any particular process, since it is obvious that all music falls somewhere between the two extremes of order and chaos and that changes in musical style involve fluctuations first toward one pole and then toward the other. Thus, "shape may, from this point of view, be regarded as a kind of stylistic 'mean' lying between the extremes of overdifferentiation and primordial homogeneity."[8] It follows from this argument, as Meyer notes,[9] that:

Weak, ambiguous shapes may perform a valuable and vital function . . . for the lack of distinct and tangible shapes and of well-articulated modes of progression is capable of arousing powerful desires for, and expectations of, clarification and improvement. This aspect of musical structure and expression is one which has unfortunately received but scant attention from music theorists, aestheticians and critics who have continually construed 'inevitability' to mean unequivocal progression. . . . Yet the fact of the matter is that some of the greatest music is great precisely because the composer has not feared to let his music tremble on the brink of chaos, thus inspiring the listener's awe, apprehension and anxiety, and, at the same time, exciting his emotions and his intellect.

[3] I. Stravinsky, *Poetics of Music* (Cambridge, Mass.: Harvard University Press, 1947), p. 5.

[4] *Ibid.*, p. 6.

[5] *Ibid.*, p. 11.

[6] *Ibid.*, pp. 23-24.

[7] *Ibid.*, p. 69.

[8] L. B. Meyer, *Emotion and Meaning in Music* (Chicago: University of Chicago Press, 1956), p. 161.

[9] *Ibid.*, p. 160.

The above passages, quoted from the recent study of musical meaning by Leonard Meyer, are a distinct contrast to discussions of the pair of opposites, order and chaos, which tend to confuse these terms with stylistic problems, if not also with problems of value. Thus, order has frequently been associated with "classicism" and its equivalents, and disorder with "romanticism" or "expressiveness." It is not necessary for our purposes to assess the *value* of order or of chaos as such, as Stravinsky does when he associates order with "the good," or as other composers such as John Cage, to cite a recent example, have attempted to do when they have set up an opposing musical aesthetic in which randomness or disorder is sought after as a desirable goal. The difficulty, obviously, is that few writers have attempted to define just what *order* is quantitatively in musical terms and have usually simply related this term in one way or another to compositional procedures which satisfy their stylistic prejudices. Moreover, few of them have ever considered it explicitly as a quantitative variable, subject to control for expressive purposes.

In considering specific examples of how ordering processes are imposed upon musical materials, we shall postulate that the most important involves choices of pitch. There are necessarily many such choices in musical composition. In the first place, one of the most fundamental is the decision to tune a scale to certain fixed pitches. The mere fact that most Western music is written for a chromatic scale tuned to even temperament is in itself a highly restrictive limitation upon random choice. The choice of a certain harmonic style imposes additional restrictions. Arguments in discussions of musical style, though seldom expressed explicitly as such, are really concerned in many ways with the question of how restrictive the selection process should be. Thus, stylistic limits in terms of pitch, for example, are easy to distinguish. Complete disorder is characterized by the random choice of any number of all possible pitches. On the other hand, complete order is characterized by the arbitrary and sole choice of some one fixed pitch.

A second basic choice process is connected with the fact that music, like language, depends upon a series of *successive* selections; in other words, that it exists in time. In fact, it is generally acknowledged that the two most fundamental dimensions of music specifically are pitch and time. The essential process of musical composition, therefore, consists of the sequential selection of a series of pitches. This process is also recognized by musicians, and again for comment, we may note that Stravinsky states that: "Music is based on temporal succession and requires alertness of memory. Consequently, music is a *chronologic* art, as painting is a *spatial* art."[10] Just as the restrictions imposed upon pitch selection lead to scales and ultimately to harmony, we find that restrictions of choice can be imposed upon the time dimension as well. This leads directly to the development of meter and rhythm and ultimately to the organization of large-scale musical structures. Moreover, the interaction of pitch selection and time-interval selection is the basis of virtually all our known procedures for musical composition involving the internal relationships tabulated by Tischler.[11]

To illustrate these points, we might consider the composition of a single melodic line, restricting our argument, as we shall throughout for the sake of simplicity, to a fixed tuning scheme, specifically, the ordinary chromatic scale. We note initially that a melodic line is a sequence of *intervals* between successive notes chosen sequentially in a time scale dictated by the choice, random or otherwise, of meter and rhythm, and that it is the sequence of *intervals* rather than of tones, or *specific pitches,* which gives a melody its characteristic profile. If a mechanism is provided whereby the successive choice of intervals can be made completely random, a random melody is produced. On the other hand, if no choice whatever is provided, the melody is a monotone. The imposition of a characteristic style between these extremes involves the choice of specific rules of melodic writing which will govern the nature of successive interval selection.

Polyphony involves the simultaneous interaction of two or more melodic lines and as such is a characteristic feature of music as distinguished from language. However, the principles of operation remain fundamentally similar, and to handle the more complex problems involved in this interaction, we require the imposition of rules of harmony and counterpoint.

In the last passage we quoted from Stravinsky's *Poetics of Music,* there is mentioned another significant issue that requires comment, namely, that "music . . . requires alertness of memory." This remark points up the fact that recognition of a musical message and, hence, the over-all organization of a musical structure depends on its existence in *time* and on comprehending it in its totality in spite of its existence in time. Musical understanding has been recognized since ancient times to involve the perception of what is going on in the immediate present, but always within the framework of what has already happened and persists in the memory. For example, Aristoxenus[12] stated that: "musical cognition implies the simultaneous

[10] Stravinsky, *op. cit.,* p. 29.
[11] H. Tischler, "The Aesthetic Experience," *The Music Review* (1956).
[12] Aristoxenus, *op. cit.,* pp. 27-30.

recognition of a permanent and a changeable element . . . for the apprehension of music depends upon these two faculties, sense perception and memory; for we must perceive the sound that is present, and remember that which is past. In no other way can we follow the phenomenon of music. . . ." St. Augustine[13] also described musical communication in these same terms when he said that listening to music depends not only on *numeri sonantes,* that is, actual music which is heard, but also upon its comparison with *numeri recordabiles,* that is, music which is remembered. This process is required in order to form a musical judgment.

The consequence of this last characteristic of musical organization is of the greatest significance, since it is at the root of our concepts and techniques of thematic repetition and development, rhythmic repetition, the need for systematic structures such as sonata form, fugue, and variation form, and, perhaps most important of all, of our ideas of tonality. Since certain experiments carried out with the Illiac involve investigation into aspects of the nature of tonality, this brings up the last point we shall consider at this stage, namely, a working definition for tonality. We shall define tonality as tonal organization based on a pitch reference point for a piece of music. A composition which uses a fixed-pitch reference point can be said to be *tonal;* if it has several such fixed reference points, it may be called *polytonal.* It is also presumably possible for the reference point to shift during the course of a composition. Lastly, if no such reference point is ascertainable, the piece can be considered *atonal.* Again, we shall not attempt to evaluate tonality as something "good" or "bad," but we shall rather treat it as a parameter to be measured and to be controlled. Moreover, if tonality in one form or another is being used to infuse coherence into a piece of music, *tones,* that is, *specific pitches, acquire significance because they are related, through specific intervals over a span of time, to a specific tonal center.* It is these long-range intervallic relationships that require memory for their recognition and which are used to build up both small- and large-scale musical structures depending upon tonal coherence as an organizational principle. It is important to separate this principle from successive interval relationships which depend much more directly only upon immediate sense perception. It is this, probably, that Aristoxenus[14] had in mind when he remarked: "Again, since intervals are not in themselves sufficient to distinguish notes—the third part of

[13] St. Augustine, *De Musica,* books I-VI (trans. by R. C. Taliaferro), (Annapolis, Md., 1939).

[14] Aristoxenus, *op. cit.,* p. 29.

our science will deal with notes [and] will consider the question of whether they are certain points of pitch, as commonly supposed, or whether they are musical functions." In spite of this early awareness of the problem, however, it is interesting to note that, historically, the concept of tonality was one of the last to be formalized in terms of conscious operating principles and can be said to be utilized consciously in its full scope perhaps only since the time of Rameau and Bach. The rules of strict counterpoint, for example, which are based largely on the compositional techniques of the Renaissance and, specifically, the sixteenth century, are almost entirely concerned with problems of successive-intervals relationships and only marginally with the question of tonality. "Sixteenth-century theorists characteristically faced the problem of chord progression as if they wore blinders that prevented them from seeing more than two chords at a time. The extent of their scope was the passage of one consonance to the next, the suspension and 'saving' of dissonances, and cadence patterns made up usually of two intervals or chords."[15] Even today, in the teaching of the theory of music, and specifically in the teaching of common practice harmony, the general problem of tonal organization is largely ignored. Basic harmony in many traditional harmony textbooks is still taught largely in terms of four-part chorale settings in the style of Bach, but with an emphasis solely on the rules of successive chord progression. It is in recognition of the lack of awareness of the necessity of utilizing logical processes which depend upon and stimulate long-range recall that music analysts such as Heinrich Schenker (1868-1935), for example, have attempted to formulate more general principles of tonality and of melodic construction in music written since 1700.

To summarize, (1) the process of musical composition requires the selection of musical materials out of a random environment. This is accomplished by a process of elimination. The extent of order imposed depends upon the nature of the restrictions imposed during the process of selection. (2) Music is organized in terms of pitch—specifically, intervals between notes—and in terms of time. Many possible interactions between these two variables are expressed in terms of traditional rules of composition. (3) Musical coherence in a musical structure depends on the exploitation of memory as well as immediate sense perception. A recognition of this principle is essential in the understanding of how proper articulation is achieved in setting up musical structures.

---

[15] C. V. Palisca, "Vincenzo Galilei's Counterpoint Treatise: A Code for the Seconda Pratica," *Journal of the American Musicological Society* (1956).

## INFORMATION THEORY

In recent years, a new scientific theory, which has received the name *information theory,* or *communication theory,* has been worked out in considerable detail, particularly in certain practical applications in the fields of telegraphy, telephony, and, in general, in problems of communication engineering. We shall now consider certain important concepts of information theory relevant to the general musical problems just reviewed and in anticipation of some of the techniques applied to generate computer music. The present discussion of information theory is abstracted primarily from two recent and authoritative books on the subject by Shannon and Weaver[16] and by Brillouin.[17]

Information theory depends upon a precise and limited definition of the word *information* which answers the question of how to define the *quantity* of information contained in a message to be transmitted. As a first step toward an answer, it is observed that for the communications engineer the technical problem is always the same, namely, to transmit "information" accurately and correctly, quite without regard to the "meaning" or "value" of the "information." It is of no concern to the engineer whether the message he transmits is nonsense or of the greatest significance. Therefore, in its current state, modern communication theory is restricted strictly to the study of the technical problems involved in transmitting a message from sender to receiver. Having accepted this limitation, we may then establish, as our second premise, that *every constraint imposed on freedom of choice immediately results in a decrease of information.* To help clarify this somewhat unusual notion, it is helpful to consider how the alphabet can be used to build up a language.[18] For this purpose, let us next introduce an additional concept of importance, namely, that we can classify communication systems roughly into three main categories: discrete, continuous, and mixed. A language consists of sequences of discrete symbols we call letters; Morse code consists of sequences of dashes and dots. Other forms of communication, however, such as paintings, photographs, or television images, are continuous. Superficially this would seem to be the case also with music. However, these continuous media are frequently converted into discrete systems, as with the half-tone reproductions of photographs and the symbolic representation of music via musical score. As

---

16 C. E. Shannon and W. Weaver, *The Mathematical Theory of Communication* (Urbana: University of Illinois Press, 1949).

17 L. Brillouin, *Science and Information Theory* (New York: Academic Press, 1956).

18 Shannon and Weaver, *op. cit.,* pp. 13-14.

Shannon and Weaver[19] define it: "A discrete channel will mean a system whereby a sequence of choices from a finite set of elementary symbols, $S_1 \ldots S_n$, can be transmitted from one point to another." Moreover, "It is not required that all possible sequences of the $S_i$ be capable of transmission on the system, certain sequences only may be allowed." Thus, to return to our consideration of language, we have twenty-seven letters in the alphabet including the space. The simplest type of sentence might be constructed by selecting letters sequentially with the choice of letters being completely random, this choice being arrived at by assigning equal probabilities to each letter of the alphabet. The result bears little resemblance to an English sentence, however, except by pure chance. The situation is one of highest potential information content: *Anything might be said.* We can, however, reduce the information content of this random language in order to achieve some higher degree of "meaning" by altering the probabilities used to select the letters of the alphabet. Thus, we can first assign probabilities based on the frequencies with which letters occur in the English language. The next step beyond this is to assign probabilities based on the frequencies with which letters occur one after the other. In this way, freedom of choice is gradually reduced, and the results begin to take on a more and more recognizable form. The decrease in information which occurs is said to be the consequence of introducing *redundancy,* which is therefore related to order as information is related to disorder. This particular example of language construction, incidentally, is worked out in some detail by Shannon and Weaver.

"Information" is thus defined as the result of "choice" and is given a statistical significance based upon probability theory. It is possible, therefore, to write algebraic expressions for the information content of a communication system. In order to do this, the information content of the system is defined purely in terms of the number of possible choices inherent in the system itself. If we know nothing about the system, in other words, if we are unable to define any of its properties, we must assume that the choice is random, which is equivalent to saying that the information content of the system is at a maximum. On the other hand, if we happen to possess some information concerning the properties of the system, it is probable that we can restrict the choice process to a situation that is less than totally random. This means that the information content of the system has been reduced, or, in other words, we might state that the information we, as observers of the system, have acquired concerning its properties has been obtained at the expense of the information content of the

19 *Ibid.,* p. 7.

system. The more information about the system we acquire, the less information the system contains. Therefore, according to Brillouin:[20]

... we consider a problem involving a certain number of possible answers, if we have no special information on the actual situation. When we happen to be in possession of some information on the problem, the number of possible answers is reduced, and complete information may even leave us with only one possible answer. Information is a function of the ratio of the number of possible answers before and after [a choice process], and we choose a logarithmic law in order to insure additivity of the information contained in independent situations.

We may now follow Brillouin[21] to define information algebraically:

Let us consider a situation in which $P_0$ different possible things might happen but with the condition that these $P_0$ possible outcomes are equally probable *a priori*. This is the initial situation, when we have no special information about the system under consideration. If we obtain more information about the problem, we may be able to specify that only one out of the $P_0$ outcomes is actually realized. *The greater the uncertainty in the initial problem is, the greater $P_0$ will be, and the larger will be the amount of information required to make the selection.* Summarizing, we have:

Initial situation: $I_0 = 0$ with $P_0$ equally probable outcomes;
Final situation: $I_1 \neq 0$, with $P_1 = 1$, i.e., one single outcome selected.
The symbol $I$ denotes information, and the definition of the information is
$$I_1 = K \ln P_0 \tag{1}$$
where $K$ is a constant and "ln" means the natural logarithm to the base $e$.
The definition of the measure of information can be generalized to cover the case when $P_0$ possibilities exist in the initial situation, while the final situation still contains $P_1$ possibilities;
Initially: $I_0 = 0$ with $P_0$ equally probable cases;
Finally: $I_1 \neq 0$ with $P_1$ equally probable cases.
In such a case we take
$$I_1 = K \ln (P_0/P_1) = K \ln P_0 - K \ln P_1 \tag{2}$$
This definition reduces to Eq. 1 when $P_1 = 1$. [Italics supplied.]

The two cases discussed by Brillouin which apply to systems narrowed down to one choice in the first case and to a number of choices in the second case depend on the assumption of equal a priori probabilities. This is the simplest condition for, as we shall see, it is also possible to have unequal a priori probabilities, probabilities conditioned by previous choices and many more complex situations.

At this point, it is crucial to note that Equations (1) and (2) bear a striking resemblance to an equation, well known to physical scien-

[20] Brillouin, *op. cit.*, Introduction.
[21] *Ibid.*, pp. 1 ff.

tists familiar with statistical mechanics, which relates thermodynamic probability and entropy. *Thermodynamic probability,* roughly, is a measure of the number of ways in which a physical system might be arranged, and *entropy* is related to this function by means of the following expression:

$$S = k \ln W \tag{3}$$

where $S$ is the entropy of the system, $W$ is the thermodynamic probability, and $k$ is Boltzmann's constant, equal to $1.36 \times 10^{-16}$ erg/ degree C. We may now relate information and entropy through the ratio $k/K$, the exact value of which depends on the units used to express information.

The question now arises as to the significance of the concept of entropy. It is essentially a measure of the degree of disorder or randomness in a physical system. Whenever a change occurs in some physical system which results in a decrease in order, the entropy of the system is said to increase. Conversely, an increase in order results in a decrease in entropy. For example, if a sample of crystalline ice is melted to form liquid water, there results an increase of entropy, because in the crystalline ice water molecules are arranged in a highly ordered lattice structure, while in liquid water these same molecules are more nearly scattered at random. Converting liquid water to steam involves yet another entropy gain, because this process causes the water molecules to become widely scattered and to move about at high velocity through a large volume of space. Scrambling an egg is an even simpler example of an entropy change. No chemical change occurs during this process, only mixing; however, after scrambling, because the resulting mixture is more random than before, the entropy content of the egg has increased. Even shuffling a sorted deck of cards can in a sense be said to bring about a change of entropy. It takes work to sort the cards into an ordered sequence, and this work can be thought of as an extraction of entropy. The problem of unscrambling an egg is also a problem involving the extraction of entropy.

In 1929, Szilard[22] recognized the close similarity between information and entropy, but the significance of this relationship was not generally recognized until it was rediscovered years later by Shannon to lead to the current development of information theory. It is now recognized that entropy is a measure of *missing information.* Thus, in the physical sciences, where all systems (except perfect crystals at absolute zero, $-273.16°C$) have positive entropy content, we find that all systems except these must of necessity be incompletely

[22] L. Szilard, "Uber die Entropieverminderung in einem thermodynamischen System bei Eingriffen intelligenter Wesen," *Z. Physik* (1929).

defined, this incompleteness being in direct relation to their entropy contents. To go back to our examples, we see that we know more about water molecules in crystalline ice than in liquid water, because, if for no other reason, we at least know more precisely where the molecules are.

We can now reproduce from Shannon and Weaver two useful propositions. Shannon and Weaver[23] note that the entropy of a communication system will be zero "if and only if all the $P_i$ but one are zero, this one having the value unity. Thus, only when we are certain of the outcome does [the entropy] vanish. Otherwise [the entropy] is positive." Moreover, "for a given [number of possible choices], [the entropy] $n$ is a maximum and equal to log $n$ when all the $P_i$ are equal, i.e., $1/n$. This is also intuitively the most uncertain situation." And lastly, "any change towards equalization of the probabilities, $P_i$, increases [the entropy]."

The definition of information as a measure of a number of choices from a random arrangement of a finite set of elements is unquestionably confusing when first met with, so it is important that it be clearly understood that by "information" we do *not* mean information in the everyday sense. "Information" in information theory is *not* the same thing as "meaning," particularly semantic meaning, or "specific knowledge about," which are definitions more nearly synonymous with the common use of the word. To clarify this point, Weaver states that:[24] "The word information in communication theory relates not so much to what you *do* say as to what you *could* say. . . . The concept of information applies not to the individual message (as the concept of meaning would) but rather to the situation as a whole."

In a similar vein, Brillouin, as previously cited, concludes:

Our definition of information is an absolute objective definition, independent of the observer. . . . The restrictions we have introduced enable us to give a quantitative definition of information and to treat information as a physically measurable quantity. . . . We define 'information' as distinct from 'knowledge' for which we have no numerical measure. . . .

Moreover, as Weaver points out:[25]

The concept of information developed in this theory at first seems disappointing and bizarre—disappointing because it has nothing to do with meaning, and bizarre because it deals not with a single message but rather with the statistical character of a whole ensemble of messages, bizarre also because in these statistical terms the two words *information* and *uncertainty* find themselves to be partners.

23 Shannon and Weaver, *op. cit.*, p. 21.
24 *Ibid.*, p. 110.
25 *Ibid.*, p. 116.

However, Weaver suggests that: "one is now, perhaps, for the first time, ready for a real theory of meaning." He attempts to set up this problem for future study by suggesting "three levels of communication," namely:[26]

Level A. How accurately can the symbols of communication be transmitted? (The technical problem.)

Level B. How precisely do the transmitted symbols convey the desired meaning? (The semantic problem.)

Level C. How effectively does the received meaning affect conduct in the desired way? (The effectiveness problem.)

In this connection, it has been stressed by Weaver that there may be a high degree of overlap between the three levels. He suggests that:[27]

A larger part of the significance [of information theory] comes from the fact that the analysis at level A discloses that this level overlaps the other levels more than one could possibly naively suspect. Thus, the theory of level A is, at least to a significant degree, also the theory of levels B and C.

Brillouin similarly recognizes two areas of investigation which lie outside current research in information theory. He points out[28] that the next problem to be defined is the problem of semantic information, i.e., whether or not a message makes sense. As noted by Brillouin, some exploratory investigations of this problem in language have apparently been carried out by Ville[29] and by Carnap and Bar-Hillel,[30] who based their work on the methods of symbolic logic, but this seems to be about the extent of current research in this area. Lastly, Brillouin recognizes the problem of "value," i.e., whether or not the message is of value to the sender or receiver. Here, he says we "invade a territory reserved for philosophy. . . . Shall we ever be able to cross this border? . . . This is for the future to decide." This is, of course, Weaver's level C, which in his estimation involves aesthetic considerations in the fine arts.[31]

26 *Ibid.*, pp. 95-96.

27 *Ibid.*, p. 98.

28 Brillouin, *op. cit.*, pp. 297 ff.

29 J. Ville, *Actualitiés sci. et ind.*, 1145:101-114, Hermann, Paris, 1951.

30 Y. Bar-Hillel and R. Carnap, "Semantic Information," *British Journal of Philosophy of Science* (1953); see also C. Cherry, *On Human Communication*, (New York: John Wiley and Sons, 1957), pp. 231-50, for a detailed discussion of his problem based on another paper by these same authors, namely: R. Carnap and Y. Bar-Hillel, "An Outline of a Theory of Semantic Information," *M.I.T., Research Lab. Electronics Tech. Rept.* 247 (1953).

31 Shannon and Weaver, *op. cit.*, p. 97.

To summarize: (1) in recent years, information theory has been applied to certain practical problems of communication engineering.[32] (2) certain authors have suggested that the concepts of information theory might well be used more generally than just in engineering problems. (3) *Information* is defined as proportional to the logarithm of the number of possible choices available when making a decision. Information is thus analogous to entropy. (4) Inasmuch as common communication systems utilize finite sets of discrete symbols, these symbols can be selected sequentially by what we will call a *stochastic process* to build up a "message." The information, or entropy, content of a communication system is at a maximum if there are the least number of restrictions upon the process of selecting successive events; specifically, the largest entropy content is obtained whenever the sequence of symbols is completely random.

## INFORMATION THEORY AND MUSIC

It is now necessary to examine how these concepts relate to the definitions of musical meaning and form previously discussed. We can start by noting that not only has Weaver suggested in general terms that information theory can be applied to the study of art, but that Pinkerton,[33] for example, has proposed that the theory might be used in studies of music. Also, fairly ambitious theoretical attempts to apply information theory to the study of music have been published by W. Meyer-Eppler[34] and A. Moles.[35] Moreover, Leonard Meyer, whose concepts were reviewed in some detail earlier in this chapter, has also recently recognized many corresponding properties between his theories of musical meaning and information theory.[36] Thus, Meyer acknowledges the equivalence between his ideas of ambiguity and precision of form and entropy variation and, secondly,

[32] In fact, it might be of interest to note that these applications have now become sufficiently extensive that a technical journal, *IRE Transactions on Information Theory,* which is devoted specifically to this subject, is now being published.

[33] R. C. Pinkerton, "Information Theory and Melody," *Scientific American,* (February, 1956).

[34] W. Meyer-Eppler, "Statistic and Psychologic Problems of Sound," *Die Reihe,* 1:55 ff.; "Informationstheorie," *Naturwissenschaften,* (1952). A review of some of Meyer-Eppler's views is also given in an article by H. Le Caine, "Electronic Music," *Proc. I.R.E.,* (1956).

[35] A. Moles, "Informationstheorie der Musik," *Nachr. Technik Fachberichte,* (1956). *Théorie de l'Information et perception esthétique,* Presses Universitaires de France, Paris, 1957; *Some Basic Aspects of an Informational Theory of Music,* unpublished manuscript; and other writings. Also private conversations between Dr. Moles and one of the present authors (L. A. H.) in Paris, June, 1957.

[36] L. B. Meyer, "Meaning in Music and Information Theory," *Journal of Aesthetics and Art Criticism,* (1957).

the importance of sequential choice processes in the building up of musical structures.

Some main points of Moles' applications of information theory to musical communication can now be summarized. Moles postulates two determining factors which permit a listener to build messages out of musical sounds, namely, *memory* and *attention,* i.e., perception. This is, of course, in accord with traditional aesthetic theory. Moles then notes that memory appears to be divided, in terms of span, into three categories: (1) instantaneous memory, (2) dated memory, and (3) undated memorization. However, it is to the problem of attention that he has directed most of his studies. He suggests that "attention" can be divided into two distinct "modes": (1) the *semantic mode* and (2) the *aesthetic mode.* The semantic mode is characterized as the "language side of music—a system of organized and standardized symbols—which can be *coded*[37]—i.e., translated into another language—the *score.*" On the other hand, the aesthetic mode "does not appeal to intellectual faculties, but to the directly sensorial ones—even sensual at the limit." Moles thus differentiates two types of structures as does Tischler and defines the term *acoustical quanta.* These quanta "make up the repertory of aesthetic symbols at a given scale of duration [and] information rate, $H_e$,—[which] can then be computed and which comes parallel to the semantic information rate, $H_s$." Moles' purpose is "to study the properties of the aesthetic message—*vs.* the semantic one, both being bound into the same sequence of acoustical sets of quanta grasped in a different manner."

One additional point made by Moles is of interest:

The fact acknowledged by many psychologists dealing with the human operator that one is unable to grasp a message of more than 10—20 bits/second,[38] (compared with the estimated maximal capacity of some hundred bits/second) implies that perception is a selection of definite symbols in the whole of the message and that these symbols, these Gestalt are not picked at random, which would simply express the utter incapacity of the listener to cope with a too original message.[39] In consequence, the structure of Music itself regarding the color, thickness and rate of originality of the musical stuff should be directly considered by the composer. This leads to the concept of "authentic composition" (Meyer-Eppler) which has recently found its way into experimental music.

[37] In relation to computers, the term 'coding' covers the process of preparing instructions for use by a computer in a language to which it can respond.

[38] A *bit* is a unit quantity of information and is a term used in digital-computer theory. (Editors' note: see fn. 2, p. 36 of this book).

[39] *I.e.,* a message with too high an entropy content.

The first point to decide, if practical musical applications are to be made for the concepts of information theory, is whether music is basically a discrete, a continuous, or a mixed communication system. We should like to propose that it is effectively a discrete system. It is thus like language, although normally more complex operationally, because in language only one symbol for an operational element is considered at a time. In music, a number of elements are normally in operation simultaneously.

There are a variety of ways in which music operates through discrete elements. Most importantly, as Helmholtz,[40] for example, has noted:

Alterations of pitch in melodies take place by intervals and not by continuous transitions. The psychological basis of this fact would seem to be the same as that which led to rhythmic subdivision periodically repeated. . . . The musical scale is as it were the divided rod, by which we measure progression in pitch, as rhythm measures progression in time. Hence, the analogy between the scale of tones and rhythm occurred to musical theoreticians of ancient as well as modern times.

We consequently find the most complete agreement among all nations that use music at all, from the earliest to the latest times, as to the separation of certain determinate degrees of tone from the possible mass of continuous gradations of sound, all of which are audible, and these degrees form the scale in which the melody moves. But in selecting the particular degrees of pitch, deviations of national taste become immediately apparent. The number of scales used by different nations and at different times is by no means small.

Almost all music notation, in fact, is based upon a definition of discrete musical elements. Thus, except possibly for such recent artifacts as some forms of electronic music (Chapter 3), we can define the basic texture of music as an assembly of discrete symbols with the few exceptions (such as continuous dynamics changes) being so simple that these are readily taken care of independently.

Secondly, restricting the number of choices should tend to increase the "meaningfulness" of messages. Thus, the most diffuse type of music is produced on the average when successive note selection is permitted to be completely random. As we shall see, music of this type is rather easily generated in a computer and *forms the basic substance from which we must fashion more characteristic structures*. Thus, we note that our operational basis is entirely in accord with Stravinsky's concepts of the logic of musical composi-

[40] H. L. M. Helmholtz, *On the Sensations of Tone,* 2nd English edition of 1885 by A. J. Ellis, based on the 4th German edition of 1877 (New York: Dover Publications, 1954), pp. 250-53.

tion discussed earlier in this chapter. Or, as noted by Helmholtz:[41] "Music alone finds an infinitely rich but totally shapeless plastic material in the tone of the human voice and artificial musical instruments which must be shaped on purely artistic principles."

Thirdly, the problem arises as to what techniques to apply to restrict successive choices if we desire to produce music less chaotic than random music. It is possible, for example, to apply statistical methods and compute transition probabilities for successive note selection based upon the analysis of some known species of music. Pinkerton worked out a simple example of how this can be done by constructing a transition-probabilities table based upon the analysis of a set of nursery tunes. Pinkerton quite correctly observed, however, that the use of such tables leads to the construction of "banal" tunes as a general rule. It is easy to see that this is bound to occur whenever a purely statistical analysis to determine mean choices is used as an aesthetic basis for computing transition probabilities. The difficulty here is an aesthetic one; if we wish to generate something besides banal music, other criteria must be sought.

In this connection, we should mention also that a similar but more thorough study has been carried out recently by Brooks, Hopkins, Neumann, and Wright.[42] Like Pinkerton, these authors subjected a sampling of simple tunes (this time hymn tunes) to statistical analysis to form transition-probability tables. However, their analysis was more elegant, since they carried out their calculations to the extent of eighth-order probabilities, i.e., to include into the calculations relationships as far as eight notes back. On the other hand, there is considerable danger in elaborating a simple eighth-order process to produce music, since aside from simple tunes such as hymn tunes, there is little music in which a fluctuation of transition probabilities from one part of a composition to another would not occur. This danger has been recognized, incidentally, by Meyer. Consequently, means are required for controlling fluctuations between randomness and order during the course of a composition.

Still another study in this same vein has been recently published by Youngblood.[43] In contrast to the above studies, Youngblood has computed sets of transition probabilities derived from the analysis of fairly complex art music. For his study, Youngblood has chosen a group of songs by Schubert, Mendelssohn, and Schumann and has compared the results obtained from the music of these three com-

[41] *Ibid.*, p. 250.
[42] F. P. Brooks, Jr., A. L. Hopkins, Jr., P. G. Neumann, and W. V. Wright, "An Experiment in Musical Composition," *IRE Trans. on Electronic Computers*, EC-6:175, 1957.
[43] J. E. Youngblood, "Style as Information," *Journal of Music Theory* (1958).

posers. He has tabulated differences as reflected in transition probabilities and information contents between the individual styles of these composers, as well as similarities which one would, of course, expect, since all three employ the same basic style of composition.

Lastly, two other recent incidents of rather simple applications of the idea of sequential-choice processes to compose music have been also reported by J. R. Pierce.[44] Thus:

J. J. Coupling has discussed stochastic composition of music in Science for Art's Sake in *Astounding Science Fiction,* Nov., 1950. [Similarly] Dr. D. Slepian of Bell experimented with stochastic composition, not using statistics but such ideas of probability as have accumulated in the minds of a group of experimenters. Thus, he had each of a group of men add to a composition after examining only one or more preceding half measures. Tape recordings of the resulting music have been played as a part of a number of talks on information theory.

Pierce himself, in collaboration with M. E. Shannon, has also worked out an example of stochastic music, this music involving common chords selected in random sequences. This particular example of stochastic music is reproduced in a recent book by Pierce.[45]

It can be seen that the various experiments to produce stochastic music thus far carried out are subject to critical limitations of one type or another. The end products, if not banal, as Pinkerton termed his results, nevertheless remain rather primitive. In designing our experiments, we were well aware of the difficulty of basing experiments utilizing these new techniques on initial operating principles which might appear on first inspection to be far removed from traditional musical procedures. An alternative procedure was to combine relevant concepts of traditional musical experience with the operating techniques derived from information theory and to take advantage of Weaver's suggestion that there is extensive overlap between the three areas of investigation relevant to information theory. In this way, we would use the stimulus provided by working with traditional music concepts in terms of new operational principles as a point of departure for formulating abstract structural bases for music synthesis.

It is interesting to note, in concluding, that attempts to apply information theory to musical problems raise in a new guise an old issue which has been a source of dispute in musical aesthetics many times in the past. It is yet another attempt to codify musical aesthetics in terms of natural law. This is, of course, an argument resorted to

[44] J. R. Pierce, letter to *Scientific American* (April 1956).
[45] J. R. Pierce, *Electrons, Waves and Messages* (Garden City: Hanover House, 1956), pp. 271-74.

by many writers ever since music was defined as an imitation of nature in ancient times. Zarlino, for example, looked "on music as an imitation of nature and endeavored to derive his teachings from natural law,"[46] i.e., in accord with Pythagorean and Platonic theory. On the other hand, Vincenzo Galilei in attacking Zarlino's teachings "considered numerical ratios irrelevant to the artist and the rules of counterpoint a product of the demands of taste, experience and aesthetic purpose."[47] More recently Helmholz remarked that:[48]

. . . to furnish a satisfactory foundation for the elementary rules of musical composition . . . we tread on new ground, which is no longer subject to physical laws alone. . . . Hence it follows—*that the system of Scales, Modes, and Harmonic Tissues does not rest solely upon inalterable natural laws, but is also, at least partly, the result of aesthetical principles, which have already changed, and will still further change, with the progressive development of humanity.* [Helmholtz's italics.]

A more subtle statement of the same basic thesis is contained in Meyer's recent book, already referred to, when he remarks[49] that three interrelated errors have continually plagued music theory, namely, *hedonism,* the philosophy that pleasure is the primary purpose of musical experience; *atomism,* which is the attempt to characterize music solely by means of its discrete elements; and *universalism,* which is "the belief that the responses obtained by experiment or otherwise are universal, natural, and necessary. This universalist approach is also related to the time-honored search for a physical quasi-acoustical explanation of musical experience—the attempt, that is, to account for musical communication in terms of vibration ratios of intervals, and the like." What effect information theory will have on this problem will be of considerable interest to watch in the future.

To summarize, music, being a nondiscursive form of communication, operates with a semantic peculiarly dependent upon technical structure as such. Therefore, the study of musical structure in terms of information theory should be a significant technique for breaking through the "semantic barrier" which seems to hamper current investigations in information theory and should perhaps also lead to an improved delineation of the aesthetic basis of musical composition. Specifically, in light of the apparent close dependence of meaning upon form in music, we suggest that Weaver's overlap, if it exists, is particularly significant in music. The aesthetic significance, or

46 O. Strunk, *Source Readings in Music History* (New York: W. W. Norton, 1959), p. 228.
47 Palisca, *op. cit.*
48 Helmholtz, *op. cit.*, pp. 250-51.
49 Meyer, *op. cit.*, p. 5.

"value," of a musical composition depends in considerable measure upon its relationship to our inner mental and emotional transitions, but this relationship is largely perceived in music through the articulation of musical forms. The articulation of musical forms can be considered the semantic content of music, and this in turn can best be understood in terms of the technical problems of musical composition. Since the articulation of musical forms is the primary problem faced by composers, it seemed most logical to start our investigation by attempting first to restate the techniques used by composers in terms both compatible with information theory and translatable into computer programs utilizing sequential-choice operations as a basis for music generation. In our investigation, as we have already noted, therefore, we first studied the traditional craft acquired by every composer, namely, counterpoint, harmony, rhythm, melodic construction, and similar basic problems. Only after results were achieved in this investigation did we feel that we could apply more experimental processes. Not unexpectedly, work of this nature soon led to speculation as to whether there exist more general principles of musical composition suitable for computer use. It is seen that in this approach we used the differentiation of internal and external relations suggested by Tischler, or alternately, the distinction between semantic and aesthetic quanta as suggested by Moles as a basic operating premise. However, we did not feel that the closer dependence of the relevant external meanings upon internal musical relationships suggested by Meyer conflicted with this experimental approach, since Meyer's analysis of musical meaning represents a broadening of these concepts rather than a departure from them.

## SOME FUTURE MUSICAL APPLICATIONS

### INTRODUCTION

It is convenient to define two general areas of interest which might be considered in applying computers to musical problems in the future. One of these we may describe as the theorist's field of interest; the other, as the composer's. The theorist analyzes music written by composers to characterize musical forms and how they operate. On the other hand, the composer is more of an empiricist who seeks out new musical forms which seem to him to be satisfactory. In attempting to suggest how various new musical projects might be started from where we have left off, we shall arbitrarily group our suggestions into these two basic categories—the first related in general to the analyst's problems, the second to the composer's.

## Applications to Music Analysis

The fundamental role of the music analyst is to verbalize specific musical problems so that aspects of musical communication can in turn be defined. In essence, the problem for the musical analyst is to find the reasons why a composer accepts or rejects musical materials, and to this end, principles of musical aesthetics such as those reviewed above have been gradually established. We have indicated, however, that much of the writing on aesthetics is not yet particularly precise—Langer's "significant form" is a case in point. We have also indicated that the investigation of specific forms, rather than general concepts, is to be preferred for the time being in seeking more precise definitions of musical concepts. This proposition follows from the argument of significant overlap of levels of communication proposed by Weaver, which we referred to above. The description of musical forms perhaps ultimately can be expressed in terms of information theory or some future equivalent, although, at the present time, application of this theory to musical analysis is perhaps still too recent to evaluate critically in any detail.

If we now tabulate various applications within this general field of interest, the following suggestions come to mind as representative examples of the large number of possible projects which might be carried out:

1. Perhaps the most obvious application of computers to musical analysis is the extension of the type of studies illustrated by the *Illiac Suite,* in which we have applied the Monte Carlo method to the problem of musical form.[50] As a consequence of coding aspects of this problem as numerical information and generating experimental results by means of a computer, a computer is made to behave as a specialized, but unbiased composing apparatus existing in a completely isolated environment, subject only to the controls and information the music analyst might wish to supply. In this application, a computer is an ideal instrument by means of which analytical ideas can be tested, since the investigator starts with certain hypotheses from which he formulates operating principles; he supplies this information to the computer; the computer then generates music based upon these principles; and the investigator then analyzes the results to further his investigation. This, of course, is essentially nothing

[50] (Editors' note: *Illiac Suite for String Quartet,* copyright under the authors' names by New Music Editions, is reproduced as the Appendix of *Experimental Music.* The *Illiac Suite* was named with reference to a high speed computer at the Digital Computer Laboratory of the University of Illinois, upon which experiments leading to the composition of the *Suite* were performed. 'Monte Carlo method' refers to a technique of obtaining approximate estimates of probability distribution characteristics by analyzing an extensive series of random numbers, according to the requirements of a given statistical problem.)

more than a standard example of experimental scientific method, but the unusual thing is that computers provide a practical experimental technique for carrying out such research in the musical field. It can reasonably be assumed that in the future the combination of these techniques with the more purely theoretical and speculative studies in the musical field, such as those by Moles, referred to above, would be profitable.

2. In addition to these more general studies, there are many specific tasks of musical analysis that could also be carried out with the aid of computers. For example, estimates of the relative degrees of order and disorder of different samples of music or different sections of given musical structures could be attempted. This is suggested since entropy seems to be a more useful variable than less well-defined concepts such as "harmonic tension." Characteristic melodic profiles for different styles could also be examined and codified. Studies of this sort would be of particular interest in musicological research, such as finding the determining characteristics of particular styles of historical interest. It is also possible that the results of such analysis could be used in a practical way to identify, to sort, and to catalogue old music—often a tedious and laborious task. Thus, for example, it might be possible to determine whether samples of music merely represent variants of one basic piece or fundamentally different pieces. With adequate analytical criteria, at least a major part of such a problem could be coded for a computer to permit automatic cross-comparisons of the samples and subsequent sorting into appropriate categories. As a specific example, at the present time we are considering a project for transcribing, sorting, and reproducing French lute music in a complete modern edition.[51] Since there is a vast quantity of this music, it has been estimated that up to ten years will be required to do the job by ordinary means. It has been suggested, however, that instruments such as the Illiac could be used to speed up the process. It should be pointed out in connection with this problem that a similar application of computers has already been made in the field of Biblical research and also in the preparation of a concordance for the new revised standard version of the Bible.[52] It has been pointed out that it took thirty years to prepare the concordance for the St. James version of the Bible, while

[51] D. Lumsden, *Un catalogue international des sources de la musique pour luth (Les lecons d'une étude des sources anglaises)*, CNRS colloque, "Le Luth et sa musique," Paris, Sept. 14, 1957; T. E. Binkley, letter to Jean Jacquot, President of CNRS, Paris, based upon comments upon Lumsden paper just referred to.

[52] A. Carpenter, "Amazing New Uses for Robot Brains," *Science Digest* (February, 1957).

for the newer Bible, the same task was carried out in nine months with the help of a computer.

It should be stressed in this connection that such a project would include the automatic conversion of old music into modern notation in score from, along with performance parts, if desired. Utilizing a computer, this older music could be worked up rather easily and after final editing could be made available in modern copy. The most efficient utilization of computers for such purposes would depend on the development of adequate scanning devices for computers which would recognize printed and even handwritten letters and numbers. At the present time, research is being carried on to produce such scanning devices. This was given recognition in a recent symposium devoted to document reading, pattern recognition, and character synthesis.[53] When these devices become generally available, it should be possible to adapt them to the scanning of musical notation. In the meanwhile, transcription of musical materials onto coded tape or punched cards is an adequate substitute technique.

Other possible practical applications in musicology might include the use of computers to realize *continuo* and figured bass in Baroque music and to complete the part writing in older music where the music has either been left incomplete or some of the parts are missing. In this last application, as a result of informed statistical style analysis, at least a highly probable realization of the missing parts could be produced.

3. Another practical application in this general area, namely, to pedagogical uses, should be mentioned. Several such applications have been suggested to the authors. Extensions of this work, such as the generation and cataloguing of such tone rows into different groups with characteristic properties, has been proposed by Robert Kelly, the author of the counterpoint method for which these tone rows are intended.[54]

The systematic generation of musical materials for teaching manuals for instrumental performance would be a second application of this type. The preparation of manuals for the guitar and the lute has also been proposed.[55] In this application, the coding would be based on guitar and lute tablature rather than standard musical notation,

[53] L. Cohn, R. A. Kirsch, L. C. Ray, and G. H. Urban, "Experimental Use of Electronic Computers in Processing Pictorial Information"; T. L. Dimond, "Devices for Reading Handwritten Characters"; A. I. Tersoff, "Automatic Registration of High-speed Character-sensing Equipment," all given at Session IX of the 1957 Eastern Joint Computer Conference, Washington, D.C., Dec. 9-13, 1957.

[54] R. Kelly, private communication.

[55] T. E. Binkley, private communication.

since tablature is in itself already a codification of the technical limitations of these instruments.

4. A final application to music analysis, we should like to mention, is the analysis of musical sounds themselves. This type of information would be particularly useful in the production of synthetic music by means of computers in conjunction with other electronic equipment. A very considerable knowledge of musical sounds and their physical constitution is, of course, available today.[56] Moreover, a large amount of information on how to process these sounds by means of electrical and electronic equipment has been built up through the development of sound-reproduction systems, broadcasting, and other commercial developments.

Musical sounds are, of course, extremely varied, and the analysis of timbre, attack, and other factors which make up these sounds becomes quite complex and is by no means completely understood. It seems possible that a computer might be useful in improving the design of sound-producing equipment in one significant way in particular. The analysis of sound could be coded as digital information, using standard techniques such as Fourier analysis and the like, and stored for computer utilization in permanent form, perhaps, on magnetic tape or equivalent high-capacity storage. Instruments such as the RCA Synthesizer might be extremely useful as primary sources for acquiring such stored information, or, alternatively, the analysis of actual sounds might be carried out in a computer by reversing the flow of information through a digital-to-analog type device.[57] Basic programs for extracting this information out of storage and building up complex sound structures could also be developed. These synthesized sound patterns could be printed out as digital results and used to process sound by means of instruments such as the Synthesizer. Or, more directly, this information could be reconverted directly to sound, using digital-to-analog conversion units.

[56] Typical books on musical acoustics are numerous and include H. L. M. Helmholtz, *On the Sensations of Tone* (New York: Dover Publications, 1954); Alexander Wood, *The Physics of Music* (Cleveland: The Sherwood Press, 1944); C. A. Culver, *Musical Acoustics,* 4th ed. (New York: McGraw-Hill, 1956); L. S. Lloyd, *Music and Sound* (New York: Oxford University Press, 1937); H. F. Olson, *Musical Engineering* (New York: McGraw-Hill, 1952).

[57] Details of the principles of operation of analog computers can be found in standard reference works. For example, I. A. Greenwood, Jr., J. V. Holdam, Jr., D. Macrae, Jr., *Electronic Instruments,* vol. 17 of the MIT Radiation Laboratory Series (New York: McGraw-Hill, 1958); G. A. Korn and T. M. Korn, *Electronic Analog Computers,* 2nd ed. (New York: McGraw-Hill, 1956). Also periodicals such as *Instruments and Automation.*

## APPLICATIONS TO MUSIC COMPOSITION

1. There are many practical problems of composition which require examination in order that the rather limited catalogue of compositional techniques thus far treated might be extended. We may note, therefore, just a few of the more urgent of these problems to illustrate the nature of what could be done: (*a*) the writing of computer programs for handling many of the traditional and contemporary harmonic practices; (*b*) the writing of more complex counterpoint programs, including programs for more contemporary counterpoint; (*c*) the correlation of elements such as rhythms and dynamics to note selection; (*d*) the use of imitation as a structural device; (*e*) the use of thematic and melodic recall and development; (*f*) the coding of factors thus far neglected, such as tempo, meter, and choice of instruments; (*g*) the writing of standard closed forms, such as variation form, fugue, song form, sonata form, etc. This last is of obvious major importance. Not only specific forms, but the more general problem of form needs to be considered here. The application of ideas such as Schenker's concept of chord prolongation and of Meyer's concept of purposeful musical motion would undoubtedly be useful in these studies, to say nothing of the possible results of analytical studies such as those proposed in the previous section. In time, it is conceivable that the handling of many elements involved in the writing of standard musical textures might be carried out relatively simply and efficiently with a computer. This would depend, of course, on the ease and precision with which these musical elements could be programmed and the information stored in sufficiently compact form. The extent to which this may become possible is, of course, a matter for speculation at present, so we can only suggest that music-writing programs might be designed to produce music efficiently by utilizing, among other things, standardized "library subroutines" for standard musical operations, much as today standard subroutines are utilized for ordinary mathematical operations. In this connection, it is worthwhile to note that the writing of the computer programs themselves may very well be made more efficient. Since the time consumed in computer programming normally requires much more time than the actual time of computation in a computer, there is intensive research today into the possibility of computers themselves generating detailed computer programs from more general sets of instructions.[58] Therefore, if these new techniques are developed, there is no reason to suppose that they could not be adapted to the coding of musical as well as mathematical problems.

[58] For example, see D. D. McCracken, *Digital Computer Programming* (New York: John Wiley and Sons, 1957), chap. 18 in particular.

2. The organization of more or less standard musical materials in relatively novel musical textures, including combinations not easy or even feasible by other means, might be carried out. Some possibilities which come readily to mind include: (a) the use of different rules or even of different styles between different voices in a polyphonic texture; (b) the inversion of rules, forbidding what is now permitted, permitting what is now forbidden; (c) the development of new rules of operation for handling musical materials, such as subjecting tone rows to complex permutations based upon the concept of these rows as arrays spaced across $12 \times 12$ unit plots of pitch versus time.

3. There might be developed sets of new organizing principles for musical elements leading to basically new musical forms. In the *Illiac Suite,* we have already provided a number of specific examples of how this can be done. The production of random musical elements, either notes, or rhythms, or scoring, is one example. This represents the opposite condition of totally organized music and, as such, becomes a formal element to be integrated into musical structures. More generally, the control of a precise degree of randomness and of the fluctuation of musical texture between order and disorder would seem to be more easily controlled by computer processing than by other means. Obviously, this development of a composing style consciously based upon this picture of musical structure could be of significance in developing an aesthetic not only related to concepts of information theory, on the one hand, but also, on the other hand, of more general significance than such relatively restricted concepts as traditional harmonic music, the tone-row technique, totally organized music, and so on. Moreover, since the codes used for the Illiac are based in part upon random-number processes, these codes permit the computer a conditional sort of "freedom of choice," this "freedom" being the equivalent of randomness. The extent of this freedom could be made to depend on how much the aesthetics of music might be expressed in the most general terms. If a large number of highly specific rules, such as the rules of strict counterpoint, are given the machine, the freedom of choice for the computer to select musical materials is quite limited. Not only is the over-all aesthetic quality highly predictable, but the specific details of the music are rarely surprising. This is equivalent to saying that the redundancy is large. However, if a computer is supplied with less restrictive rules, then neither the general aesthetic effect nor the specific musical results are necessarily so predictable. One possible consequence of this is that the composer might no longer be preoccupied with selecting specific notes of the scale, specific rhythms,

and other such details, but rather with more generalized sets of symbols, which would be used in turn for the generation and arrangement of the musical details in accord with the musical "message." This could result in a very different attitude toward specific musical details, and they might cease to have the importance we now attach to them. In fact, these details could easily be varied over wide limits within the same essential "composition," just as we now permit, to a greater or lesser extent, variability in the interpretation of music by performing musicians and yet recognize that this does not destroy the uniqueness of a musical composition. It is only fair to note, however, that if such a development were to occur, it would be a radical departure from the attitude prevailing at the present time.

Among the few experiments of this type not involving computers that seem to have been carried out recently are compositions of students of John Cage, such as Morton Feldman, who has written a composition entitled *Intersection No. 3, for Strings, Woodwinds, and Solo Cello*. In this work, Feldman permits a high degree of improvisatory choice by the performers, since the "score" is set down upon graph paper rather than in conventional notation.[59] A somewhat similar, but less extreme experiment has also recently been carried out by Gunther Schuller in a string quartet composed for the 1957 Contemporary Arts Festival at the University of Illinois.[60]

4. Another project might be the systematic study of microtone music. In the past, because of the difficulties of understanding and building systematic harmonic relationships in microtone systems such as quarter-tone music and complex tunings employing microtone intervals to secure just intonation in all keys, and performance difficulties, this field has largely been neglected. Moreover, in the few examples of microtone music we have heard, the smaller intervallic movements seem to fulfill a coloristic rather than a functional purpose. The use of quarter-tones in Bartók's *Violin Concerto* and in Julian Carillo's *Preludio a Cristobol Colombo,* to cite two examples, seem to be cases in point. With suitable sound production means, however, a systematic study of the harmonic and contrapuntal relationships in microtone music could be carried out by means of computers. Similar studies could be carried out also on unusual scales and tuning systems, or even variable tuning systems in which tunings could be changed during the course of "performance." Variable tuning, of course, is the ideal technique for securing just intonation in all keys.

[59] H. Cowell, "Current Chronicle, New York," *The Musical Quarterly* (1952).
[60] W. S. Goldthwaite, "Current Chronicle, Urbana, Illinois," *The Musical Quarterly* (1957).

5. Perhaps the most significant application of computers would be the combination of computers with synthetic electronic and tape music. This obviously is a natural and complementary combination, since with computer music we are primarily concerned with organizing musical materials, while with synthetic music we are concerned more directly with the production of sound. Certain specific rather immediate results can be predicted. In future experimentation with computer music, the advantages of being able to produce the results directly in sound as well as in score form are obvious. Not only would the results be analyzed more efficiently, but the means would be available for producing quickly and efficiently the final desired musical end result. Moreover, in view of certain of the other projects outlined above, the experimentation would no longer have to be confined to musical materials for conventional scales, tunings, and instruments.

A related application of considerable interest in this combined area of computer and electronic music would be the realization of music too difficult or too complex for performance by live performers. Not an inconsiderable amount of modern music verges on being almost too difficult to perform. Charles Ives' *Fourth Symphony,* for example, is a case in point, to say nothing of a large body of more recent works. It would seem that the threshold level of our ability to perceive complex rhythms and tonal combinations exceeds present performance capacities.

6. It should be mentioned, although not directly as a consequence of the present computer experiments, that certain mechanical aids to the composer might be effected by means of a computer. In particular, one great help would be the copying of parts from scores to eliminate what is now very tedious and time-consuming work. This could be readily accomplished once the scanning devices referred to earlier come into use. Moreover, these scanning devices could be used to read composer's written scores and convert them into sound as well as into printed parts.

7. It is also necessary to take note of one less attractive possibility, but one which must also at least be mentioned, since it is so often suggested. This is the efficient production of banal commercial music. For example, it is not difficult to conceive of programs for writing music of this sort to generate songs for juke-box consumption and similar uses, probably at a highly efficient and rapid rate. All applications of this sort, however, are nonartistic and fall outside the area of problems of aesthetic interest. Belonging in a somewhat similar category is the frequently asked question of whether synthetic Beethoven, Bartók, or Bach might also be produced by computers. The answer to this would seem to depend on the degree to

which the elements of the styles of these composers could be verbalized, i.e., coded in a form suitable for computer programming. Appropriate statistical analysis of Beethoven's music might conceivably lead to the production of synthetic average Beethoven, just as, in a sense, the application of strict counterpoint rules can yield a reasonable simulation of average sixteenth-century style, *quite independently of whether computers or normal composing techniques are employed.* The goal rather than the means appears objectionable here, however. The conscious imitation of other composers, by any means, novel or otherwise, is not a particularly stimulating artistic mission. Moreover, this type of study is, in the final analysis, a logical tautology, since it produces no information not present initially. The statistical aspect of the problem should not be permitted to obscure this point. Reduced to its extreme case, this process would revert to coding exactly the content of a specific and particular piece of music, feeding this information into a computer, and obtaining back from the computer exactly the same piece of music. It is obvious that nothing is accomplished by such an operation.

# CHAPTER 4

# The Chess Machine

### ALLEN NEWELL

The modern general-purpose computer can be characterized as the embodiment of a three-point philosophy: (1) There shall exist a way of computing anything computable; (2) The computer shall be so fast that it does not matter how complicated the way is; and (3) Man shall be so intelligent that he will be able to discern the way and instruct the computer.

Sufficient experience with the large machines has accumulated to reveal the peculiar difficulties associated with these points. There has been a growing concern over problems which violate them, and instead satisfy the condition that (1) The relevant information is inexhaustible; (2) The set of potential solutions is neither enumerable nor simply representable; (3) The processing to be accomplished is unknown until other processing is done; and (4) An acceptable solution is required within a limited time.

Most design problems, including programming a computer, are of this nature; so are the very complex information processing tasks like translating languages or abstracting scientific articles. The current arguments about thinking machines and general-purpose robots also revolve about whether computers can deal with problems of this general nature.

The problem of playing good chess certainly falls into this class of ultracomplicated problems. It is a useful type case for general discussion because the nature of the task and the complexities surrounding it are common knowledge. Further, it already has something of a history.[1]

[1] C. E. Shannon, "Programming a Computer for Playing Chess," *Phil. Mag.* (March 1950), pp. 256-75; M. Weinberg, "Mechanism in Neurosis," *American Scientist* (January 1951), pp. 74-98; P. I. Richards, "On Game Learning Machines," *Scientific Mon.* (April 1952), pp. 201-05; C. S. Strachey, "Logical or Nonmathematical Programmes," *Proc. Ass. Computing Machinery* (September 1952), pp. 46-49.

The aim of this effort, then, is to program a current computer to learn to play good chess. This is the means to understanding more about the kinds of computers, mechanisms, and programs that are necessary to handle ultracomplicated problems. The limitation to current computers provides the constant reminder that the heart of the problem lies in the limitation of resources, both memory and time. This aim would be somewhat ambitious even if all the details were available. The paper will actually be limited to presenting an over-all schema which appears feasible, and relating it to some of the critical problems which must be solved. The reference to learning expresses the conviction that the only way a machine will play good chess is to learn how. Although learning considerations have been prominent in the thinking and motivation behind the machine, attention will have to be restricted to the performance system; that is, to those features which are necessary in order to play the game. However, some of the learning potentialities implicit in the performance system will be discussed.

The work presented here represents the early phases of an attempt to actually construct such a program for the JOHNNIAC, one of Rand's high speed computers.

Before starting it is desirable to give some additional conditions of the problem. From now on the computer with program will be called the "machine," and the various parts of what it does will be called "mechanisms." The problem is not to construct a machine which can induct the rules of chess by playing it; it will be instructed concerning the legalities. Finally, the machine is only to do the job of one man; it will require an outside opponent, human or otherwise.

PROBLEMS

As everyone knows,[2] it is possible in principle to determine the optimal action for a given chess position. First compute out all continuations to the bitter end. See whether they win, lose, or draw; and then work backwards on the assumption that the opponent will always do what is best for him and you will do what is best for you.

The difficulty, of course, is that this "in principle" solution requires a rather unnerving amount of computing power, and doesn't give any clues about what to do if you don't have it. It will provide us, however, with a short checklist of problems which must be solved if the computing requirements are ever to shrink to a reasonable size.

The most striking feature of the "in principle" solution is the tremendous number of continuations. This is accounted for by both the number of new consequences that appear at each additional move

[2] J. von Neumann and O. Morgenstern, *Theory of Games and Economic Behavior,* 2nd ed. (Princeton, N.J.: Princeton University Press, 1947).

into the future, and the large number of moves required to explore to the end. This provides two problems:

1. The consequences problem, or which of the possibilities that follow from a given proposed action should be examined;
2. The horizon problem, or how far ahead to explore.

The possibility that one might stop looking at some intermediate position only raises a third problem:

3. The evaluation problem, or how to recognize a good position when you see one.

Another feature of the "in principle" solution is the identical examination of all the possible alternative actions. Despite the similarity in describing both present and future moves, it is worth while to keep distinct the actions that are actually available at a move, and from which a choice must be made; and the future consequences of these actions, which may include, among other things, limitations on the alternatives available in the future. Hence, we have:

4. The alternatives problem, or which actions are worth considering.

These four problems, consequences, horizon, evaluation, and alternatives, will be sufficient to keep us aware of the difficulties as we search for a set of mechanisms to play chess. Solutions must be found to all of them if the machine is to play good chess with reasonable resources.

## OVERVIEW

There is a common pattern to the solutions to be described here. In all of them the machine uses very partial and approximate methods. It is as if the machine consisted of a vast collection of rules of thumb. Each rule is a much oversimplified expression of how the machine should behave with respect to some particular aspect of the problem. The rules are of all kinds: chess principles to follow, measurements to make, what to do next, how to interpret rules of thumb, and so on. These are so organized that they form the necessary qualifications and additional specifications for each other. Each rule is essentially a machine program. At any particular instant the machine is under the control of some such rule, or shunting between rules under the control of a master program.

The main effort of the paper is devoted to describing how such a set of rules can be defined and organized to achieve solutions to the four problems, and thus provide a schema for a machine which puts all these pieces together to play chess. Only minor effort is devoted to indicating the detailed structure of these programs at the level of machine code.

One aspect of the underlying coding does require attention, and is dealt with at the end of the paper. The large number of rules, their complexity, and the necessity for adding new ones and modifying old ones, implies the use of a fairly extensive general-purpose language. That is, all these rules are to be given in this language or pseudo-code, as it might also be called. Hence, each use of a rule must be preceded by an interpretive step. However, a few programs suffice for using any and all of the rules that might be required in the machine.

## PRELIMINARIES

Let us start by providing the machine with a few basic facilities. Each chessman and each square of the chessboard needs a name, suitably coded into binary bits. A fixed set of addresses is set aside to hold the current position. This can be given as a list of the men with the squares they occupy, including a "zero" square if the man is off the board. The machine can accept an opponent's action by reading a punched card. This can be given as a list of the men which have been moved, along with their new locations. Thus an action involving a capture has two terms: one giving the new location of the man that captured, and a second giving the location of the captured man as the zero square, that is, off the board. The machine obtains the new position by substituting in the old one, which is already stored. It can also output its own action on a punched card.

The machine must also be equipped to answer an array of elementary questions that recur constantly, such as, "Can a given man move to a given square?" or, "What man is blocking the Queen Pawn?" Each of these questions can be answered by a straightforward and not-too-lengthy investigation of the current position. The number of actual programs needed is within reasonable bounds since the more complicated questions are combinations of the more elementary ones.

Assume, then, that the machine has these basic capabilities. They have solved none of the four problems.

## GOALS AND TACTICS

Suppose, in the midst of a game, the machine (which is White) has stored in a suitable place the following expression:

$$att(BKB, WKR).$$

The machine interprets this as: "Attack the Black King-Bishop with the White King-Rook." Attack will be considered to mean a successful attack, which in turn means that the attacking man (here, the

Rook) is capable of capturing the object of the attack (here, the Bishop) with a relative gain in material after the smoke of engagement has cleared. Thus, for a given position, the attack is either successful or not; and the machine can determine this by a sequence of those elementary programs given it earlier. Call such an expression a goal, which is either achieved or not achieved for any given position.

Now, suppose the machine were to start tracing out continuations. It could determine at each new position it arrived at whether or not the goal was achieved. If it is, the machine could stop searching. This might provide a solution to the horizon problem: have a goal and only explore continuations until a position is reached where the goal is achieved.

The machine can represent such a set of continuations as a branching net, or tree, of actions. Each action is linked by some kind of indexing to the immediately preceding action, and to each action is associated by this indexing a number of other actions that might possibly follow. Such a tree is a tactic for a given goal if it always terminates in positions that achieve that goal. Further, a tactic will always indicate a single action for the machine to take, and many actions for the opponent.

But if the machine has a goal like "attack the Black King," it is right back with the original difficulty of searching for continuations which end in checkmate. This merely indicates that in general one can hardly expect to find a tactic for a given goal. But on the other hand, one sometimes will: men do get captured and games do get won.

By some means let the machine acquire in memory a second goal, which is indexed to the first:

$$blk \ (BQ, BKB) \rightarrow att(BKB, WKR).$$

The machine interprets this as: "Block the Black Queen's ability to recapture where the Black King-Bishop is." If this ability to recapture was in fact one of the deterrents to taking the Bishop with the Rook, then achievement of this second goal could be considered as an intermediate aid to achievement of the attack. Such a goal will be called a subgoal. It may itself have subgoals, and thus the machine may acquire rather large networks of goals.

Now, instead of trying to construct a tactic for the attack goal, the machine can search for a tactic for the subgoal of blocking. Perhaps it will find one. If it cannot, then it needs either other subgoals for the attack or some subgoals for the block.

The single large search for winning positions has been replaced by two searches, each terminating the other. The machine searches for intermediate goals; it stops this search when it finds subgoals it can achieve. It determines the question of achievement by a search for particular sequences of action. This search terminates with a completed tactic, that is, when the sequences end in goal achievement.

But when to stop if the tactic search continues to be unsuccessful? The mechanism of subgoal formation operates only if the signal has been given to terminate further search for a tactic. Before discussing this, it is appropriate to consider another aspect of the total problem, which, after a twist or two, will lead back to this same decision problem.

### LIKELIHOODS

The mechanisms introduced so far have only yielded a solution to the horizon problem. For instance, they do not provide a solution for the consequences problem. It would still seem the machine would examine all branches at any given future move it arrived at. Thus, tactics might be short, but they would have very large spreads.

Suppose the machine had some other goals in its memory labeled "opponent's goals." For example, the machine might have:

$$ctl(Q5).$$

The machine interprets this as, "Control the Queen five square," and takes as a definition of achievement for the opponent that he could win an engagement if White tried to occupy the square or capture a Black man who did occupy it. If the machine considered this goal to be one of the opponent's important goals, then clearly, any opponent's action which achieved this goal would be relatively likely to occur. Or would it? It certainly depends to what degree the machine's representations of the opponent's goals correspond to the opponent's real goals or whatever other mechanisms guide his actions.

The machine must now be equipped with all the apparatus for collecting evidence, forming hypotheses, verifying them, and making inferences from them. At least in some rudimentary form these will all be required to develop and maintain a running model of the opponent's intentions.

If such a set of mechanisms were available to the machine, then, within certain limits of accuracy, it could assign likelihoods to the various alternatives by inference from the model. These likelihoods provide a solution to half the problem of consequences: how to know which consequences to examine at any position that is the opponent's move. Examine those alternatives which seem most likely.

A rather large number of mechanisms are involved. First, each action that the opponent makes must be classified as stemming from some goal or goals. Somewhere in memory let there be stored some expressions like:

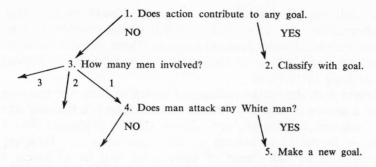

1. Does action contribute to any goal.

NO  YES

3. How many men involved?  2. Classify with goal.

3  2  1

4. Does man attack any White man?

NO  YES

5. Make a new goal.

These expressions are coded in the language spoken of earlier. The machine starts with expression 1 and interprets it. This instructs the machine to test each of the opponent's goals to see if the action contributes to it. This term is used in a narrow sense: only men who can capture contribute to an attack; only men who command the square contribute to its control. Thus, in the example, "control Queen five," the machine would determine if the action had resulted in any new man commanding the Queen five square. If the answer is yes, the machine proceeds to expression 2. When interpreted, this instructs the machine to classify the action as stemming from the goal to which it contributes. This ends the decision process. But as usual, the answer could also be no; the first rule does not suffice to classify the action. The machine then proceeds to expression 3, interprets it, and counts the number of men who changed in the current action. Finding the number to be one, which means that nothing complicated like a capture, promotion, or castle occurred, it proceeds to expression 4. The machine is now instructed to see if the man which moved can be considered as attacking some new man, and if so to read expression 5, which instructs the machine to create a new goal. Notice that this alternative is considered only if the action has failed to be consistent with any of the goals already hypothesized as accounting for the opponent's action.

So far only a mechanism for classification and possible introduction of new goals has been described. It should be remarked about this mechanism that the content of the expressions is much less important at this juncture than the general schema. Other expressions and more of them could just as well be used. Instead of describing the rest of the mechanisms needed to complete this component, it is necessary to move on to other key pieces. The undescribed elements will be constructed in the same vein. For instance, there will be expressions for obtaining likelihoods like, "How often has a goal been contributed to recently," and "High activity implies continued activity is likely."

## UTILITY

Even admitting the machine can assign likelihoods to the opponent's alternatives, this solves only the half of the problem of consequences associated with opponent's moves. There remains the other half: how to know which of the machine's possibilities to explore when searching for a tactic.

Consistent with the design philosophy emerging here, the machine will have a section of memory devoted to expressions in the language that are relevant to this problem. These will be organized into a decision net in the same fashion as the expressions for classifying opponent's actions. The object of such a net will be to assign a utility to future machine actions that could be explored in trying to complete tactics. This utility would be expected to reflect a complex of factors. The feature to note is not just the possibility of such nets, but the kinds of relevant information that now are available to be used.

The most important kind, I think, is that every man has associated with it the functions that it is performing. These associations occur by means of the goal structure. Suppose there is a subgoal that the King-Knight supports the King-Bishop; that is, can retaliate by recapturing any man that captures the Bishop. This serves as a statement that the Knight has a function to perform. Any goal whose tactic depends on moving the Knight into a new position must compete with the goal which already has the Knight supporting the Bishop. The machine can determine this by a simple search of its goals. Therefore a reasonable decision net would recommend exploration of this Knight's moves only as a last resort.

The vision of a large collection of small reasons why various moves should have low utility for exploration raises a caution. We do not want the machine to spend all its time examining the future actions of committed men; yet if it were never to do this, it could overlook real opportunities and might even gradually paralyze itself by the accumulation of commitments. The solution, of course, is the random element. The difficulty with random search in a complex environment is that in reasonable time scales, nothing will ever be discovered. Therefore, randomness should be introduced into the decision nets only in small and well controlled amounts. The machine should rarely search for combinations which sacrifice a Queen and Rook to no apparent gain only to develop a mate eight moves later.

### LEVEL OF ASPIRATION

By now we have finally returned to the decision problem stated earlier. There are devices for stopping the search for tactics if successful. There are devices for differentiating the various directions of search. These are likelihoods for the opponent's moves, and utilities for the machine's. But there exists no stop rule in the face of continued difficulties.

To find a solution we turn to a phenomenon well known in the human sciences: levels of aspiration. The fundamental reason why the machine must terminate the search is limitation of resources, in this case mostly computing time. By a level-of-aspiration type solution is meant the introduction into the machine of the limitation of resources as an explicit mechanism. That is, various expressions will exist in the machine which measure and utilize the information about the amount of resources available. Thus, the limitations will no longer function as absolute constraints; the way in which they affect the machine is partially within the machine's control.

For tactics a suitable measure, correlated with computing time but more appropriate to the task, is the likelihood of a position. As the machine explores into the future, selecting one possible action after another, the likelihoods compound like probabilities so that the ultimate likelihood diminishes as actions get further into the future, or are reached through lower-likelihood actions.

The machine sets out on a tactic search with a predetermined level of final likelihood. It gradually extends the tree of actions until each terminal position has fallen below this level; then it stops. If, now, the aggregate likelihood of reaching a position of goal achievement lies above another predetermined aspiration level, the machine considers the tactic adequate. If not, it returns to the goal structure and develops some additional goals, as described earlier.

TRANSFORMATION RULES

Nothing has yet been said about how all these subgoals are generated. The structure of the mechanism is clear; it will consist of more rules of thumb. There will exist a set of expressions in the language which function like the rules of inference in logic: they allow us to derive new expressions from old ones. They are of the form, "For a goal of type A, try a subgoal of type B." For example, "For att $(x, y)$ try def $(y)$." This expresses the fact that there is some merit to defending the men who are involved in carrying out an attack. If this transformation rule, as it is called, were applied prior to the opponent's actual attack on the attackers, this would constitute a fine example of anticipatory response.

The machine must examine its goal structure to determine the types of goals for which it requires new subgoals. It selects out those transformation rules which might be relevant; that is, where the structure of the goals in the net fits the specifications of the first part, or premise, of the transformation rule. Several possible rules may be obtained. It seems appropriate to introduce a random element to guide the final choice, since the inference expressed by the rules is rather a loose one. The weights assigned to each rule will be functions of experience, so that rules which work get chosen relatively often.

We have again arrived at a place where the important question is the actual content of these expressions. Certainly, if the rules are poor the machine will play terrible chess. Its operation will bear little relation to the objective game situation. Again, other problems are more important. No solution has yet been described for either the evaluation or the alternatives problem. It will be appropriate to consider evaluations next.

### EVALUATIONS

It may seem that somehow the evaluation problem has an implicit solution in the array of mechanisms postulated so far. The problem is to relate a position to the winning of the game. Since the machine uses intermediate goals, the problem now is to relate positions to these subgoals. It seems that the tactics do provide this relation. If a sequence of actions in a tactic results, sometime, in the given position, then the likelihood of achieving that tactic's goal from the position is known. The machine spend time computing it when generating the tactic.

The immediate difficulty with this is that it relates a position to a goal only if it occurs in that goal's tactics. This provides no evaluation for the other goals. Hence, it is only a partial solution since the problem of evaluation is assessing the relation to the ultimate goal, which is winning. In order to make playing possible, the machine has replaced the single remote goal with a large number of more immediate ones. Thus, for the machine the problem is: for any given goal, determine the likelihood of achievement from any given position.[3]

The solution exists for the special case where the position occurs in the tactic of the goal. Consider two other special cases. First, suppose the goal were achieved for the given position. It would receive a likelihood of one if we think of likelihoods as similar to probabilities. Second, suppose a goal were not achieved, had no tactic, and no subgoals. It would receive a likelihood of zero, since

[3] Throughout the paper I have very carefully used the term "likelihood," instead of "probability." The logical status of the entities referred to is not at all clear since the machine uses the measured likelihoods to determine action which in turn determines whether the move or position will ever occur; that is, what the likelihood "really" is.

its achievement rests solely with coincidence or the opponent, both equally bad bets.

These special cases provide the basis for a solution of the evaluation problem. If the machine generates goals as described, then at any instant all the terminal elements belong to one of the three special cases. This is so since the situations not covered by the special cases all involve a goal having subgoals, which means they cannot be terminal elements. The terminal evaluations are a set of boundary conditions, from which, step by step, evaluations can be assigned throughout the goal structure.

In the general case, the problem will be to compute the likelihood of a goal, given the likelihoods of all its subgoals. It is here that the relation of subgoal is given operational significance. The machine operates as if the following principle were true: if $g_1$ is a subgoal of $g_2$, then an increase in the likelihood of achievement of $g_1$ produces an increase in the likelihood of achievement of $g_2$. It interprets its experience in this light, so that contrary instances are treated as implying that the subgoal is a poor one.

The laws of combination of likelihoods must have several simple properties, mostly those implied by the principle above. Other than this, it may not make too much difference; simple linear combination may do admirably.

Although some of the details have not been enumerated, the machine now has the mechanisms for evaluation. The result is a large set of numbers, one for each goal. The reason why more combination is not required, or perhaps not even desirable, leads to the problem of alternatives.

## ALTERNATIVES

Clearly, the machine is interested only in alternatives that further its goals. Now, goals are general statements, and the tactic is the bridge provided to pass between the goals and the very particular current situation. Tactics provide actions that lead to goal achievement. At any moment, then, there are a certain number of tactics and these yield an equal number of alternatives (not necessarily all distinct), all of which are worth considering since they each further some part of the machine's goal structure.

This would be a solution to the alternatives problem if this set were always adequate. It can hardly be expected to be so at all times. For instance, right after a very unexpected move by the opponent there may be no tactics left at all.

The solution lies in more levels of aspiration, partial efforts and iteration. For each alternative, the machine computes the goal evaluations for the new position that would follow if the alternative were chosen. This yields an evaluation of each alternative's effect throughout the goal structure. Although this evaluation appears to be only one move deep, it is fundamentally grounded in the tactics, which extend much further into the future.

The decision is now made whether to make the available set suffice, or whether to return and work some more: to add and modify the goals and tactics. This is a level-of-aspiration type of decision, which will depend not only on whether the alternatives are "good enough," but also on how much time remains, and whether the move is crucial. Only if the decision is made not to explore and expand further, is the best alternative picked from the limited set and punched into the card as the machine's actual move.

The term "best alternative," is used in a very casual way. The evaluations consist of many numbers, at least one for each goal. It is clear that if a single alternative dominates all others, it should be chosen. It is also fairly clear than an alternative which achieves a very important subgoal is to be preferred over one which only increases the likelihood of a few very subordinate ones. But basically this is a multiple value situation, and in general no such simple rules can be expected to indicate a single best action. The problem for the machine is not to somehow obtain a magic formula to solve the unsolvable but to make a reasonable choice with least effort and proceed with more productive work. There are other ways to deal with the problem; for instance, include conflict as a fundamental consideration in the decision to explore further.

Thus, at each move the machine can be expected to iterate several times until it achieves an alternative that it likes, or until it runs out of time and thus loses the game by not being smart enough or lucky enough.

PERFORMANCE SCHEMA

The pieces now exist to give an over-all schema for the performance system of the chess-learning machine. This is a set of mechanisms which is sufficient to enable the machine to play chess. There is no learning in this system; it will play no better next time because it played this time. If the content of all the expressions required is appropriate, it will play good chess; if they are not, it will play very poor chess.

This performance system is highly adaptive. A goal structure peculiar to each play of the game is generated during the course of play. Tactics reflect the minute detail of the current situation. This short-run adaptability is not to be confused with learning which would permanently affect the way the machine would play in the future.

Fig. 1 gives the schema of operation. Rather than present as systematic and complete a representation as possible, attention has been given to relating the elements discussed so far. The rectangles represent the major kinds of information in the system. These may be viewed as memories. The arrows indicate processes that operate on one kind of information to produce another. The small writing by these arrows relates these processes to key words used earlier. Some of the main decisions are put in circles, since it makes the diagram easier to follow. The programs for carrying out most of these processes are the various nets, like the classification net. For the sake of clarity, these are not shown as explicit kinds of information, although they certainly occupy a large part of the computer's memory.

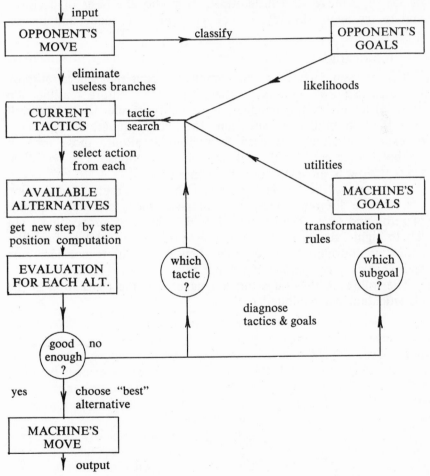

Fig. 1—Schematic flow diagram for performance system.

Each sequence always starts with an opponent's move being received (at the top). The process continues (downward) by a series of straightforward computations until the question is reached whether the situation is "good enough." This is the fundamental question. If the answer is yes, the machine has only to choose from among the available alternatives and play, thus ending the sequence (down). So far the effort spent is nominal. If, however, the answer is no, the machine proceeds to the modification and extension of the goals and tactics (to the right and up). This part is of indeterminate duration and effort and utilizes all of the complex apparatus that has been built up. Following this, the machine again attempts to produce a move (downward again). This is the fundamental cycle: to try to decide on a move with little effort, to modify the basis of decision, and to try again. Finally, of course, a move is made and the sequence stops.

LANGUAGE

It is necessary to add a few comments about the general-purpose language required to make a machine of this nature feasible. An essential feature of this language is its ability to refer to itself as well as to the "external" chess situation. The only languages of this power of expression that have been formalized at all are those used in symbolic logic such as the calculus of propositions.[4] The one illustrated below is an adaptation for computer use.

Each symbol has a binary code, although, for efficiency's sake, not all have different codes. An expression, then, is a long sequence of zeros and ones. The expression is decodable by proceeding from left to right: knowing which symbols have been found so far gives sufficient information to determine how many bits to consider next and what class of symbols it belongs to.

The following illustrates this language. It is the translation of the classification net exhibited earlier.

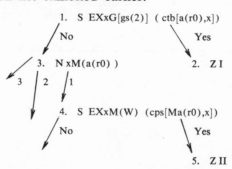

1. S EXxG[gs(2)] ( ctb[a(r0),x])
    No          Yes
3. N xM(a(r0) )          2. Z I
    3   2   1
4. S EXxM(W) (cps[Ma(r0),x])
    No          Yes
5. Z II

[4] R. Carnap, *Logical Syntax of Language* (New York: Harcourt, Brace, 1937).

*Mental Skills*    86

Consider expression 1 as an example. *In toto* it means, "Does the action contribute to any goal?" A question in the symbolic language is a sentence without its truth value. The machine interprets the missing value as an instruction to determine it; that is, to obtain the answer to the question. Expression 1, then, starts with "S" to identify itself as a sentence. (Expression 3 has an "N," and its value would be a number.) "EX $x$ G" means, "there exists an $x$ which is a goal." The "gs(2)" in parentheses gives additional specifications on the range of $x$. The machine will only search gs(2) which is the opponent's goal structure. The last parentheses contain the predicate, "contribute" symbolized by "ctb." Its arguments are first, an action, "a(r0)," the "r0" standing for relative time zero so the machine will always look at the current action; and then a goal, *"x,"* which is the variable over which the machine will search.

The machine interpretation and execution of such an expression runs along lines very similar to those used in algebraic coding schemes. The machine has programs for determining the truth or falsity of each individual predicate, here only the "ctb." Truth values are combined, with due regard for brackets, by the laws of "and," "or," and "not," depending on which occur in the expression. The machine interprets "EX" as making the sentence true if for any of the goals considered it obtains "true" for ctb.

LEARNING

The section is limited to some remarks on the requirements for learning and the potentialities for it that exist in the machine.

The large number of highly interrelated mechanisms involved in the performance of the machine indicates a major difficulty. Consider the hundreds of expressions which each determine a highly specific rule of action. How is it possible to have a set that actually fits together to produce effective chess play? The assumption that man can discern which sets will work seems rather untenable; there are too many effects and hidden consequences. Learning seems to offer a solution.

At any given time the machine has a set of expressions, which work tolerably well over some restricted range of environments. The machine generates a few extensions of or modifications to its current set. These are incorporated if their use provides an improvement in performance. The features to note about this learning process are, first, that it gradually extends the set of expressions, and second, that expressions get admitted only if they "fit in" with the others already there. Thus, given that an appropriate training sequence of games are played, the machine will grow itself a set of expressions of sufficient complexity to play good chess.

Many of the mechanisms necessary to provide this learning are already in the machine. First, it is necessary to measure the effects of one mechanism on another. The machine is already able to perform any test or measurement given by a network of expressions. All that is required is that the expressions refer to the appropriate internal parts of the machine and ask the right questions. The language is powerful enough to do this. These nets also allow diagnosis of which parts of a complex mechanism are causing the undesirable effects. Memory is needed to keep performance records, and mechanisms are needed to collect and classify these records; all of this is already possible. The possibilities for new mechanisms are limited only by the modes of expression of the language, since the specific behavior of the performance system is determined by the content of expressions. Finally, the search for new mechanisms is quite similar to obtaining subgoals for goals. That is, there would be sets of transformation rules to give the types of modifications that might prove useful for a given type of expression.

The problem of sample-size requires mention: How large a sample of experience is necessary to obtain learning? Or better: How much information about the effects of behavior is necessary to successfully modify the behavior? Chess affords a good example of this problem. It is extremely doubtful whether there is enough information in "win, lose, or draw" when referred to the whole play of the game to permit any learning at all over available time scales. There is too much behavior. For learning to take place, each play of the game must yield much more information. This is exactly what is achieved by breaking the problem into components. The unit of success is the goal. If a goal is achieved, its subgoals are reinforced; if not, they are inhibited. (Actually, what is reinforced is the transformation rule that provided the subgoal.) This is so whether the game is ultimately won or lost. Each play gives learning information about each goal that is generated. This also is true of the other kinds of structure: every tactic that is created provides information about the success or failure of tactic search rules; every opponent's action provides information about success or failure of likelihood inferences; and so on. The amount of information relevant to learning increases directly with the number of mechanisms in the chess playing machine.

CONCLUSION

"As every design engineer knows, the only difference between a good design and the actual machine is time and effort." This adage is a byword in the field of robots and thinking machines. The scheme presented here is not far from a "good design." One can estimate the man-hours necessary to draw up the detailed flow diagrams from which machine coding follows as routine chore. But this is not sufficient. These mechanisms are so complicated that it is impossible to predict whether they will work. The justification for the present article is the intent to see if *in fact* an organized collection of rules of thumb can "pull itself up by its bootstraps" and learn to play good chess.

# CHAPTER 5

# Toward Mechanical Mathematics

HAO WANG

*Abstract: Results are reported here of a rather successful attempt at proving all theorems, totalling near 400, of Principia Mathematica which are strictly in the realm of logic, viz., the restricted predicate calculus with equality. A number of other problems of the same type are discussed. It is suggested that the time is ripe for a new branch of applied logic which may be called "inferential" analysis, which treats proofs as numerical analysis does calculations. This discipline seems capable, in the not too remote future, of leading to machine proofs of difficult new theorems. An easier preparatory task is to use machines to formalize proofs of known theorems. This line of work may also lead to mechanical checks of new mathematical results comparable to the debugging of a program.*

INTRODUCTION

If we compare calculating with proving, four differences strike the eye: (1) Calculations deal with numbers; proofs, with propositions. (2) Rules of calculation are generally more exact than rules of proof. (3) Procedures of calculation are usually terminating (decidable, recursive) or can be made so by fairly well-developed methods of approximation. Procedures of proof, however, are often nonterminating (undecidable or nonrecursive, though recursively enumerable), indeed incomplete in the case of number theory or set theory, and we do not have a clear conception of approximate methods in theorem-proving. (4) We possess efficient calculating procedures, while with proofs it frequently happens that even in a decidable theory, the decision method is not practically feasible. Although short-cuts are the exception in calculations, they seem to be the rule with proofs in so far as intuition, insight, experience, and other vague and not easily imitable principles are applied. Since the proof procedures are so complex or lengthy, we simply cannot manage unless we somehow discover peculiar connections in each particular case.

Undoubtedly it is such differences that have discouraged responsible scientists from embarking on the enterprise of mechanizing significant portions of the activity of mathematical research. The writer, however, feels that the nature and the dimension of the difficulties have been misrepresented through uncontrolled speculation and exaggerated because of a lack of appreciation of the combined capabilities of mathematical logic and calculating machines.

Of the four differences, the first is taken care of either by quoting Gödel representations of expressions or by recalling the familiar fact that alphabetic information can be handled on numerical (digital) machines. The second difference has largely been removed by the achievements of mathematical logic in formalization during the past eighty years or so. Item (3) is not a difference that is essential to the task of proving theorems by machine. The immediate concern is not so much theoretical possibility as practical feasibility. Quite often a particular question in an undecidable domain is settled more easily than one in a decidable region, even mechanically. We do not and cannot set out to settle all questions of a given domain, decidable or not, when, as is usually the case, the domain includes infinitely many particular questions. In addition, it is not widely realized how large the decidable subdomains of an undecidable domain (e.g., the predicate calculus) are. Moreover, even in an undecidable area, the question of finding a proof for a proposition known to be a theorem, or formalizing a sketch into a detailed proof, is decidable theoretically. The state of affairs arising from the Gödel incompleteness is even less relevant to the sort of work envisaged here. The purpose here is at most to prove mathematical theorems of the usual kind, e.g., as exemplified by treatises on number theory, yet not a single "garden-variety" theorem of number theory has been found unprovable in the current axiom system of number theory. The concept of approximate proofs, though undeniably of a kind other than approximations in numerical calculations, is not incapable of more exact formulation in terms of, say, sketches of and gradual improvements toward a correct proof.

The last difference is perhaps the most fundamental. It is, however, easy to exaggerate the degree of complexity which is necessary, partly because abstract estimates are hardly realistic, partly because so far little attention has been paid to the question of choosing more efficient alternative procedures. There will soon be occasion to give illustrations to these two causes of exaggeration. The problem of introducing intuition and experience into machines is a bit slippery. Suffice it to say for the moment, however, that we have not realized that much of our basic strategies in searching for proofs is mechanizable, because we had little reason to be articulate on such matters until large, fast machines became available. We are in fact faced with a challenge to devise methods of buying originality with plodding, now that we are in possession of slaves which are such persistent plodders. In the more advanced areas of mathematics, we are not likely to succeed in making the machine imitate the man entirely. Instead of being discouraged by this, however, one should view it as a forceful reason for experimenting with mechanical mathematics. The human inability to command precisely any great mass of details sets an intrinsic limitation on the kind of thing that is done in mathematics and the manner in which it is done. The superiority of machines in this respect indicates that machines, while following the broad outline of paths drawn up by man, might yield surprising new results by making many new turns which man is not accustomed to taking.

It seems, therefore, that the general domain of algorithmic analysis can now begin to be enriched by the inclusion of inferential analysis as a younger companion to the fairly well established but still rapidly developing leg of numerical analysis.

The writer began to speculate on such possibilities in 1953, when he first came into contact with calculating machines. These vague thoughts were afterwards appended to a paper on Turing machines.[1] Undoubtedly many people have given thought to such questions. As far as the writer is aware, works more or less in this area include Burks-Warren-Wright,[2] Collins,[3] Davis,[4] Newell-Shaw-Simon, Gelernter.[5] Of these, the most extensively explained and most widely known is perhaps that of Newell-Shaw-Simon, a series of reports and articles[6] written since 1956. Their work is also most immediately

[1] H. Wang, "A Variant to Turing's Theory of Computing Machines," *Journal ACM,* **4,** 88-92 (January 1957).

[2] A. W. Burks, D. W. Warren, and J. B. Wright, "An Analysis of a Logical Machine Using Parenthesis-Free Notation," *Mathematical Tables and Other Aids to Computation,* **8,** 53-57 (April 1954).

[3] G. E. Collins, "Tarski's Decision Method for Elementary Algebra," *Proceedings of the Summer Institute of Symbolic Logic at Cornell University,* p. 64 (1957).

[4] M. Davis, "A Program for Presburger's Algorithm," *ibid.,* p. 215.

[5] H. Gelernter, "Theorem Proving by Machine," *ibid.,* p. 305.

[6] For example, A. Newell, J. C. Shaw, and H. A. Simon, "Empirical Explorations of the Logic Theory Machine: A Case Study in Heuristics," Report P-951, Rand Corporation, March, 1957, 48 pp.

relevant to the results to be reported in this paper. It will, therefore, not be out of place if we indicate the basic differences in the respective approaches and the specific advances beyond their work.

They report[7] that their program LT on JOHNNIAC was given the task of proving the first 52 theorems of *Principia Mathematica* of Whitehead and Russell: "Of the 52 theorems, proofs were found for a total 38. . . . In 14 cases LT failed to find a proof. Most of these unsuccessful attempts were terminated by time or space limitations. One of these 14 theorems we know LT cannot prove, and one other we believe it cannot prove." They also give as examples that a proof for *2.45 was found in 12 minutes and a report of failure to prove *2.31 was given after 23 minutes.

The writer wrote three programs last summer on an IBM 704. The first program provides a proof-decision procedure for the propositional calculus which prints out a proof or a disproof according as the given proposition is a theorem or not. It was found that the whole list of over 200 theorems of the first five chapters of *Principia Mathematica* were proved within about 37 minutes, and 12/13 of the time is used for read-in and print-out, so that the actual proving time for over 200 theorems was less than 3 minutes. The 52 theorems chosen by Newell-Shaw-Simon are among the easier ones and were proved in less than 5 minutes (or less than ½ minute if not counting input-output time.) In particular, *2.45 was proved in about 3 seconds and *2.31 in about 6 seconds. The proofs for these two theorems and some more complex proofs are reproduced in Appendix I as they were printed out on the machine.

The other two programs deal with problems not considered by Newell-Shaw-Simon in their published works. The second program instructs the machine to form propositions of the propositional calculus from basic symbols and select nontrivial theorems. The speed was such that about 14,000 propositions were formed and tested in one hour, storing on tape about 1000 theorems. The result was disappointing in so far as too few theorems were excluded as being trivial, because the principles of triviality actually included in the program were too crude.

The third program was meant as part of a larger program for the whole predicate calculus with equality which the writer did not have time to complete during 1958. The predicate calculus with equality takes up the next five chapters of *Principia Mathematica* with a total of over 150 theorems. The third program as it stands can find and print out proofs for about 85 per cent of these theorems in about an hour. The writer believes that slight modifications in the program

[7] *Ibid.*, p. 26 and p. 28.

will enable the machine to prove all these theorems within 80 minutes or so. The full program, as envisaged, will be needed only when we come to propositions of the predicate calculus which are much harder to prove or disprove than those in this part of *Principia Mathematica*.

It will naturally be objected that the comparison with the program of Newell-Shaw-Simon is unfair, since the approaches are basically different. The writer realizes this but cannot help feeling, all the same, that the comparison reveals a fundamental inadequacy in their approach. There is no need to kill a chicken with a butcher's knife. Yet the net impression is that Newell-Shaw-Simon failed even to kill the chicken with their butcher's knife. They do not wish to use standard algorithms such as the method of truth tables,[8] because "these procedures do not produce a proof in the meaning of Whitehead and Russell. One can invent 'automatic' procedures for producing proofs, and we will look at one briefly later, but these turn out to require computing times of the orders of thousands of years for the proof of *2.45." It is, however, hard to see why the proof of *2.45 produced by the algorithms to be described in this paper is less acceptable as a proof, yet the computing time for proving *2.45 is less than ¼ second by this algorithm. To argue the superiority of "heuristic" over algorithmic methods by choosing a particularly inefficient algorithm seems hardly just.

The word "heuristic" is said to be synonymous with "the art of discovery," yet often seems to mean nothing else than a partial method which offers no guarantees of solving a given problem. This ambiguity endows the word with some emotive meaning that could be misleading in further scientific endeavors. The familiar and less inspiring word "strategy" might fare better.

While the discussions by Newell-Shaw-Simon are highly suggestive, the writer prefers to avoid hypothetical considerations when possible. Even though one could illustrate how much more effective partial strategies can be if we had only a very dreadful general algorithm, it would appear desirable to postpone such considerations till we encounter a more realistic case where there is no general algorithm or no efficient general algorithm, e.g., in the whole predicate calculus or in number theory. As the interest is presumably in seeing how well a particular procedure can enable us to prove theorems on a machine, it would seem preferable to spend more effort on choosing the more efficient methods rather than on enunciating more or less familiar generalities. And it is felt that an emphasis on mathematical logic is unavoidable, because it is just as essential

[8] *Ibid.,* p. 8 and p. 10.

in this area as numerical analysis is for solving large sets of simultaneous numerical equations.

The logical methods used in this paper are along the general line of cut-free formalisms of the predicate calculus initiated by Herbrand[9] and Gentzen.[10] Ideas of Hilbert-Bernays,[11] Dreben,[12] Beth,[13] Hintikka,[14] Schütte[15] and many others on these formulations, as well as some from standard decision methods for subdomains of the predicate calculus presented by Church[16] and Quine,[17] are borrowed. The special formulations actually used seem to contain a few minor new features which facilitate the use on machines. Roughly speaking, a complete proof procedure for the predicate calculus with equality is given which becomes a proof-decision procedure when the proposition to be proved or disproved falls within the domain of the propositional calculus or that of the "$AE$ predicate calculus" [those propositions which can be transformed into a form in which no existential quantifier governs any universal quantifier] which includes the monadic predicate calculus as a subdomain.

The treatment of the predicate calculus by Herbrand and Gentzen enables us to get rid of every "Umweg" (cut or *modus ponens*) so that we obtain a cut-free calculus in which, roughly speaking, for every proof each of the steps is no more complex than the conclusion. This naturally suggests that, given any formula in the predicate calculus, we can examine all the less complex formulae and decide whether it is provable. The reason that this does not yield a decision procedure for the whole predicate calculus is a rule of contraction which enables us to get rid of a repetition of the same formula. As a result, in searching for a proof or a disproof, we may fail in some case because we can get no proof, no matter how many repetitions we introduce. In such a case, the procedure can never come to an end, although we do not know this at any finite stage. While this situation does not preclude completeness, it does exclude a decision procedure.

[9] J. Herbrand, *Recherches sur la Théorie de la Démonstration*, Traveaux de la Société des Sciences de Varsovie, No. 33, 1930, 128 pp.

[10] G. Gentzen, "Untersuchungen über das Logische Schliessen," *Math. Zeitschrift*, **39**, 176-210, 405-431 (1934-35).

[11] D. Hilbert and P. Bernays, *Grundlagen der Mathematik*, vol. II, Berlin, 1939.

[12] B. Dreben, "On the Completeness of Quantification Theory," *Proc. Nat. Acad. Sci. U.S.A.*, **38**, 1047-1052 (1952).

[13] E. W. Beth, *La Crise de la Raison et la Logique*, Paris et Louvain, 1957.

[14] K. J. J. Hintikka, "Two Papers on Symbolic Logic," *Acta Philos. Fennica*, **8**, 7-55 (1955).

[15] K. Schütte, "Ein System des Verknupfenden Schliessens," *Archiv f. Math. Logik u. Grundlagenforschung*, **2**, 375-387 (1955).

[16] A. Church, *Introduction to Mathematical Logic, I*. Princeton, 1956.

[17] W. V. Quine, *Methods of Logic*, New York, 1950.

Now if we are interested in decidable subdomains of the predicate calculus, we can usually give suitable reformulations in which the rule of contraction no longer occurs. A particularly simple case is the propositional calculus. Here we can get a simple system which is both a complete proof procedure and a complete decision procedure. The completeness receives a very direct proof, and as a decision procedure it has an advantage over usual procedures in that if the proposition tested is provable, we obtain a proof of it directly from the test. This procedure is coded in Program I. Moreover, it is possible to extend the system for the propositional calculus to get a proof-decision procedure for the $AE$ predicate calculus, which has the remarkable feature that in searching for a proof for a given proposition in the "miniscope" form, we almost never need to introduce any premise which is longer than its conclusion. This procedure is coded in Program III.

A rather surprising discovery, which tends to indicate our general ignorance of the extensive range of decidable subdomains, is the absence of any theorem of the predicate calculus in *Principia* which does not fall within the simple decidable subdomain of the $AE$ predicate calculus. More exactly, there is a systematic procedure of separating variables to bring a proposition into the "miniscope" form, a term to be explained below. Since this procedure can be easily carried out by hand or by machine for these particular theorems, every theorem in the predicate calculus part of *Principia* can then be proved by the fairly simple Program III.

Originally the writer's interest was in formalizing proofs in more advanced domains, such as number theory and differential calculus. It soon became clear that for this purpose a pretty thorough mechanization of the underlying logic is a necessary preliminary step. Now that this part is near completion, the writer will discuss in the concluding part of this paper some further possibilities that he considers to be not too remote.

## THE PROPOSITIONAL CALCULUS (SYSTEM P)

Since we are concerned with practical feasibility, it is preferable to use more logical connectives to begin with when we wish actually to apply the procedure to concrete cases. For this purpose we use the five usual logical constants $\sim$ (not), & (conjunction), v (disjunction), $\supset$ (implication), $\equiv$ (biconditional), with their usual interpretations.

A propositional letter $P$, $Q$, $R$, $M$ or $N$, et cetera, is a formula (and an "atomic formula"). If $\phi$, $\psi$ are formulae, then $\sim \phi$, $\phi$ & $\psi$, $\phi$ v $\psi$, $\phi \supset \psi$, $\phi \equiv \psi$ are formulae. If $\pi$, $\rho$ are strings of formulae (each, in particular, might be an empty string or a single formula) and $\phi$ is a formula, then $\pi, \phi, \rho$ is a string and $\pi \to \rho$ is a sequent which, intuitively speaking, is true if and only if either some formula in the string $\pi$ (the "antecedent") is false or some formula in the string $\rho$ (the "consequent") is true, i.e., the conjunction of all formulae in the antecedent implies the disjunction of all formulae in the consequent.

There are eleven rules of derivation. An initial rule states that a sequent with only atomic formulae (proposition letters) is a theorem if and only if a same formula occurs on both sides of the arrow. There are two rules for each of the five truth functions—one introducing it into the antecedent, one introducing it into the consequent. One need only reflect on the intuitive meaning of the truth functions and the arrow sign to be convinced that these rules are indeed correct. Later on, a proof will be given of their completeness, i.e., all intuitively valid sequents are provable, and of their consistency, i.e., all provable sequents are intuitively valid.

*P1.* Initial rule: if $\lambda$, $\zeta$ are strings of atomic formulae, then $\lambda \to \zeta$ is a
   theorem if some atomic formula occurs on both sides of the arrow.

In the ten rules listed below, $\lambda$ and $\zeta$ are always strings (possibly empty) of atomic formulae. As a proof procedure in the usual sense, each proof begins with a finite set of cases of *P1* and continues with successive consequences obtained by the other rules. As will be explained below, a proof looks like a tree structure growing in the wrong direction. We shall, however, be chiefly interested in doing the steps backwards, thereby incorporating the process of searching for a proof.

*P2a.* Rule $\to \sim$: If $\phi, \zeta \to \lambda, \rho$, then $\zeta \to \lambda, \sim \phi, \rho$.
*P2b.* Rule $\sim \to$: If $\lambda, \rho \to \pi, \phi$, then $\lambda, \sim \phi, \rho \to \pi$.
*P3a.* Rule $\to$ &: If $\zeta \to \lambda, \phi, \rho$ and $\zeta \to \lambda, \psi, \rho$, then $\zeta \to \lambda, \phi \,\&\, \psi, \rho$.
*P3b.* Rule & $\to$: If $\lambda, \phi, \psi, \rho \to \pi$, then $\lambda, \phi \,\&\, \psi, \rho \to \pi$.
*P4a.* Rule $\to$ v: If $\zeta \to \lambda, \phi, \psi, \rho$, then $\zeta \to \lambda, \phi \lor \psi, \rho$.
*P4b.* Rule v $\to$: If $\lambda, \phi, \rho \to \pi$ and $\lambda, \psi, \rho \to \pi$, then $\lambda, \phi \lor \psi, \rho \to \pi$.
*P5a.* Rule $\to \supset$: If $\zeta, \phi \to \lambda, \psi, \rho$, then $\zeta \to \lambda, \phi \supset \psi, \rho$.
*P5b.* Rule $\supset \to$: If $\lambda, \psi, \rho \to \pi$ and $\lambda, \rho \to \pi, \phi$, then $\lambda, \phi \supset \psi, \rho \to \pi$.
*P6a.* Rule $\to \equiv$: If $\phi, \zeta \to \lambda, \psi, \rho$ and $\psi, \zeta \to \lambda, \phi, \rho$, then $\zeta \to \lambda,$
      $\phi \equiv \psi, \rho$.
*P6b.* Rule $\equiv \to$: If $\phi, \psi, \lambda, \rho \to \pi$ and $\lambda, \rho \to \pi, \phi, \psi$, then $\lambda, \phi \equiv \psi,$
      $\rho \to \pi$.

The rules are so designed that given any sequent, we can find the first logical connective, i.e., the leftmost symbol in the whole sequent that is a connective, and apply the appropriate rule to eliminate it, thereby resulting in one or two premises which, taken together, are equivalent to the conclusion. This process can be repeated until we reach a finite set of sequents with atomic formulae only. Each connective-free sequent can then be tested for being a theorem or not, by the initial rule. If all of them are theorems, then the original sequent is a theorem and we obtain a proof; otherwise we get a counterexample and a disproof. Some simple examples will make this clear.

For example, given any theorem of *Principia*, we can automatically prefix an arrow to it and apply the rules to look for a proof. When the main connective is $\supset$, it is simpler, though not necessary, to replace the main connective by an arrow and proceed. For example:

*2.45.  $\vdash\ :\sim (P \vee Q) \cdot \supset \cdot \sim P,$
*5.21:  $\vdash\ :\sim P\ \&\sim Q \cdot \supset \cdot P \equiv Q$

can be rewritten and proved as follows.

| | |
|---|---|
| *2.45    $\sim (P \vee Q) \to\ \sim P$ | (1) |
|      (1) $\to\ \sim P, P \vee Q$ | (2) |
|      (2) $P \to P \vee Q$ | (3) |
|      (3) $P \to P, Q$ | |
|         VALID | |

QED

| | |
|---|---|
| *5.21.    $\to\ \sim P\ \&\sim Q \cdot \supset \cdot P \equiv Q$ | (1) |
|      (1) $\sim P\ \&\sim Q \to P \equiv Q$ | (2) |
|      (2) $\sim P, \sim Q \to P \equiv Q$ | (3) |
|      (3) $\sim Q \to P \equiv Q, P$ | (4) |
|      (4) $\to P \equiv Q, P, Q$ | (5) |
|      (5) $P \to Q, P, Q$ | |
|         VALID | |
|      (5) $Q \to P, P, Q$ | |
|         VALID | |

QED

These proofs should be self-explanatory. They are essentially the same as the proofs printed out by the machine, except that certain notational changes are made both to make the coding easier and to avoid symbols not available on the machine printer. The reader may wish to read the next section, which explains these changes, and then compare these with more examples of actual print-outs reproduced in Appendix I. It is believed that these concrete examples will greatly assist the understanding of the procedure if the reader is not familiar with mathematical logic.

PROGRAM 1 : THE PROPOSITIONAL CALCULUS *P*

There is very little in the program which is not straightforward. To reserve the dot for other purposes and to separate the numbering from the rest, we write, for example, 2*45/ instead of *2.45.

*Toward Mechanical Mathematics*     99

For the other symbols, we use the following dictionary:

| | |
|---|---|
| $-$ | $\rightarrow$ |
| $B$ | $\equiv$ |
| $C$ | $\&$ |
| $D$ | v |
| $F$ | $\sim$ |
| $I$ | $\supset$ |

Moreover, we use a modified Polish notation by putting, for example, $CFP \cdot FQ$ instead of $\sim P \& \sim Q$. By putting the connective at the beginning, we can more easily search for it. The use of dots for grouping makes it easier to determine the two halves governed by a binary connective. The reader will have no difficulty in remembering these notational changes if he compares the examples *2.45 and *5.21 with the corresponding proofs in the new notation given in Appendix I.

With the longer examples in Appendix I, the reader will observe that the numbers on the right serve to identify the lines, while the numbers on the left serve to identify the conclusions for which the numbered lines are premises. Essentially each proof is a tree structure. Since we have to arrange the lines in a one-dimensional array, there is a choice among various possible arrangements. The one chosen can be seen from the example 4*45 given in Appendix I. The tree structure would be:

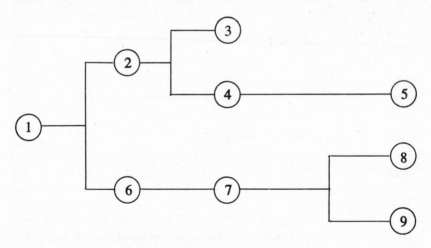

and the one-dimensional arrangement we use is:
(1), (1,2), (2,3), (2,4), (4,5), (1,6), (6,7), (7,8), (7,9).

The whole program has about 1000 lines. The length of the sequents to be tested is deliberately confined to 72 symbols, so that each sequent can be presented by a single punched card. Although this restriction can be removed, it makes the coding considerably easier and gives ample room for handling the problems on hand. Thus, for instance, the longest theorem of the propositional calculus in *Principia*, 5*24, has only 36 symbols. When presented with any punched card, the program enables the machine to proceed as follows.

Copy the card into the reserved core storage COL1 to COL72 (72 addresses in all) in the standard *BCD* notation, i.e., a conventional way of representing symbols by numbers, one symbol in each address. Append the number 1 at the last address, viz., COL72. Search for the arrow sign. If it does not occur, then the line is regarded as ordinary prose, printed out without comment, and the machine begins to study the next card. In particular, the machine stops if the card is blank. If the arrow sign occurs, then the machine marks all symbols before the arrow sign as negative and proceeds to find the earliest logical connective. According as it is *F*, *C*, *D*, *I*, or *B*, the machine turns to *RTNF*, *RTNC*, *RTND*, *RTNI*, or *RTNB*. In each case the proper rule is applied according as whether the connective is before or after the arrow.

After COL1 to COL72, 144 addresses are reserved for getting the one or two premises. As soon as the premises are found according to the proper rule, the original line is printed out and the first premise is shifted into COL1 to COL72 and gets the next number for its identification. If there is a second premise, it has to be shifted away to the idle section and wait for its turn. When the line in COL1 to COL72 contains no more logical connectives, the machine goes to a COMPARE routine to determine whether there is a formula occurring on both sides of the arrow or not and prints the line out with VALID or NOT VALID appended to it. Then it looks at the idle section to see whether any earlier premises remain there. If there is, it moves the first line there into COL1 to COL72 and pushes the remaining lines of the idle section to fill up the vacancy. If there is no more line left then it concludes, according as whether all final sequents are valid, that the original sequent is a theorem (QED) or not (NOT VALID). When the original sequent is not a theorem, the conjunction of all the resulting nonvalid connective-free sequents amounts to a conjunctive normal form of the original sequent.

PROGRAM II: SELECTING THEOREMS IN THE PROPOSITIONAL CALCULUS

A natural question to ask is "Even though the machine can prove theorems, can it select the theorems to be proved?" A very crude experiment in this direction was made with some quite preliminary results. These will be reported here, not for their intrinsic interest, but for suggesting further attempts on the same line. The motive is quite simple: by including suitable principles of triviality, the machine will only select and print out less trivial theorems. These may in turn suggest further principles of triviality; after a certain stage, one would either arrive at essentially the same theorems which have already been discovered and considered interesting, or find in addition a whole crowd of interesting new theorems.

The machine has been made to form a fairly large class of propositions (sequents) and select "interesting" theorems from them. At first all formulae with exactly six symbols containing at most the propositional letters $P$, $Q$, $R$ are formed. These come to a total of 651, of which 289 are basic and 362 are trivial variants obtainable from the basic ones by renaming the propositional letters. Of these 651 formulae, 107 are theorems. The program enables the machine to form these formulae, one stored in a single address, and select the theorems among them, prefixing each with a minus sign.

Then the machine is to form all non-ordered pairs $(\pi, \rho)$ such that either $\pi$ or $\rho$ is (or both are) among the 289 basic formulae and for each pair $(\pi, \rho)$, the sequents $\pi \to \rho$, $\rho \to \pi$, $\pi, \rho \to$, $\to \pi, \rho$, when neither $\pi$ nor $\rho$ is a theorem. When $\pi$, $\rho$ are the same, $\pi \to \rho$, $\rho \to \pi$, $\to \pi, \rho$ are not formed. These are the only principles of triviality which are included. Thus, the distinction between basic formulae and their variants avoids the necessity of testing that large number of sequents which are variants of other tested sequents. Moreover, if either $\pi$ or $\rho$ is a theorem, $\to \pi, \rho$ is a trivial consequence, $\pi, \rho \to$ is a trivial variant of $\rho$, $\rho \to$ or $\pi$, $\pi \to$; moreover, then $\pi \to \rho$ (or $\rho \to \pi$) is a theorem, and a trivial one, if and only if $\rho$ (or $\pi$) is a theorem. Finally, $\pi \to \pi$ is always a trivial theorem.

It was at first thought that these crude principles are sufficient to cut down the number of theorems to a degree that only a reasonably small number of theorems remain. It turns out that there are still too many theorems. The number of theorems printed out after running the machine for a few hours is so formidable that the writer has not even attempted to analyze the mass of data obtained. The number of sequents to be formed is about half a million, of which about $1/14$ are theorems. To carry out the whole experiment would take about 40 machine hours.

The reason that such a high portion are theorems comes from the bias in our way of forming sequents. If we view an arbitrary truth table with $n$ proposition letters, since the table gives a theorem if and only if every row gets the value true and there are $2^n$ rows, the probability of getting a theorem is $\frac{1}{2}^{(2^n)}$. In particular, if $n = 3$, we get $1/256$. However, the sequents $\pi \to \rho$, $\rho \to \pi$, $\to \pi, \rho$, $\pi, \rho \to$ amount to $\sim \pi \vee \rho$, $\sim \rho \vee \pi$, $\rho \vee \pi$, $\sim \rho \vee \sim \pi$, each being a disjunction. Hence, the probability is much higher since the probability of $\phi \vee \psi$ being true is $\frac{3}{4}$. If there are three proposition letters, we have $(\frac{3}{4})^8$, which is about $1/10$. The few crude principles of triviality, besides cutting the sequents to be tested to less than half, reduces this percentage to about $1/14$. It would seem clear that other principles of triviality should be devised and included, e.g. if $\pi \equiv \rho$ and $\Theta(\pi)$ are theorems, $\Theta(\rho)$ is a trivial consequence which need not be recorded.

## COMPLETENESS AND CONSISTENCY OF THE SYSTEMS $P$ AND $P_s$

A simple proof for the consistency and the completeness of the system $P$ is possible. Since, however, such considerations become even shorter if fewer truth-functional connectives are used, a system $P_s$ based on the single-stroke| connective (not both) will be given and proved consistent, as well as complete. It will then be clear that a similar proof applies to the system $P$.

The formulae and sequents are specified as with the system $P$ except that the clause on forming new formulae is now merely: if $\phi$ and $\psi$ are formulae, then $\phi \mid \psi$ is a formula. There are only three rules:

$P_s1$. Same as $P1$.

If $\lambda$ and $\zeta$ are (possibly empty) strings of atomic formulae, then:

$P_s2$. If $\phi, \psi, \zeta \rightarrow \lambda, \rho$, then $\zeta \rightarrow \lambda, \phi \mid \psi, \rho$.

$P_s3$. If $\lambda, \rho \rightarrow \pi, \phi$ and $\lambda, \rho \rightarrow \pi, \psi$,
   then $\lambda, \phi \mid \psi, \rho \rightarrow \pi$.

*Consistency of the Calculus $P_s$.* One can easily verify by the intended interpretation of the arrow and the comma that $P_s1$ is valid, i.e., true in every interpretation of the atomic formulae, that the conclusion of $P_s2$ is valid if (and only if) its premise is, and that the conclusion of $P_s3$ is valid if (and only if) its premises are. It follows that every provable sequent is valid.

*Completeness of the Calculus $P_s$.* We wish to prove that every sequent, if valid, is provable. Given any sequent, we find the earliest non-atomic formula, if any, in the antecedent, and apply $P_s3$ in reverse direction, thereby obtaining two premises, each with less occurrences of $\mid$. If there is no $\mid$ in the antecedent, we find the earliest, if any, occurrence of $\mid$ in the consequent and apply $P_s2$ in reverse direction. We then repeat the same procedure with the results thus obtained. This process will be continued with each sequent until $\mid$ no longer occurs. Since there are only finitely many occurrences of $\mid$ in each sequent, this process always comes to an end and then we have a finite class of sequents in which only atomic formulae occur. Now the original sequent is valid if and only if every sequent in the class is. But a sequent with only atomic formulae is valid if and only if it is a case of $P_s1$, and we can decide effectively in each case whether this is so. Hence, the calculus is complete and we have a decision procedure for provability which yields automatically a proof for each provable sequent.

It is convenient, though not necessary, to add the equality sign $=$ before introducing quantifiers. This procedure serves to stress the fact that equality is more elementary than quantifiers, even though customarily quantifiers are presented prior to equality. The changes needed to reach this system from the system $P$ are rather slight. Variables $X$, $Y, Z, S, T, U, V, W$, et cetera, are now taken as terms, and the domain of atomic formulae are extended to include all expressions of the form $\alpha = \beta$ when $\alpha$ and $\beta$ are terms.

The only additional rules necessary for equality are an extension of the initial rule $P1$ so that in addition to the rules $P1$ to $P6b$ of the system $P$, we now have: If $\lambda$, $\zeta$ are strings (possibly empty) of atomic formulae, then:

$P7$. $\lambda \rightarrow \zeta$ is a theorem if there is a term $\alpha$ such that $\alpha = \alpha$ occurs in $\zeta$.

$P8$. $\lambda \rightarrow \zeta$ is a theorem if $\alpha = \beta$ occurs in $\lambda$ and $\lambda \rightarrow \zeta'$ is a theorem, where $\zeta'$ is obtained from $\zeta$ by substituting $\alpha$ (or $\beta$) for some or all occurrences of $\beta$ (or $\alpha$).

It is quite easy to extend Program I to obtain a program for the system $P_e$. The writer, however, did not write a separate program for $P_e$ but includes such a program as a part in Program III. This part enables the machine to proceed exactly as in Program I except that, in testing whether a sequent of atomic formulae is a theorem, the machine does not stop if the sequent is not a theorem by the initial rule $P1$ but proceeds to determine whether the sequent can be shown to be a theorem by using the additional initial rules $P7$ and $P8$. To distinguish sequents of atomic formulae which are valid truth-functionally from those which become valid only after applying $P7$ or $P8$, the former case is marked with VA only, while the latter case is marked in addition by $=$. Examples of print-outs are given in Appendix III.

The longish example *13.3 is included to make a minor point. It has been suggested that it would be interesting if the machine discovers mistakes in *Principia*. This example may be said to reveal a mistake in *Principia* in the following sense. The authors of *Principia* proved this theorem by using *10.13 and *10.221 from the predicate calculus. From the discussion attached to the proof of this theorem, it seems clear that the authors considered this as a theorem which presupposes tne predicate calculus. Yet in the proof printed out by the machine, no appeal to anything beyond the system $P$, i.e., no appeal even to the additional rules $P7$ and $P8$ is made. This is revealed by the fact that all the sequents of atomic formulae, viz., lines 6, 10, 14, 18, 24, 28, 32, 36 in the proof, are marked with VA without that additional $=$ sign. At first the writer thought this indicates a mistake in the program. An examination of the theorem shows, however, that *13.3 is indeed a theorem of the propositional calculus. In fact, Program I alone would yield essentially the same proof.

## PRELIMINARIES TO THE PREDICATE CALCULUS

Thus far an attempt has been made to avoid heavy technicalities from symbolic logic. A few more exact definitions seem necessary, however, when one comes to the predicate calculus.

Formulae, terms, and sequents of the full predicate calculus are specified as follows. Basic symbols are $=$ ; the five truth-functional connectives; the quantification symbols for "all" and "some"; proposition letters $P, Q, R$, et cetera; predicate letters $G, H, J, K$, et cetera; variables $X, Y, Z$, et cetera; function symbols $f, g, h$, et cetera; numerals $1, 2, \ldots , 9$, et cetera; dots or parentheses for grouping. Terms are: (i) a variable is a term; (ii) a numeral is a term; (iii) if $\alpha, \beta$, et cetera are terms and $\sigma$ a function symbol, then $\sigma \alpha, \sigma \alpha \beta$, et cetera, are terms. A variable or a numeral is a simple term; other terms are composite. The five truth-functional connectives and two quantification symbols are called logical constants. Atomic formulae are: (i) proposition letters; (ii) $\alpha = \beta$, when $\alpha, \beta$ are terms; (iii) $G \alpha, H \alpha \beta$, et cetera, where $\alpha, \beta$, et cetera are terms. Formulae are: (i) atomic formulae are formulae; (ii) if $\phi, \psi$ are formulae, $\sim \phi, \phi \vee \psi, \phi \supset \psi$, $\phi \equiv \psi, \phi \& \psi, (E \alpha)\phi, (\alpha)\phi$ are formulae, where $\alpha$ is a variable. A string may be empty or a single formula, and if $\pi, \rho$ are nonempty strings $\pi, \rho$ is a string. Given any two strings $\pi$ and $\rho, \pi \rightarrow \rho$ is a sequent.

Intuitively the scope of a logical constant is clear. In mechanical terms, the method of finding the scope of a logical constant in a given formula depends on the notation. According to the notation actually chosen for the machine, $\phi \vee \psi, \phi \& \psi, \phi \supset \psi, \phi \equiv \psi$ are written as $D\phi - \psi, C\phi - \psi, I\phi - \psi, B\phi - \psi$, with the blank filled in by a string of dots whose number is one larger than the longest string in $\phi$ and $\psi$ except that no dot is used when both $\phi$ and $\psi$ are proposition letters. Given a sequent, the scope of a logical constant $\Gamma$ standing at the beginning of a whole formula in the sequent is the entire formula minus $\Gamma$. If $\Gamma$ is singulary, that is, $\sim$ or one of the two quantification symbols, the scope of the next logical constant $\Gamma'$ in the formula, if any, is the whole remaining part of the formula minus $\Gamma'$. If $\Gamma$ is binary, then its scope breaks into two parts at the longest string of dots in the scope and each part, if containing a logical constant at all, must begin with one, say $\Gamma'$, whose scope is the whole part minus $\Gamma'$. This gives a mechanizable inductive definition of the scope of every logical constant

*Toward Mechanical Mathematics* 105

in any sequent. A logical constant $\Gamma$ is said to "govern" a logical constant $\Gamma'$, if $\Gamma'$ falls within the scope of $\Gamma$.

To avoid the explicit use of the prenex normal form, i.e., the form in which all quantifiers in a formula stand at its beginning, it is desirable to introduce, after Herbrand,[18] the sign of every quantifier in a sequent. Two simple preliminary operations will be performed on a given sequent before calculating the signs of the quantifiers in it. First, distinct quantifiers are to get distinct variables, even when one quantifier does not govern the other; moreover, the free variables in the sequent are not used as variables attached to explicit quantifiers. This simplifies the elimination of quantifiers afterwards. Second, all occurrences of $\equiv$ which govern any quantifiers at all are eliminated by either of two simple equivalences: $\phi \equiv \psi$ if and only if $(\phi \,\&\, \psi) \vee (\sim \phi \,\&\, \sim \psi)$, or, alternatively, $(\sim \phi \vee \psi) \,\&\, (\sim \psi \,\phi)$.

The positive and negative parts of any formula in the sequent are defined thus: (i) (an occurrence of) $\phi$ is a positive part of (the same occurrence of) $\phi$; (ii) if $\phi$ is a positive (a negative) part of $\psi$, then $\phi$ is a negative (a positive) part of $\sim \psi$; (iii) if $\phi$ is a positive (a negative) part of $\psi$ or of $\chi$ then $\phi$ is a positive (a negative) part of $\psi \vee \chi$; (iv) similarly with $\phi$ and $\psi \,\&\, \chi$; (v) if $\phi$ is a positive (a negative) part of $\psi$, then $\phi$ is a positive (a negative) part of $(\alpha)\psi$; (vi) similarly with $\phi$ and $(E\alpha)\psi$; (vii) if $\phi$ is a positive (a negative) part of $\psi$, then $\phi$ is a positive (a negative) part of $\chi \supset \psi$, and a negative (a positive) part of $\psi \supset \chi$. Any formula $\phi$ in a sequent is a positive or negative part of the sequent according as (i) it is a positive (a negative) part of a whole formula in the consequent (the antecedent), or (ii) it is a negative (a positive) part of a whole formula in the consequent (the antecedent). Any quantifier $(\alpha)$ with the scope $\phi$ in a given sequent is positive (negative) in the sequent if and only if $(\alpha)\,\phi$ is a positive (a negative) part of the sequent; $(E\alpha)$ is positive (negative) if and only if $(E\alpha)\,\phi$ is a negative (a positive) part of the sequent; the different occurrences of a same free variable $\alpha$ in the sequent also make up a positive quantifier (as if $(\alpha)$ were put at the head of the whole sequent).

This involved definition can be illustrated by an example:

Ex.0. $(X) (GXY \supset (\sim GXX \,\&\, (EZ) HXZ))$,
$(W) ((\sim GWW \,\&\, (EU) HWU) \supset GWY)$
$\to \sim (EV)HYV$.

In this example, $(X)$ is a negative quantifier, $(EZ)$ is positive, $(W)$ is negative, $(EU)$ is negative, $(EV)$ is positive. For instance, $(EU) HWU$ is positive in $\sim GWW \,\&\, (EU) HWU$ but negative in $(\sim GWW \,\&\, (EU) HWU) \supset GWY$ and $(W)(\sim GWW \,\&\, (EU) HWU) \supset GWY)$, which is

18 Herbrand, *op. cit.*, p. 21.

a whole formula in the antecedent. Hence, $(EU) HWU$ is positive in the sequent. Hence, $(EU)$ is negative. The assignment of signs to quantifiers coincides with the result in a prenex normal form; positive for universal, negative for existential. Thus, one prenex form of Ex. 0 is:

$(Y) (EX) (EW) (EU) (Z) (V)\{[(GXY \supset$
$(\sim GXX \& HXZ))$
$\&((\sim GWW \& HWU) \supset GWY)] \supset \sim HYV\}.$

Another useful but involved concept is "miniscope" forms of a formula of the predicate calculus. It is in a sense the opposite of the prenex form, which generally gives every quantifier the maximum scope. Since the interweaving of quantifiers and variables is the main factor determining the complexity of a formula of the predicate calculus, it is not hard to see that separating variables and reducing the ranges of quantifiers may help to simplify the problem of determining whether a formula is a theorem. The unfortunate part is that sometimes it can be a very complicated process to get a formula into the miniscope form.

It is easier to explain the notion for a formula in which $\equiv$ and $\supset$ no longer occur (say, eliminated by usual definitions) so that the only truth-functional connectives are $\sim$, $\&$, $\mathbf{v}$. Such a formula is said to be in the miniscope form if and only if: (i) an atomic formula $\phi$ is in the miniscope form; (ii) if $\phi$ in $(\alpha)\phi$ (or $(E\alpha)\phi$) is a disjunction (a conjunction) of formulae, each of which is in the miniscope form and either contains $\alpha$ or contains no free variable at all, then $(\alpha)\phi$ (or $(E\alpha)\phi$) is in the miniscope form; (iii) if $\phi$ and $\psi$ are in the miniscope form, so are $\sim \phi$, $\phi \mathbf{v} \psi$, $\phi \& \psi$; (iv) if $\phi$ in $(\alpha)\phi$ (or $(E\alpha)\phi$) begins with $(E\beta)$ (or $(\beta)$) and is in the miniscope form, so is $(\alpha)\phi$ (or $(E\alpha)\phi$); (v) a formula beginning with a string of quantifiers of the same kind is in the miniscope form if every formula obtained by permuting these quantifiers and then dropping the first, is in the miniscope form. One procedure for bringing a formula into the miniscope form is explained in detail by Quine.[19] In what follows, only parts of Quine's procedure will be used and explained, the machine will follow quite different procedures if the formulae in a given sequent are not easily brought into the miniscope form.

### THE SYSTEM $Qp$ AND THE $AE$ PREDICATE CALCULUS

A specially simple decision procedure is available for many of those sequents not containing function symbols in which each formula is in the miniscope form and in the $AE$ form, i.e., no positive quantifier is governed by a negative quantifier. The procedure can be extended by two preliminary steps and described as follows.

[19] Quine, *op. cit.*, pp. 101-107.

*Step 1*. Bring every formula into the miniscope form and at the same time apply the truth-functional rules *P2-P6b*, whenever possible. In general, we obtain a finite set of sequents which all are theorems if and only if the original sequent is.

*Step 2*. Test each sequent and decide whether it is in the *AE* form. If this is so for all the sequents, then they and the original sequent all fall within the *AE* predicate calculus, and we proceed to decide each sequent by continuing with Step 3. If this is not so for some sequent, then the original sequent does not belong to the *AE* predicate calculus and has to be treated by appealing to a richer system *Q* to be described below.

*Step 3*. For a sequent in the *AE* predicate calculus, drop all quantifiers and replace all the variables attached to negative quantifiers by numerals, one numeral for each quantifier. The resulting sequent contains no more quantifiers.

*Step 4*. Apply the truth-functional rules to obtain a finite set of sequents which contain no more logical constants. Test each sequent by the initial rules and retain only the non-valid ones.

*Step 5*. List all the variables and numerals occurring in this last set of sequents of atomic formulae, make all possible substitutions of the variables for the numerals in the sequents, (substitute $X$ for the numerals if no variables occur) and test each time whether the resulting sequents are all valid. The initial sequent of Step 3 is a theorem if there is a substitution which makes all the sequents in the finite set theorems.

*Step 6*. The original sequent is a theorem if all the sequents obtained by Step 1 are theorems by Steps 3 to 5.

This completes the description of *Qp*. It is possible to formulate this system more formally, as derived from the basic system $P_e$, by adding additional explicit rules. But the result would be rather lengthy and a bit artificial. Since the above less explicit formulation conforms to the general theoretical requirements of a formal system, we shall not give a formally more pleasing description.

### PROGRAM III: THE *AE* PREDICATE CALCULUS

This program was originally intended to embody the procedure *Qp*. But the preliminary part of bringing a formula into the miniscope form has not been debugged. It is now clear that just for the purpose of proving all the theorems of the predicate calculus in *Principia*, it is not necessary to include all the rules for bringing a formula into a miniscope form. Indeed, only about 5 per cent of the theorems need such rules at all, and only rather simple ones.

There are, however, a few other differences between Program III and the procedure described above. Instead of eliminating all quantifiers at once according to their signs, quantifiers are treated on the same basis as the truth-functional connectives with two rules for each. If $\lambda$ and $\zeta$ are (possibly empty) strings of atomic formulae and i is a new numeral, $v$ is a new variable:

Rule $\rightarrow \forall$: If $\zeta \rightarrow \lambda, \phi\, v, \pi$, then $\zeta \rightarrow \lambda, (\alpha)\, \phi\, \alpha, \pi$.

Rule $\rightarrow \exists$: If $\zeta \rightarrow \lambda, \phi\, i, \pi$, then $\zeta \rightarrow \lambda, (E\,\alpha)\, \phi\, \alpha, \pi$.

Rule $\forall \rightarrow$: If $\lambda, \phi\, i, \rho \rightarrow \pi$, then $\lambda, (\alpha)\, \phi\, \alpha, \rho \rightarrow \pi$.

Rule $\exists \rightarrow$: If $\lambda, \phi\, v, \rho \rightarrow \pi$, then $\lambda, (E\,\alpha)\, \phi\, \alpha, \rho \rightarrow \pi$

These rules make for uniformity in the whole procedure except that precaution should be taken that the same quantifier, when recurring at different places on account of truth-functional reductions, should still be replaced by the same variables or numerals, although when the replacement is by a numeral, the difference is not vital. When this precaution is not taken, it can happen that certain theorems of the *AE* predicate calculus do not get proofs. This in fact happened with Program III, which failed to yield proofs for *10.3, *10.51, *10.55, *10.56, *11.37, *11.52, *11.521, *11.61, for no other reason than this.

A less serious defect in Program III is that truth-functional reductions are not always made as often as possible before eliminating quantifiers. This has the defect that several separate problems are sometimes treated as one whole problem and the running time required for getting a proof becomes unnecessarily long. In four special cases, viz., *10.22, *10.29, *10.42, *10.43, this defect in fact results in the failure to get a proof, even though a proof for each can be found by Program III, if all possible truth-functional reductions are made before eliminating quantifiers. Both this and the preceding defects of Program III can easily be amended. The reason for dwelling so long on them is to illustrate how machines can assist mathematical research in revealing theoretical defects in preliminary formulations of general procedures.

Since the present methods do not use axioms and definitions, the axioms and definitions of *Principia* are rewritten as theorems. The resulting augmented list of theorems in *Principia* (*9 to *13) from the predicate calculus with equality, has a total number of 158 members. Of these, 139 can be proved by Program III as it stands, although some of them require unnecessarily long running time, e.g., *11.21 and *11.24. If we make the few minor modifications mentioned above, the running time for all becomes reasonably short and the 12 theorems listed in the last two paragraphs become provable. Altogether there are only 7 of the 158 theorems which stand in need of some preliminary simple steps to get the formulae into the miniscope form: *11.31, *11.391, *11.41, *11.57, *11.59, *11.7, *11.71. The rules needed to take care of these cases are three:

(i)   Replace $(\alpha)\, (\phi\, \alpha\, \& \, \psi\, \alpha)$ by $(\alpha)\, \phi\, \alpha\, \& \, (\alpha)\, \psi\, \alpha$.

(ii)  Replace $(E\alpha)(\phi \alpha \vee \alpha)$ by $(E\alpha) \phi \alpha \vee (E \alpha) \psi \alpha.$

(iii) Replace $(\alpha) (\chi \alpha \supset (\phi \alpha \mathbin{\&} \psi \alpha))$ by

$$(\alpha) (\chi \alpha \supset \phi \alpha) \mathbin{\&} (\alpha) (\chi \alpha \supset \psi \alpha).$$

Hence, to summarize, Program III can be somewhat modified to prove all the 158 theorems of *Principia*, with the modified program doing the following. Given a sequent, see whether the rules (i) (ii), (iii) are applicable and apply them if so. Then make all truth-functional simplifications by the rules *P2-P6b*. This in general yields a finite set of sequents. If every one is in the *AE* form and either contains no more than one positive quantifier or is in the miniscope form, then the original sequent is often decidable by the method; otherwise it is beyond the capacity of the method. If the former is the case, proceed to decide each sequent either by eliminating all quantifiers at once, as in Step 3 of the preceding section, or by mixing the application of the rules *P2-P6b* with the rules $\rightarrow \vee$, $\rightarrow \exists$, $\forall \rightarrow$, $\exists \rightarrow$. Finally, use Steps 4 and 5 of the preceding section.

## CONCLUSIONS

The original aim of the writer was to take mathematical textbooks such as Landau on the number system,[20] Hardy-Wright on number theory,[21] Hardy on the calculus,[22] Veblen-Young on projective geometry,[23] the volumes by Bourbaki, as outlines and to make the machine formalize all the proofs (fill in the gaps). The purpose of this paper is to report work done recently on the underlying logic, as a preliminary to that project.

The restricted objective has been met by a running program for the propositional calculus and a considerable portion of the predicate calculus. Methods for dealing with the whole predicate calculus by machine have been described fairly exactly. A summary of results and a comparison with previous work in this field were given in the introductory section and will not be repeated here.

The writer sees the main interest of the work reported here, not so much in getting a few specific results which in some ways are stronger than expected (e.g., the fast speed attained and the relatively small storage needed), as in illustrating the great potentiality of machines in an apparently wide area of research and development. Various problems of the same type come to mind.

Decision procedures for the intuitionistic and modal propositional

[20] E. Landau, *Grundlagen der Analysis*, Leipzig, 1930.

[21] G. H. Hardy and E. M. Wright, *Introduction to the Theory of Numbers*, Oxford, 1954.

[22] G. H. Hardy, *A Course of Pure Mathematics*, various editions.

[23] O. Veblen and J. W. Young, *Projective Geometry*, 1910.

calculi are available but often too lengthy to be done by hand.[24] It seems possible and desirable to code these procedures in a manner similar to the classical systems of logic. The intuitionistic predicate calculus with its decidable subdomains, such as all those propositions which are in the prenex form, may also be susceptible to analogous treatment. Since the efficiency of the proof-decision procedure in Program I depends on the elimination of *modus ponens* (rule of detachment), a related question of logic is to devise cut-free systems for various partial and alternative systems of the propositional calculus.

A good deal of work has been spent in constructing various systems of the propositional calculus and of modal logic. The questions of completeness and independence are often settled by methods which are largely mechanizable and even of no great complexity. This suggests that many of the results in this area, such as those reported by Prior,[25] can be obtained by mechanical means. Given a system, in order to determine the independence and completeness (i.e., non-independence of all axioms of some given complete system) of its axioms, we may simultaneously grind out proofs and matrices used for independence proofs and stop when we have either obtained a derivation or a matrix that establishes the independence of the formula under consideration. It is true that Linial and Post[26] have proved the undecidability of this class of problems so that we cannot be sure that we can always settle the particular question in each case. Nonetheless, we may expect this procedure to work in a large number of cases. The only practical difficulty is that, in grinding out proofs, the rules of *modus ponens* makes the matter rather unwieldy. When equivalent cut-free formulations are available, this mechanical aid to such simple mathematical research would become more feasible. Alternatively, the strategies devised by Newell-Shaw-Simon may find here a less wasteful place of application.

A mathematically more interesting project is to have machines develop some easy number theory. Here there are two possible alternative approaches: use quantifiers or avoid quantifiers. It is known in mathematical logic that ordinary number theory can be developed largely without appeal to quantifiers. Thus, from the discussions in the body of the paper, it is clear that quantifiers serve essentially to replace an indeterminate class of function symbols. In number theory, these function symbols can usually be replaced by specific function symbols introduced by recursive definitions. Since these are

[24] See, e.g., G. Kreisel and H. Putnam, "Ein Unableitbarsbeweismethode," *Arkiv f. Math. Logik u. Grundlagenforschung,* **3,** 74-78 (1957).

[25] A. N. Prior, *Formal Logic,* Oxford, 1954.

[26] S. Linial and E. L. Post, "Recursive Unsolvability of Axioms Problems of the Propositional Calculus," *Bull. Am. Math. Soc.,* **55,** 50 (1949).

more specific and often intuitively more familiar, it seems quite plausible that avoiding quantifiers would be an advantage. On the other hand, it may be better to use existential quantifiers but avoid mixing quantifiers of both kinds ("all" and "some"), since that is the main source of the complexity of the predicate calculus.

If one wishes to prove that the square root of 2 is not a rational number, this can be stated in the free-variable form as: $2Y^2 \neq X^2$, and a proof can be written out without use of quantifiers. On the other hand, if one wishes to prove that there are infinitely many primes, it seems natural to state the theorem as:

$(EX)$ $(Y < X \ \& \ X$ is a prime$)$.

Essentially, the usual proof gives us a simple recursive function $f$, such that

$Y < fY \ \& \ fY$ is a prime

is true. But before we get the proof and the required function, it is convenient to use the quantifier $(EX)$ which serves to express the problem that a yet unknown function is being sought for.

In this connection, it may be of interest to make a few general remarks on the nature of expansive features in different proof procedures. The attractive feature of the system $P$ as a proof procedure is that, given a sequent, all the lines in a proof for it are essentially parts of the sequent. As a result, the task of searching for a proof is restricted in advance so that, at least in theory, we can always decide whether a proof exists or not. This contrasts sharply with those proof procedures for the propositional calculus which make use of the *modus ponens*. There, given $q$, we wish to search for $p$, such that $p$ and $p \supset q$ are theorems. There is no restriction on the length and complexity of $p$. The cut-free formulation achieves a method such that for every proof by the expansive method there is a corresponding proof in this method without expansion, and vice versa.

Since there is no decision procedure for the predicate calculus or current number theory, it follows that expansive features cannot be eliminated entirely from these disciplines. The cut-free formulation for the predicate calculus concentrates the expansive feature in one type of situation: viz., a conclusion $(EX) \ FX$ may come from $F1$ or $F2$ or et cetera. The method $Q$ given above further throws together all such expansions for a given sequent to be proved or disproved at the end of the process. These devices have the advantage that, for more efficient partial methods or strategies, one may direct the search mainly to one specific region which contains the chief source of expansion.

If number theory is developed with no appeal to quantifiers, the above type of expansion is avoided. It is not possible, however, to avoid in general another type of expansion. Thus we can conclude $X=Y$ from $fX=fY$, but given $X$ and $Y$, there are in general infinitely many candidates for the function $f$, so that trying to find an $f$ which leads to $X=Y$ through $fX=fY$ is an expansive procedure. So much for different expansive features.

Other possibilities are set theory and the theory of functions. In these cases, it seems desirable to use a many-sorted predicate calculus[27] as the underlying logic. While this is in theory not necessary, it will presumably make for higher efficiency.

As is well known, all standard formal systems can be formulated within the framework of the predicate calculus. In general, if a theorem $p$ is derived from the axioms $A_1, \cdots, A_n$, then the sequent $A_1, \cdots, A_n \to p$ is a theorem of the predicate calculus. In particular, if a system with finitely many axioms is inconsistent, the negation of the conjunction of all its axioms is a theorem of the predicate calculus. (The restriction on finitely many axioms is, incidentally, not essential since in most cases we can reformulate a formal system to use only finitely many axioms, with substantially the same theorems.) Specker has proved[28] that Quine's *New Foundations* plus the axiom of choice is inconsistent. Hence, the negation of the conjunction of these (finitely many) axioms is a theorem of the predicate calculus. If a sufficiently efficient program for the predicate calculus on a sufficiently large machine yields, unaided, a proof of this, we would be encouraged to try to see whether the system without the axiom of choice might also be inconsistent. If a system is indeed inconsistent, then there would be a chance that a proof of this fact can be achieved first by a machine.

So far little is said about specific strategies. In number theory, we are often faced with the problem of choosing a formula to make induction on. Here an obvious strategy would be to try first to use as the induction formula the whole conclusion, and then the various subformulae of the conclusion to be established. When faced with a conclusion $(EX)FX$, it seems usually advantageous to try terms occurring elsewhere in the known part of the proof, or their variants, in order to find $\alpha$ such that $F\alpha$. Polya's book[29] contains various suggestions on strategies for developing number theory which will presumably be useful when one gets deeper into the project of mechanizing number theory. Efficient auxiliary procedures such as the one already mentioned by Dunham-Fridshal-Sward for the propositional calculus will undoubtedly be of use in shortening running time, when

[27] See, e.g., Church, *op. cit.*, p. 339.
[28] E. P. Specker, "The Axiom of Choice in Quine's New Foundations for Mathematical Logic," *Proc. Nat. Acad. Sci. U.S.A.* **39,** 972-975 (1953).
[29] G. Polya, *Mathematics and Plausible Reasoning*, Oxford, 1954.

one tries to formalize proofs or prove theorems in more advanced domains.

While formalizing known or conjectured proofs and proving new theorems are intimately related, it is reasonable to suppose that the first type of problem is much easier for the machine. That is why the writer believes that machines may become of practical use more quickly for mathematical research, not by proving new theorems, but by formalizing and checking outlines of proofs. This proof formalization could be developed, say, from textbooks to detailed formulations more rigorous than *Principia,* from technical papers to textbooks, or from abstracts to technical papers.

The selection of interesting conjectures or theorems and useful definitions is less easily mechanizable. For example, Program II described above gives only very crude results. It should be of interest to try to get better results along the same line. In more advanced domains, however, the question seems to have a complexity of a different order.

If we use a machine to grind out a large mass of proofs, then there seems to be some mechanical test as to the importance and centrality of concepts and theorems. If a same theorem or a same expression occurs frequently, then we may wish to consider the theorem interesting or introduce a definition for the expression. This is, however, a rather slippery criterion. The finite number of proofs printed out at a given time may form a class that is determined on the ground of some formal characteristic of an accidental nature. Unless there is some acceptable norm in advance for ordering the proofs to be obtained, one can hardly justify in this way the claim that certain theorems are interesting.

A more stable criterion may be this: A formula which is short but can be proved only by long proofs is a "deep" theorem. A short expression which is equivalent only to very long expressions is a "rich" concept.

In the normal situations, of course, we have less restricted objective guidance. There is a fixed body of concepts and theorems which is for good reasons regarded as of special interest (the "archive of mathematical knowledge built up by the cumulative effort of the human intellect"). For such a body it is theoretically possible to select important theorems and concepts mechanically, as well as to find elegant alternative proofs. However, even in this case, one is looking backwards. It is not easy to find a forward-looking mechanizable criterion for mathematical centrality. For example, the nice criterion of ranges of application is hard to render articulate.

In one special kind of mathematics, one discipline is developed from another. For example, theories of natural numbers and real numbers can be developed from set theory. If theorems are generated mechanically from set theory, then any set of theorems isomorphic with the axioms for real numbers (or natural numbers) determines expressions which may be taken as definitions for the basic concepts of the theory of real numbers (or natural numbers). In such a case, one can claim that machines can discover definitions too.

It has often been remarked that the machine can do only what it is told. While this is true, one might be misled by an ambiguity. Thus the machine can be told to make a calculation, find a proof, or choose a "deep" theorem, et cetera. The main problem of using rather than building machines is undoubtedly to express more things in mechanical terms.

The limitation of machines has been seen as revealed by its inability to write love letters. That depends on the quality of the love letters to be composed. If one takes the common sort of love letter taught in manuals of effective letter-writing, the machine can certainly write some useful love letters more quickly than it can prove an interesting theorem. If the image of Don Juan in some films is to be believed, the machine can surely be taught to repeat the few sentences of flattery to every woman.

If experimenting with a machine to see what it can do is compared with the usual type of scientific research, it seems more like engineering than physics, in so far as we are not dealing with natural objects but man-made gadgets, and we are applying rather than discovering theories. On the other hand, calculating machines are rather unique among man-made things in that their potentialities are far less clear to the maker than are other gadgets. In trying to determine what a machine can do, we are faced with almost the same kind of problem as in animal or human psychology. Or, to quote Dunham, we are almost trying to find out what a machine is.

The suspiciously aggressive term "mechanical mathematics" is not unattractive to a mathematical logician. A common complaint among mathematicians is that logicians, when engaged in formalization, are largely concerned with pointless hairsplitting. It is sufficient to know that proofs can be formalized. Why should one take all the trouble to show exactly how such formalizations are to be done, or even to carry out actual formalizations? Logicians are often hard put to give a very convincing justification of their occupation and preoccupation. One lame excuse which can be offered is that they are of such a temperament as to wish to tabulate all scores of all baseball players just to have a complete record in the archives. However, the machines seem to supply, more or less after the event, one good reason for formalization. While many mathematicians have never learned the predicate calculus, it seems hardly possible for the machine to do much mathematics without first dealing with the underlying logic in some explicit manner. While the human being gets bored and confused with too much rigour and rigidity, the machine requires entirely explicit instructions.

It seems as though logicians had worked with the fiction of man as a persistent and unimaginative beast who can only follow rules blindly, and then the fiction found its incarnation in the machine. Hence, the striving for inhuman exactness is not pointless, senseless, but gets direction and justification. One may even claim that a new life is given to the Hilbert program of the *Entscheidungs-problem* which von Neumann thought was thoroughly shattered by Gödel's discoveries. Although a universal decision procedure for all mathematical problems is not possible, formalization does seem to promise that machines will do a major portion of the work that takes up the time of research mathematicians today.

### APPENDIX I: A SAMPLE FROM PRINT-OUTS BY PROGRAM I

| | |
|---|---|
| $2*45/FDPQ-FP$ | 1 |
| $1/-FP, DPQ$ | 2 |
| $2/P-DPQ$ | 3 |
| $3/P-P, Q$ | 4 |
| VALID | 4 |
| | QED |
| $5*21/-ICFP . FQ .. BPQ$ | 1 |
| $1/CFP . FQ-BPQ$ | 2 |
| $2/FP, FQ-BPQ$ | 3 |
| $3/FQ-BPQ, P$ | 4 |
| $4/-BPQ, P, Q$ | 5 |
| $5/P-Q, P, Q$ | 6 |
| VALID | 6 |
| $5/Q-P, P, Q$ | 7 |
| VALID | 7 |
| | QED |
| $2*31/DP . DQR-DPQ, R$ | 1 |
| $1/P-DPQ, R$ | 2 |
| $2/P-P, Q, R$ | 3 |
| VALID | 3 |
| $1/DQR-DPQ, R$ | 4 |
| $4/Q-DPQ, R$ | 5 |

```
5/Q−P, Q, R                                          6
   VALID                                             6
4/R−DPQ, R                                           7
7/R−P, Q, R                                          8
   VALID                                             8
                                           QED

4*45/−BP . . CP . DPQ                                1
1/P−CP . DPQ                                         2
2/P−P                                                3
   VALID                                             3
2/P−DPQ                                              4
4/P−P, Q                                             5
   VALID                                             5
1/CP . DPQ−P                                         6
6/P, DPQ−P                                           7
7/P, P−P                                             8
   VALID                                             8
7/P, Q−P                                             9
   VALID                                             9
                                           QED

5*22/−BFBPQ . . . DCP . FQ . . CQ . FP               1
                                           QED
5*23/−BBPQ . . . DCPQ . . CFP . FQ                   1
                                           QED
5*24/−BFDCPQ . . CFP . FQ . . . DCP . FQ . . CQ . FP  1
                                           QED
7. PRELIMINARY TO PREDICATE CALCULUS                 1
7*1/IG2 . H2, GX, KX−CH3 . K3                         1
1/H2, GX, KX−CH3 . K3                                2
2/H2, GX, KX−H3                                       3
   NOT VALID                                         3
2/H2, GX, KX−K3                                       4
   NOT VALID                                         4
1/GX, KX−CH3 . K3, G2                                5
5/GX, KX−H3, G2                                       6
   NOT VALID                                         6
5/GX, KX−K3, G2                                       7
   NOT VALID                                         7
                                     NOT VALID
```

*13. IDENTITY                                                        1
$13*1/=XY-IGX.GY$                                                    1
$1/GX,=XY-GY$                                                  $= VA$  2
   QED

$13*12/=XY-BGX.GY$                                                   1
$1/GX,=XY-GY$                                                  $= VA$  2
$1/GY,=XY-GX$                                                  $= VA$  3
   QED

$13*13/GX,=XY-GY$                                              $= VA$  1
   QED

$13*14/GX, FGY-F=XY$                                                 1
$1/GX-F=XY, GY$                                                      2
$2/=XY, GX-GY$                                                 $= VA$  3
   QED

$13*15/-=XX$                                                   $= VA$  1
   QED

$13*16/-B=XY.=YX$                                                    1
$1/=XY-=YX$                                                    $= VA$  2
$1/=YX-=XY$                                                    $= VA$  3
   QED

$13*17/=XY,=YZ-=XZ$                                            $= VA$  1
   QED

$13*171/=XY,=XZ-=YZ$                                           $= VA$  1
   QED

$13*172/=YX,=ZX-=YZ$                                           $= VA$  1
   QED

$13*18/=XY, F=XZ- F=YZ$                                         •      1
$1/=XY-F=YZ,=XZ$                                                     2
$2/=YZ,=XY-=XZ$                                                $= VA$  3
   QED

$13*194/-BCGX.=XY...CGX..CGY.=XY$                                    1
$1/CGX.=XY-CGX..CGY.=XY$                                             2
$2/GX,=XY-CGX..CGQ.=XY$                                              3

† (Editors' note: Appendices II, IV, V, VI, and VII of the original article are not reproduced here.)

$3/GX,=XY-GX$        VA 4

$3/GX,=XY-CGY.=XY$        5

$5/GX,=XY-GY$        $=$ VA 6

$5/GX,=XY-=XY$        VA 7

$1/CGX..CGY.=XY-CGX.=XY$        8

$8/GX.CGY.=XY-CGX.=XY$        9

$9/GX, GY,=XY-CGX.=XY$        10

$10/GX, GY,=XY-GX$        VA 11

$10/GX, GY,=XY-=XY$        VA 12

   QED

 

$13*3/DGY.FGY-BDGX.FGX..D=XY.F=XY$        1

$1/GY-BDGX.FGX..D=XY.F=XY$        2

$2/DGX.FGX, GY-D=XY.F-XY$        3

$3/GX, GY-D=XY.F=XY$        4

$4/GX, GY-=XY, F=XY$        5

$5/=XY, GX, GY-=XY$        VA 6

$3/FGX, GY-D=XY.F=XY$        7

$7/GY-D=XY.F=XY, GX$        8

$8/GY-=XY, F=XY, GX$        9

$9/=XY, GY-=XY, GX$        VA 10

$2/D=XY. F=XY, GY-DGX.FGX$        11

$11/=XY, GY-DGX, FGX$        12

$12/=XY, GY-GX, FGX$        13

$13/GX,=XY, GY-GX$        VA 14

$11/F=XY, GY-DGX.FGX$        15

$15/GY-DGX. FGX,=XY$        16

$16/GY-GX, FGX,=XY$        17

$17/GX, GY-GX,=XY$        VA 18

$1/FGY-BDGX.FGX..D=XY.F=XY$        19

$19/-BDGX.FGX..D=XY.F=XY, GY$        20

$20/DGX.FGX-D=XY.F=XY, GY$        21

$21/GX-D=XY.F=XY, GY$        22

$22/GX-=XY, F=XY, GY$        23

$23/=XY, GX-=XY, GY$        VA 24

$21/FGX-D=XY.F=XY, GY$        25

$25/-D=XY.F=XY, GY, GX$        26

$26/-=XY, F=XY, GY, GX$        27

$27/=XY-=XY, GY, GX$        VA 28

$20/D=XY.F=XY-DGX.FGX, GY$        29

$29/=XY-DGX.FGX, GY$        30

$30/=XY-GX, FGX, GY$        31

$31/GX,=XY-GX, GY$        VA 32

$$29 \mid F = XY - DGX . FGX, GY \qquad 33$$
$$33 \mid -DGX, FGX, GY, = XY \qquad 34$$
$$34 \mid -GX, FGX, GY, = XY \qquad 35$$
$$35 \mid GX - GX, GY, = XY \qquad VA\ 36$$

QED

# CHAPTER 6

## Remarks on Mechanical Mathematics

LUDWIG WITTGENSTEIN

I

117. In what sense is logical argument a compulsion?—"After all you grant *this* and *this; so* you must also grant *this*!" That is the way of compelling someone. That is to say, one can in fact compel people to admit something in this way.—Just as one can e.g. compel someone to go over there by pointing over there with a bidding gesture of the hand.

Suppose in such a case I point with two fingers at once in different directions, thus leaving it open to the man to go in which of the two directions he likes,—and another time I point in only *one* direction; then this can also be expressed by saying: my first order did not compel him to go just in *one* direction, while the second one did. But this is a statement to tell us what kind of orders I gave; not the way they operate, not whether they do in fact compel such-and-such a person, i.e. whether he obeys them.

118. It looked at first as if these considerations were meant to shew that 'what seems to be a logical compulsion is in reality only a psychological one'—only here the question arose: am I acquainted with both kinds of compulsion, then?!

Imagine that people used the expression: "The law § . . . punishes a murderer with death." Now this could only mean: this law runs so and so. That form of expression, however, might force itself on us, because the law is an instrument when the guilty man is brought to punishment.—Now we talk of 'inexorability' in connexion with people who punish. And here it might occur to us to say: "The law is *inexorable*—men can let the guilty go, the law executes him." (And even: "the law *always* executes him.")—What is the use of such a form of expression?—In the first instance, this proposition only says that such-and-such is to be found in the law, and human beings some-times do not go by the law. Then, however, it does give us a picture of a single inexorable judge, and many lax judges. That is why it serves to express respect for the law. Finally, the expression can also be so used that a law is called inexorable when it makes no provision for a possible act of grace, and in the opposite case it is perhaps called 'discriminating'.

Now we talk of the 'inexorability' of logic; and think of the laws of logic as inexorable, still more inexorable than the laws of nature. We now draw attention to the fact that the word "inexorable" is used in a variety of ways. There correspond to our laws of logic very general facts of daily experience. They are the ones that make it possible for us to keep on demonstrating those laws in a very simple way (with ink on paper for example). They are to be compared with the facts that make measurement with a yardstick easy and useful. This suggests the use of precisely these laws of inference, and now it is *we* that are inexorable in applying these laws. Because we '*measure*'; and it is part of measuring for everybody to have the same measures. Besides this, however, inexorable, i.e. *unambiguous* rules of inference can be distinguished from ones that are not unambiguous, I mean from such as leave an alternative open to us.

119. "But I can infer only what actually does follow."—That is to say: what the logical machine really does produce. The logical ma-chine—that would be an all-pervading ethereal mechanism.—We must give warning against this picture.

Imagine a material harder and more rigid than any other. But if a rod made of this stuff is brought out of the horizontal into the vertical, it shrinks; or it bends when set upright and at the same time it is so hard that there is no other way of bending it.—(A mechanism made of this stuff, say a crank, connecting-rod and crosshead. The different way the crosshead would move.)

Or again: a rod bends if one brings a certain mass near it; but it is completely rigid in face of all forces that we subject it to. Imagine that the guide-rails of the crosshead bend and then straighten again as the crank approaches and retreats. My assumption would be, how-ever, that no particular external force is necessary to cause this. This behaviour of the rails would give an impression as of something alive.

When we say: "If the parts of the mechanism were quite rigid, they would move so and so," what is the criterion for their being quite rigid? Is it that they resist certain forces? Or that they do move so and so?

Suppose I say: "This is the law of motion of the crosshead (the correlation of its position and the position of the crank perhaps) when the lengths of the crank and connecting-rod remain constant." This presumably means: If the crank and crosshead keep these relative positions, I say that the length of the connecting-rod remains constant.

120. "If the parts were quite rigid this is how they would move"; is that a hypothesis? It seems not. For when we say: "Kinematics describes the movements of the mechanism on the assumption that its parts are completely rigid," on the one hand we are admitting that this assumption never squares with reality, and on the other hand it is not supposed to be in any way doubtful that completely rigid parts would move in this way. But whence this certainty? The question here is not really one of certainty but of something stipulated by us. We do not *know* that bodies would move in these ways if (by such and such criteria) they were quite rigid; but (in certain circumstances) we should certainly *call* 'rigid' such parts as did move in those ways.—Always remember in such a case that geometry (or kinematics) does not specify any method of measuring when it talks about the same, or constant, length.

When therefore we call kinematics the theory, say, of the movement of perfectly rigid parts of a mechanism, on the one hand this contains an indication as to (mathematical) method—we stipulate certain distances as the lengths of machine parts that do not alter—and on the other hand an *indication* about the application of the calculus.

121. The hardness of the logical *must*. What if one were to say: the *must* of kinematics is much harder than the causal *must* compelling a machine part to move like *this* when another moves like *this*?—

Suppose we represented the movement of the 'perfectly rigid' mechanism by a cinematographic picture, a cartoon film. Suppose this picture were said to be *perfectly hard,* and this meant that we had taken this picture as our method of description—whatever the facts may be, however the parts of the real mechanism may bend or expand.

122. The machine (its structure) as symbolizing its action: the action of a machine—I might say at first—seems to be there in it from the start. What does that mean?—

If we know the machine, everything else, that is its movement, seems to be already completely determined.

"We talk as if these parts *could* only move in this way, as if they could not do anything else."

How is this—do we forget the possibility of their bending, breaking off, melting, and so on? Yes; in *many* cases we don't think of that at all. We use a machine, or the picture of a machine, to symbolize a particular action of the machine. For instance, we give someone such a picture and assume that he will derive the movement of the parts from it. (Just as we can give someone a number by telling him that it is the twenty-fifth in the series 1, 4, 9, 16, . . . .)

"The machine's action seems to be in it from the start" means: you are inclined to compare the future movements of the machine in definiteness to objects which are already lying in a drawer and which we then take out.

But we do not say this kind of thing when we are concerned with predicting the actual behaviour of a machine. Here we do not in general forget the possibility of a distortion of the parts and so on.

We do talk like that, however, when we are wondering at the way we can use a machine to symbolize a given way of moving—since it can also move in quite *different* ways.

Now, we might say that a machine, or the picture of it, is the first of a series of pictures which we have learnt to derive from this one.

But when we remember that the machine could also have moved differently, it readily seems to us as if the way it moves must be contained in the machine-as-symbol far more determinately than in the actual machine. As if it were not enough here for the movements in question to be empirically determined in advance, but they had to be really—in a mysterious sense—already *present*. And it is quite true: the movement of the machine-as-symbol is predetermined in a different sense from that in which the movement of any given actual machine is predetermined.

II

1. 'A mathematical proof must be perspicuous.' Only a structure whose reproduction is an easy task is called a "proof". It must be possible to decide with certainty whether we really have the same proof twice over, or not. The proof must be a configuration whose exact reproduction can be certain. Or again: we must be sure we can exactly reproduce what is essential to the proof. It may for example be written down in two different handwritings or colours. What goes to make the reproduction of a proof is not anything like an exact reproduction of a shade of colour or a hand-writing.

It must be easy to write down *exactly* this proof again. This is where a written proof has an advantage over a drawing. The essentials of the latter have often been misunderstood. The drawing of a Euclidian proof may be inexact, in the sense that the straight lines are not straight, the segments of circles not exactly circular, etc. etc. and at the same time the drawing is still an exact proof; and from this it can be seen that this drawing does not—e.g.—demonstrate that such a construction results in a polygon with five equal sides; that what it proves is a proposition of geometry, not one about the properties of paper, compass, ruler and pencil.

[Connects with: proof a *picture* of an experiment.]

2. I want to say: if you have a proof-pattern that cannot be taken in, and by a change in notation you turn it into one that can, then you are producing a proof, where there was none before.

Now let us imagine a proof for a Russellian proposition stating an addition like '$a + b = c$,' consisting of a few thousand signs. You will say: Seeing whether this proof is correct or not is a purely external difficulty, of no mathematical interest. ("One man takes in easily what someone else takes in with difficulty or not at all" etc. etc..)

The assumption is that the definitions serve merely to abbreviate the expression for the convenience of the calculator; whereas they are part of the calculation. By their aid expressions are produced which could not have been produced without it.

3. But how about the following: "While it is true that we cannot—in the ordinary sense—multiply 234 by 537 in the Russellian calculus, still there is a Russellian calculation corresponding to this multiplication."—What kind of correspondence is this? It might be like this: we can carry out this multiplication in the Russellian calculus too, only in a different symbolism,—just as, as we should certainly say, we can carry it out in a different number system. In that case, then, we could e.g. solve the practical problems for which we use that multiplication by means of the calculation in the Russellian calculus too, only in a more roundabout way.

Now let us imagine the cardinal numbers explained as 1, $1 + 1$, $(1 + 1) + 1$, $((1 + 1) + 1) + 1$, and so on. You say that the definitions introducing the figures of the decimal system are a mere matter of convenience; the calculation $703000 \times 40000101$ could be done in that wearisome notation too. But is that true?—"Of course it's true! I can surely write down, construct, a calculation in that notation corresponding to the calculation in the decimal notation."—But how do I know that it corresponds to it? Well, because I have derived it from the other by a given method.—But now if I look at it again half an hour later, may it not have altered? For one cannot command a clear view of it.

Now I ask: could we also find out the truth of the proposition $7034174 + 6594321 = 13628495$ by means of a proof carried out in the first notation?—Is there such a proof of this proposition?—The answer is: no.

### 4. But still doesn't Russell teach us *one* way of adding?

Suppose we proved by Russell's method that $(\exists a \ldots g) (\exists a \ldots l) \supset (\exists a \ldots s)$ is a tautology; could we reduce our result to $g + l$'s being $s$? Now this presupposes that I can take the three bits of the alphabet as representatives of the proof. But does Russell's proof shew this? After all I could obviously also have carried out Russell's proof with groups of signs in the brackets whose sequence made no characteristic impression on me, so that it would not have been possible to represent the group of signs between brackets by its last term.

Even assuming that the Russellian proof were carried out with a notation such as $x_1 x_2 \ldots x_{10} x_{11} \ldots x_{100} \ldots$ as in the decimal notation, and there were 100 members in the first pair of brackets, 300 in the second and 400 in the third, does the proof itself shew that $100 + 300 = 400$?—What if this proof led at one time to this result, and at another to a different one, for example $100 + 300 = 420$? What is needed in order to see that the result of the proof, if it is correctly carried out, always depends solely on the last figures of the first two pairs of brackets?

But still for small numbers Russell does teach us to add; for then we take the groups of signs in the brackets in at a glance and we can take *them* as numerals; for example '*xy*', '*xyz*', '*xyzuv*'.

Thus Russell teaches us a new calculus for reaching 5 from 2 and 3; and that is true even if we say that a logical calculus is only—frills tacked on to the arithmetical calculus.

The *application* of the calculation must take care of itself. And that is what is correct about 'formalism'.

The reduction of arithmetic to symbolic logic is supposed to shew the point of application of arithmetic, as it were the attachment by means of which it is plugged in to its application. As if someone were shewn, first a trumpet without the mouthpiece—and then the mouthpiece, which shews how a trumpet is used, brought into contact with the human body. But the attachment which Russell gives us is on the one hand too narrow, on the other hand too wide; too general and too special. The calculation takes care of its own application.

We extend our ideas from calculations with small numbers to ones with large numbers in the same kind of way as we imagine that, if the distance from here to the sun *could* be measured with a footrule, then we should get the very result that, as it is, we get in a quite different way. That is to say, we are inclined to take the measurement of length with a footrule as a model even for the measurement of the distance between two stars.

And one says, e.g. at school: "If we imagine rulers stretching from here to the sun . . ." and seems in this way to explain what we understand by the distance between the sun and the earth. And the use of such a picture is all right, so long as it is clear to us that we can measure the distance from us to the sun, and that we cannot measure it with footrules.

5. Suppose someone were to say: "The only real proof of 1000 + 1000 = 2000 is after all the Russellian one, which shews that the expression . . . is a tautology"? For can I not prove that a tautology results if I have 1000 members in each of the two first pairs of brackets and 2000 in the third? And if I can prove that, then I can look at it as a proof of the arithmetical proposition.

In philosophy it is always good to put a *question* instead of an answer to a question.

For an answer to the philosophical question may easily be unfair; disposing of it by means of another question is not.

Then should I put a *question* here, for example, instead of the answer that that arithmetical proposition cannot be proved by Russell's method?

6. The proof that $\overset{1}{(\ )}\overset{2}{(\ )} \supset \overset{3}{(\ )}$ is a tautology consists in always crossing out a term of the third pair of brackets for a term of (1) or (2). And there are many methods for such collating. Or one might even say: there are many ways of establishing the success of a 1-1 correlation. One way, for example, would be to construct a star-shaped pattern for the left-hand side of the implication and another one for the right-hand side and then to compare these in their turn by making an ornament out of the two of them.

Thus the rule could be given: "If you want to know whether the numbers A and B together actually yield C, write down an expression of the form . . . and correlate the variables in the brackets by writing down (or trying to) the proof that the expression is a tautology".

My objection to this is *not* that it is arbitrary to prescribe just this way of collating, but that it cannot be established in this way that 1000 + 1000 = 2000.

7. Imagine that you had written down a 'formula' a mile long, and you shewed by transformation that it was tautologous ('if *it* has not altered meanwhile', one would have to say). Now we *count* the terms in the brackets or we divide them up and make the expression into one that can be taken in, and it comes out that there are 7566 terms in the first pair of brackets, 2434 in the second, 10000 in the third. Now have I proved that $2434 + 7566 = 10000$?—That depends—one might say—on whether you are certain that the counting has really yielded the number of terms which stood between the brackets in the course of the proof.

Could one say: "Russell teaches us to write as many variables in the third pair of brackets as were in the first two together"? But really: he teaches us to write a variable in (3) for every variable in (1) and (2).

But do we learn from this what number is the sum of two given numbers? Perhaps it is said: "Of course, for in the third pair of brackets we have the paradigm, the prototype of the new number". But in what sense is $|\,|\,|\,|\,|\,|\,|\,|\,|\,|\,|\,|\,|\,|\,|\,|$ the paradigm of a number? Consider how it can be used as such.

16. It is not logic—I should like to say—that compels me to accept a proposition of the form $(\exists\quad)\,(\exists\quad) \supset (\exists\quad)$, when there are a million variables in the first two pairs of brackets and two million in the third. I want to say: logic would not compel me to accept any proposition at all in this case. Something *else* compels me to accept such a pr oposition as in accord with logic.

Logic compels me only so far as the logical calculus compels me.

But surely it is essential to the calculus with 1000000 that this number must be capable of resolution into a sum $1 + 1 + 1 \ldots$ , and in order to be certain that we have the right number of units before us, we can number the units:
$$\underset{1\quad 2\quad 3\quad 4 \qquad\qquad 1000000}{1 + 1 + 1 + 1 + \ldots + 1}$$
This notation would be like: '100,000.000,000' which also makes the numeral surveyable. And I can surely imagine someone's having a great sum of money in pennies entered in a book in which perhaps they appear as numbers of 100 places, with which I have to calculate. I should now begin to translate them into a surveyable notation, but still I should call them 'numerals', should treat them as a record of numbers. For I should even regard it as the record of a number if someone were to tell me that $N$ has as many shillings as this vessel will hold peas. Another case again: "He has as many shillings as the Song of Songs has letters".

17. The notation '$x_1$, $x_2$, $x_3$, ...' gives a shape to the expression '($\exists$...)', and so to the R-proved tautology.

Let me ask the following question: Is it not conceivable that the 1-1 correlation could not be trustworthily carried out in the Russellian proof, that when, *for example,* we try to use it for adding, we regularly get a result contradicting the usual one, and that we blame this on fatigue, which makes us leave out certain steps unawares? And might we not then say:—if only we didn't get tired we should get the same result—? Because *logic* demands it? Does it demand it, then? Aren't we here rectifying logic by means of another calculus?

Suppose we took 100 steps of the logical calculus at a time and now got trustworthy results, while we don't get them if we try to take all the steps singly—one would like to say: the calculation is still based on unit steps, since 100 steps at a time is defined by means of unit steps.—But the definition says: to take 100 steps at a time is the same thing as . . ., and yet we take the 100 steps at a time and *not* 100 unit steps.

Still, in the shortened calculation I am obeying a *rule*—and how was this rule justified?—What if the shortened and the unshortened proof yielded different results?

18. What I am saying surely comes to this: I can e.g. define '10' as '1 + 1 + 1 + 1...' and '100 × 2' as '2 + 2 + 2...' but I cannot therefore necessarily define '100 × 10' as '10 + 10 + 10...', nor yet as '1 + 1 + 1 + 1....'

I can find out that 100 × 100 equals 10000 by means of a 'shortened' procedure. Then why should I not regard *that* as the original proof procedure?

A shortened procedure tells me what *ought* to come out with the unshortened one. (Instead of the other way round.)

19. "But the calculation is surely based on the unit steps...." Yes; but in a different way. For the procedure of proof is a different one.

I could say for example: 10 = 1 + 1 + 1 + 1 + 1 + 1 + 1 + 1 + 1 + 1 *and in like manner* 100 = 10 + 10 + 10 + 10 + 10 + 10 + 10 + 10 + 10 + 10. Have I not based the definition of 100 on the successive addition of 1? But in the same way as if I had added 100 units? Is there any need at all in my notation for a sign of the form—'1 + 1 + 1...' with 100 components of the sum?

The danger here seems to be one of looking at the shortened procedure as a pale shadow of the unshortened one. The rule of counting is not counting.

20.   What does taking 100 steps of the calculus 'at once' consist in? Surely in one's regarding, not the unit step, but a different step, as decisive.

In ordinary addition of whole numbers in the decimal system we make steps in units, steps in tens, etc. Can one say that the procedure is founded on one of only making unit steps? One might justify it like this: the result of the addition does indeed look so—'7583'; but the explanation of this sign, its meaning, which must ultimately receive expression in its application too, is surely of this sort: $1 + 1 + 1 + 1 + 1$ and so on. But is it so? Must the numerical sign be explained in this way, or this explanation receive expression implicitly in its application? I believe that if we reflect it turns out that that is not the case.

Calculating with graphs or with a slide-rule.

Of course when we check the one kind of calculation by the other, we normally get the same result. But if there are several kinds—who says, if they do not agree, which is the proper method of calculation, with its roots at the source of mathematics?

30.   A proof leads me to say: this *must* be like this.—Now, I understand this in the case of a Euclidean proof or the proof of '25 times $25 = 625$', but is it also like this in the case of a Russellian proof, e.g. of '$\vdash p \supset q . p : \supset : q$'? What does 'it *must* be like this' mean here in contrast with 'it is like this'? Should I say: "Well, I accept this expression as a paradigm for all non-informative propositions of this form"?

I go through the proof and say: "Yes, this is how it *has* to be; I must fix the use of my language in *this* way".

I want to say that the *must* corresponds to a track which I lay down in language.

38.   Accepting a proof: one may accept it as the paradigm of the pattern that arises when *these* rules are correctly applied to certain patterns. One may accept it as the correct derivation of a rule of inference. Or as a correct derivation from a correct empirical proposition; or as the correct derivation from a false empirical proposition; or simply as the correct derivation from an empirical proposition, of which we do not know whether it is true or false.

But now can I say that the conception of a proof as 'proof of constructability' of the proved proposition is in some sense a simpler, more primary, one than any other conception?

Can I therefore say: "Any proof proves *first and foremost* that this formation of signs must result when I apply these rules to these formations of signs"? Or: "The proof proves first and foremost that this formation can arise when one operates with these signs according to these transformation-rules".—

This would point to a geometrical application. For the proposition whose truth, as I say, is proved here, is a geometrical proposition—a proposition of grammar concerning the transformations of signs. It might for example be said: it is proved that it makes *sense* to say that someone has got the sign . . . according to these rules from . . . and . . .; but no sense etc. etc.

Or again: when mathematics is divested of all content, it would remain that certain signs can be constructed from others according to certain rules.—

The least that we have to accept would be: that these signs etc. etc.—and accepting this is a basis for accepting anything else.

I should now like to say: the sequence of signs in the proof does not necessarily carry with it any kind of acceptance. If however we do begin by accepting, this does not have to be 'geometrical' acceptance.

A proof could surely consist of only two steps: say one proposition '$(x).fx$' and one '$fa$'—does the correct transition according to a rule play an important part here?

39. *What* is unshakably certain about what is proved?

To accept a proposition as unshakably certain—I want to say—means to use it as a grammatical rule: this removes uncertainty from it.

"Proof must be capable of being taken in" really means nothing but: a proof is not an experiment. We do not accept the result of a proof because it results once, or because it often results. But we see in the proof the reason for saying that this *must* be the result.

What *proves* is not that this correlation leads to this result—but that we are persuaded to take these appearances (pictures) as models for what it is like if. . . .

The proof is our new model for what it is like if nothing gets added and nothing taken away when we count correctly etc. But these words shew that I do not quite know what the proof is a model of.

I want to say: with the logic of *Principia Mathematica* it would be possible to justify an arithmetic in which $1000 + 1 = 1000$; and all that would be necessary for this purpose would be to doubt the sensible correctness of calculations. But if we do not doubt it, then it is not our conviction of the truth of logic that is responsible.

When we say in a proof: "This *must* come out"—then this is not for reasons that we do not *see*.

It is not our getting this result, but its being the end of this route, that makes us accept it.

What convinces us—*that* is the proof: a configuration that does not convince us is not the proof, even when it can be shewn to exemplify the proved proposition.

That means: it must not be necessary to make a physical investigation of the proof-configuration in order to shew us what has been proved.

65. Are the propositions of mathematics anthropological propositions saying how we men infer and calculate?—Is a statute book a work of anthropology telling how the people of this nation deal with a thief etc.?—Could it be said: "The judge looks up a book about anthropology and thereupon sentences the thief to a term of imprisonment"? Well, the judge does not USE the statute book as a manual of anthropology.

66. The prophecy does *not* run, that a man will get *this* result when he follows this rule in making a transformation—but that he will get this result, when we *say* that he is following the rule.

What if we said that mathematical propositions were prophecies in *this* sense: they predict what result members of a society who have learnt this technique will get in agreement with other members of the society? '25 × 25 = 625' would thus mean that men, if we judge them to obey the rules of multiplication, will reach the result 625 when they multiply 25 × 25.—That this is a correct prediction is beyond doubt; and also that calculating is in essence founded on such predictions. That is to say, we should not call something 'calculating' if we could not make such a prophecy with certainty. This really means: calculating is a technique. And what we have said pertains to the essence of a technique.

67. This consensus belongs to the essence of *calculation,* so much is certain. I.e.: this consensus is part of the phenomenon of our calculating.

In a technique of *calculating* prophecies must be possible.

And that makes the technique of calculating similar to the technique of a *game,* like chess.

But what about this consensus—doesn't it mean that *one* human being by himself could not calculate? Well, *one* human being could at any rate not calculate just *once* in his life.

It might be said: all *possible* positions in chess can be conceived as propositions saying that they (themselves) are *possible* positions, or again as prophecies that people will be able to reach these positions by moves which they agree in saying are in accordance with the rules. A position *reached* in this way is then a proved proposition of this kind.

"A calculation is an experiment."—A calculation can be an experiment. The teacher makes the pupil do a calculation in order to see whether he can calculate; that is an experiment.

When the stove is lit in the morning, is that an experiment? But it could be one.

And in the same way moves in chess are *not* proofs either, and chess positions are not propositions. And mathematical propositions are not positions in a game. And in *this* way they are not prophecies either.

68. If a calculation is an experiment, then what is a mistake in calculation? A mistake in the experiment? Surely not; it would have been a mistake in the experiment, if I had not observed the *conditions* of the experiment—if, e.g., I had made someone calculate when a terrible noise was going on.

But why should I not say: while a mistake in calculating is not a *mistake* in the experiment, still, it is a *miscarriage* of the experiment—sometimes explicable, sometimes inexplicable?

69. "A calculation, for example a multiplication, is an experiment: *we do not know what will result* and we learn it once the multiplication is done."—Certainly; nor do we know when we go for a walk where exactly we shall be in five minutes' time—but does that make going for a walk into an experiment?—Very well; but in the calculation I surely wanted from the beginning to know what the result was going to be; *that* was what I was interested in. I am, after all, curious about the result. Not, however, as what I am *going* to say, but as what I *ought* to say.

But isn't this just what interests you about this multiplication—how the generality of men will calculate? No—at least not usually—even if I am running to a common meeting point with everybody else.

But surely this is just what the calculation shews me experimentally —where this meeting point is. I as it were start myself working and see where I get. And the correct multiplication is the pattern of the way we all work, when we are set like *this*.

*Experience* teaches that we all find this calculation correct.

We start ourselves off and get the result of the calculation. But now—I want to say—we aren't interested in having—under such and such conditions say—actually produced this result, but in the pattern of our working; it interests us as a convincing, harmonious, pattern— not, however, as the result of an experiment, but as a *path*.

We say, not: "So *that's* how we go!", but: "So *that's* how it goes!"

III

45. You want to say that every new proof alters the concept of proof in one way or another.

But then by what principle is something recognized as a new proof? Or rather there is certainly no 'principle' here.

46. Now ought I to say: "we are convinced that the same result will always come out"? No, that is not enough. We are convinced that the same *calculation* will always come out, be calculated. Now is *that* a mathematical conviction? No—for if it were not always the same that was calculated, we could not conclude that the calculation yields at one time one result and at another time another.

We are *of course* also convinced that when we repeat a calculation we shall repeat the pattern of the calculation.—

47. Might I not say: if you do a multiplication, in any case you do not find the mathematical fact, but you do find the mathematical proposition? For what you *find* is the non-mathematical fact, and in this way the mathematical proposition. For a mathematical proposition is the determination of a concept following upon a discovery.

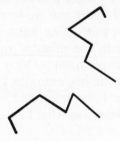

You *find* a new physiognomy. Now you can e.g. memorize or copy it.

A *new* form has been found, constructed. But it is used to give a new concept together with the old one.

The concept is altered so that this *had* to be the result.

I find, not the result, but that I reach it.

And it is not this route's beginning here and ending here that is an empirical fact, but my having gone this road, or some road to this end.

48. But might it not be said that the *rules* lead this way, even if no one went it?

For that is what one would like to say—and here we see the mathematical machine, which, driven by the rules themselves, obeys only mathematical laws and not physical ones.

I want to say: the working of the mathematical machine is only the *picture* of the working of a machine.

The rule does not do work, for whatever happens according to the rule is an interpretation of the rule.

## IV

1. It is of course clear that the mathematician, in so far as he really is 'playing a game' *does not infer*. For here 'playing' must mean: *acting* in accordance with certain rules. And it would already be something outside the mere game for him to infer that he could act in this way according to the general rule.

2. Does a calculating machine *calculate?*

Imagine that a calculating machine had come into existence by accident; now someone accidentally presses its knobs (or an animal walks over it) and it calculates the product $25 \times 20$.

I want to say: it is essential to mathematics that its signs are also employed in *mufti*.

It is the use outside mathematics, and so the *meaning* of the signs, that makes the sign-game into mathematics.

Just as it is not logical inference either, for me to make a change from one formation to another (say from one arrangement of chairs to another) if these arrangements have not a linguistic function apart from this transformation.

3. But is it not true that someone with no idea of the meaning of Russell's symbols could *work over* Russell's proofs? And so could in an important sense test whether they were right or wrong?

A human calculating machine might be trained so that when the rules of inference were shewn it and perhaps exemplified, it read through the proofs of a mathematical system (say that of Russell), and nodded its head after every correctly drawn conclusion, but shook its head at a mistake and stopped calculating. One could imagine this creature as otherwise perfectly imbecile.

We call a proof something that can be worked over, but can also be copied.

4. If mathematics is a game, then playing some game is doing mathematics, and in that case why isn't dancing mathematics too?

Imagine that calculating machines occurred in nature, but that people could not pierce their cases. And now suppose that these people use these appliances, say as we use calculation, though of that they know nothing. Thus e.g. they make predictions with the aid of calculating machines, but for them manipulating these queer objects is experimenting.

These people lack concepts which we have; but what takes their place?

Think of the mechanism whose movement we saw as a geometrical (kinematic) proof: clearly it would not normally be said of someone turning the wheel that he was proving something. Isn't it the same with someone who makes and changes arrangements of signs as a game; even when what he produces could be seen as a proof?

To say mathematics is a game is supposed to mean: in proving, we need never appeal to the meaning of the signs, that is to their extra-mathematical application. But then what does appealing to this mean at all? How can such an appeal be of any avail?

Does it mean passing out of mathematics and returning to it again, or does it mean passing from *one* method of mathematical inference to another?

What does it mean to obtain a new concept of the surface of a sphere? How is it then a concept of the surface of a *sphere?* Only in so far as it can be applied to real spheres.

How far does one need to have a concept of 'proposition', in order to understand Russellian mathematical logic?

9. We only see how queer the question is whether the pattern $\phi$ (a particular arrangement of digits e.g. '770') will occur in the infinite expansion of $\pi$, when we try to formulate the question in a quite common or garden way: men have been trained to put down signs according to certain rules. Now they proceed according to this training and we say that it is a problem whether they will *ever* write down the pattern $\phi$ in following the given rule.

But what are you saying if you say that one thing is clear: either one will come on $\phi$ in the infinite expansion, or one will not?

It seems to me that in saying this you are yourself setting up a rule or postulate.

What if someone were to reply to a question: 'So far there is no such thing as an answer to this question'?

So, e.g., the poet might reply when asked whether the hero of his poem has a sister or not—when, that is, he has not yet decided anything about it.

The question—I want to say—changes its status, when it becomes decidable. For a connexion is made then, which formerly *was not there*.

Of someone who is trained we can ask 'How *will* he interpret the rule for this case?', or again 'How *ought* he to interpret the rule for this case?'—but what if no decision about this question has been made?—Well, then the answer is, not: 'he ought to interpret it in such a way that $\phi$ occurs in the expansion' or: 'he ought to interpret it in such a way that it does not occur', but: 'nothing has so far been decided about this'.

However queer it sounds, the further expansion of an irrational number is a further expansion of mathematics.

We do mathematics with concepts.—And with certain concepts more than with other ones.

I want to say: it *looks* as if a ground for the decision were already there; and it has yet to be invented.

Would this come to the same thing as saying: in thinking about the technique of expansion, which we have learnt, we use the false picture of a completed expansion (of what is ordinarily called a "row") and this forces us to ask unanswerable questions?

For after all in the end every question about the expansion of $\sqrt{2}$ must be capable of formulation as a practical question concerning the technique of expansion.

And what is in question here is of course not merely the case of the expansion of a real number, or in general the production of mathematical signs, but every analogous process, whether it is a game, a dance, etc., etc..

10. When someone hammers away at us with the law of excluded middle as something which cannot be gainsaid, it is clear that there is something wrong with his question.

When someone sets up the law of excluded middle, he is as it were putting two pictures before us to choose from, and saying that one must correspond to the fact. But what if it is questionable whether the pictures can be applied here?

And if you say that the infinite expansion must contain the pattern $\phi$ or not contain it, you are so to speak shewing us the picture of an unsurveyable series reaching into the distance.

But what if the picture began to flicker in the far distance?

11. To say of an unending series that it does *not* contain a particular pattern makes sense only under quite special conditions.

That is to say: this proposition has been given a sense for certain cases.

Roughly, for those where it is in the *rule* for this series, not to contain the pattern. . . .

Further: when I calculate the expansion further, I am deriving new rules which the series obeys.

"Good,—then we can say: 'It must either reside in the rule for this series that the pattern occurs, or the opposite'." But is it like that?— "Well, doesn't the rule of expansion *determine* the series completely? And if it does so, if it allows of no ambiguity, then it must implicitly determine *all* questions about the structure of the series."—Here you are thinking of finite series.

"But surely all members of the series from the 1st up to 1,000th, up to the $10^{10}$-th and so on, are determined; so surely *all* the members are determined." That is correct if it is supposed to mean that it is not the case that e.g. the so-and-so-many'th is *not* determined. But you can see that *that* gives you no information about whether a particular pattern is going to appear in the series (if it has not appeared so far). *And so we can see* that we are using a misleading *picture.*

If you want to know more about the series, you have, so to speak, to get into another dimension (as it were from the line into a surrounding plane).—But then isn't the plane *there,* just like the line, and merely something to be *explored,* if one wants to know what the facts are?

No, the mathematics of this further dimension has to be invented just as much as any mathematics.

In an arithmetic in which one does not count further than 5 the question what $4 + 3$ makes doesn't yet make sense. On the other hand the problem may very well exist of giving this question a sense. That is to say: the question makes *no more* sense than does the law of excluded middle in application to it.

17. 'The pattern is in the series or it is not in the series' means: either the thing looks like *this* or it does not look like this .

How does one know what is meant by the opposite of the proposition "$\phi$ occurs in the series", or even of the proposition "$\phi$ does not occur in the series"? This question sounds like nonsense, but does make sense all the same.

Namely: how do I know that I understand the proposition "$\phi$ occurs in this series"?

True, I can give examples illustrating the use of such statements, and also of the opposite ones. And they are examples of there being a rule prescribing the occurrence in a definite region or series of regions, or determining that such an occurrence is excluded.

If "you do it" means: you must do it, and "you do not do it" means: you must not do it—then "Either you do it, or you do not" is not the law of excluded middle.

Everyone feels uncomfortable at the thought that a proposition can state that such-and-such does not occur in an infinite series—while on the other hand there is nothing startling about a command's saying that this must not occur in this series however far it is continued.

But what is the source of this distinction between: "however far you go you will never find this"—and "however far you go you must never do this"?

On hearing the proposition one can ask: "how can we know anything like that?" but nothing analogous holds for the command.

The statement seems to overreach itself, the command not at all.

Can we imagine all mathematical propositions expressed in the imperative? For example: "Let $10 \times 10$ be 100."

And if you now say: "Let it be like this, or let it not be like this", you are not pronouncing the law of excluded middle—but you are pronouncing a *rule*. (As I have already said above.)

18. But is this really a way out of the difficulty? For how about all the other mathematical propositions, say '$25^2 = 625$'; isn't the law of excluded middle valid for these *inside* mathematics?

How is the law of excluded middle applied?

"Either there is a rule that prescribes it, or one that forbids it."

Assuming that there is no rule forbidding the occurrence,—why is there then supposed to be one that prescribes it?

Does it make sense to say: "While there isn't any rule forbidding the occurrence, as a matter of fact the pattern does not occur"?—And if this does not make sense, how can the opposite make sense, namely, that the pattern does occur?

Well, when I say it occurs, a picture of the series from its beginning up to the pattern floats before my mind—but if I say that the pattern does *not* occur, then no such picture is of any use to me, and my supply of pictures gives out.

What if the rule should bend in use without my noticing it? What I mean is, that I might speak of different spaces in which I use it.

The opposite of "it must not occur" is "it can occur". For a finite segment of the series, however, the opposite of "it must not occur in it" seems to be: "it must occur in it".

The queer thing about the alternative "$\phi$ occurs in the infinite series or it does not", is that we have to imagine the two possibilities individually, that we look for a distinct idea of each, and that *one* is not adequate for the negative and for the positive case, as it is elsewhere.

19. How do I know that the general proposition "There is . . ." makes sense here? Well, if it can be used to tell something about the technique of expansion in a language game.

In *one* case what we are told is: "it must not occur"—i.e.: if it occurs you calculated wrong.

In one case what we are told is: "it can occur", i.e., no such interdict exists. In another: "it must occur in such-and-such a region (always in this place in these regions)". But the opposite of this seems to be: "it must not occur in such-and-such places"—instead of "it *need* not occur there".

But what if the rule were given that, e.g., everywhere where the formation rule for $\pi$ yields 4, any arbitrary digit other than 4 can be put in its place?

Consider also the rule which forbids one digit in certain places, but otherwise leaves the choice open.

Isn't it like this? The concepts of infinite decimals in mathematical propositions are not concepts of series, but of the unlimited technique of expansion of series.

We learn an endless technique: that is to say, something is done for us first, and then we do it; we are told rules and we do exercises in following them; perhaps some expression like "and so on *ad inf.*" is also used, but what is in question here is not some gigantic extension.

*These* are the facts. And now what does it mean to say: "$\phi$ either occurs in the expansion, or does not occur"?

# Selected Bibliography for Part II

1. Alt, F. L. (ed.), *Advances in Computers*. New York: Academic Press, 1960, Vol. 1.
2. Ashby, W. R., "Can a Mechanical Chess-Player Outplay its Designer?," *The British Journal for the Philosophy of Science*, Vol. 3 (1952-53), pp. 44-57.
3. Bernstein, A., and Roberts, M. deV., "Computer v. Chess-player," *Scientific American*, Vol. 198 (1958), pp. 96-105.
4. Birkhoff, G. D., *Aesthetic Measure*. Cambridge: Harvard University Press, 1933.
5. Brooks, F. P., Hopkins, A. L., Neumann, P. G., and Wright, W. V., "An Experiment in Musical Composition," *Institute of Radio Engineers Transactions on Electronic Computers*, EC-6 (September 1957), pp. 175-182.
6. Gelernter, H., "Realization of a Geometry Theorem Proving Machine," *Proceedings of the International Conference on Information Processing*. Paris: UNESCO House, 1959, pp. 273-282. Reprinted in *Computers and Thought*, Feldman and Feigenbaum (eds.).
7. Gilmore, P. C., "A program for the production from axioms, of proofs for theorems derivable within the first order predicate calculus," *Proceedings of the International Conference on Information Processing*, Paris: UNESCO House, 1959, pp. 265-273.
8. Koppel, H., "Digital Computer Plays NIM," *Electronics*, Vol. 25 (November 1952), pp. 155-157.
9. Newell, A., Shaw, J. C., and Simon, H. A., "Chess-playing Programs and the Problem of Complexity," *IBM Journal of Research and Development*, Vol. 2 (October 1958), pp. 320-335. Reprinted in *Computers and Thought*, Feldman and Feigenbaum (eds.).
10. Parkinson, G. H. R., "The Cybernetic Approach to Aesthetics," *Philosophy*, Vol. 36 (January 1961), pp. 49-61.
11. Perry, J. W., Kent, A., and Berry, M. M., *Machine Literature Searching*. New York: Interscience Publishers, Inc., 1956.
12. Pinkerton, R. C., "Information Theory and Melody," *Scientific American*, Vol. 194 (February 1956), pp. 77-86.
13. Polya, G., *Patterns of Plausible Inference*, Vol. 2 of *Mathematics and Plausible Reasoning*. Princeton: Princeton University Press, 1954.
14. Rashevsky, N., "The Neural Mechanism of Logical Thinking," *Bulletin of Mathematical Biophysics*, Vol. 8 (1946), pp. 29-40.
15. Samuel, A. L., "Some Studies in Machine Learning Using the Game of Checkers," *IBM Journal of Research and Development*, Vol. 3 (July 1959), pp. 210-229.
16. Searle, H., "Concrete Music," *Grove's Dictionary of Music and Musicians*, E. Blom (ed.). New York: St. Martin's Press, Vol. 9, 1954, pp. 571-572.
17. Shannon, C. E., "Programming a Computer to Play Chess," *Philosophical Magazine*, Vol. 41 (1950), pp. 356-375.
18. Wang, H., "Proving Theorems by Pattern Recognition I," *Communication of the Association for Computing Machinery*, Vol. 3 (April 1960), pp. 220-234.

## Part III

*Perceptual Acts*

# CHAPTER 7

# Sensation and Observation

GILBERT RYLE

It is no part of the object of this book to swell the ranks of theories of knowledge in general, or of theories of perception in particular. It is, rather, one of its motives to show that a lot of the theories that go by those names are, or embody, unwanted para-mechanical hypotheses. When theorists pose such 'wires and pulleys' questions as, 'How are past experiences stored in the mind?', 'How does a mind reach out past its screen of sensations to grasp the physical realities outside?', 'How do we subsume the data of sense under concepts and categories?', they are apt to pose these problems as if they were problems about the existence and interconnections of hidden bits of ghostly apparatus. They talk as if they were doing something like speculative anatomy or even counter-espionage.

Since, however, we do not regard the fact that a person has a sensation as a fact about his mind, whereas the fact that he observes something and the fact that he tends not to observe things of certain sorts do belong to the description of his mental operations and powers, it is proper to say more about this difference.

We use the verb "to observe' in two ways. In one use, to say that someone is observing something is to say that he is trying, with or without success, to find out something about it by doing at least some looking, listening, savouring, smelling or feeling. In another use, a person is said to have observed something, when his exploration has been successful, i.e., that he has found something out by some such methods. Verbs of perception such as 'see,' 'hear,' 'detect,' 'discriminate' and many others are generally used to record observational successes, while verbs like 'watch,' 'listen,' 'probe,' 'scan' and 'savour' are used to record observational undertakings, the success of which may be still in question. Hence it is proper to speak of someone watching carefully and successfully, but not of his seeing carefully or successfully, of his probing systematically, but not of his discovering systematically, and so on. The simple-seeming assertion 'I see a linnet' claims a success, where 'I am trying to make out what is moving' reports only an investigation.

In our present inquiry it will sometimes be convenient to use the ambiguous word 'observe' just because it can be used as well to signify discovery as to signify search. The words 'perception' and 'perceive' which are often used as cardinal in these inquiries, are too narrow since they cover only achievements, as do the specific verbs of perception, 'see,' 'hear,' 'taste,' 'smell' and, in one sense, 'feel.'

It has already been remarked that observing entails having at least one sensation, though having sensations does not entail observing.[1] We might now ask, "What more is there in observing than having at least one sensation?' But this formulation of the question is misleading, since it suggests that visually observing a robin consists in both having at least one visual sensation and doing or having something else as well, i.e., in two states or processes coupled together, as humming and walking can be coupled together; and this need not be the case. There is a crucial difference between doing something with heed and doing it, e.g., in absence of mind, but this difference does not consist in heeding being a concomitant act, occurring in another 'place.'[2] So we should ask, not, 'What is an observer doing besides having sensations?', but, 'What does the description of an observer embody over and above the description of him as having those sensations?' This point will be important before long.

We should begin by dismissing a model which in one form or other dominates many speculations about perception. The beloved but spurious question, 'How can a person get beyond his sensations to apprehension of external realities?' is often posed as if the situation were like this. There is immured in a windowless cell a prisoner, who has lived there in solitary confinement since birth. All that comes to him from the outside world is flickers of light thrown upon his cell-walls and tappings heard through the stones; yet from these observed flashes and tappings he becomes, or seems to become, apprised of unobserved football-matches, flower-gardens and eclipses of the sun. How then does he learn the ciphers in which his signals are arranged, or even find out that there are such things as ciphers?

[1] *The Concept of Mind,* pp. 203 ff. (all footnotes in this section have been supplied by the editors).
[2] Argued in Chapter V (Section 4), *loc. cit.*

How can he interpret the messages which he somehow deciphers, given that the vocabularies of those messages are the vocabularies of football and astronomy and not those of flickers and tappings?

This model is of course the familiar picture of the mind as a ghost in a machine, about the general defects of which nothing more need be said. But certain particular defects do need to be noticed. The use of this sort of model involves the explicit or implicit assumption that, much as the prisoner can see flickers and hear tappings, but cannot, unfortunately, see or hear football matches, so we can observe our visual and other sensations, but cannot, unfortunately, observe robins. But this is doubly to abuse the notion of observation. As has been shown, on the one had, it is nonsense to speak of a person witnessing a sensation, and, on the other, the ordinary use of verbs like 'observe,' 'espy,' 'peer at' and so on is in just such contexts as 'observe a robin,' 'espy a ladybird' and 'peer at a book.'[3] Football matches are just the sorts of things of which we do catch glimpses; and sensations are the sorts of things of which it would be absurd to say that anyone caught glimpses. In other words, the prison model suggests that, in finding out about robins and football matches, we have to do something like inferring from sensations, which we do observe, to birds and games, which we never could observe; whereas in fact it is robins and games that we observe, and it is sensations that we never could observe. The question, 'How do we jump from descrying or inspecting sensations to becoming apprised of robins and football matches?' is a spurious how-question.

Now there is no unique and central problem of perception. There is a range of partially overlapping questions, most of which will cease to be intriguing, the moment that a few of them have been cleared up. We can illustrate certain of the problems which belong to this range in this way. To describe someone as finding a thimble is to say something about his having visual, tactual or auditory sensations, but it is to say more than that. Similarly to describe someone as trying to make out whether what he sees is a chaffinch or a robin, a stick or a shadow, a fly on the window or a mote in his eye, is to say something about his visual sensations, but it is to say more than that. Finally, to describe someone as 'seeing' a snake that is not there, or as 'hearing' voices, where all is silent, seems to be saying something about his images, if not about his sensations, but it is to say more than that. What more is being said? Or, what is the specific force of such descriptions in respect of which they differ both from one another and from 'neat' descriptions of sensations, supposing that we could produce such descriptions? The questions,

3 Reference is to Chapter VII (Section 3), *loc. cit.*

that is, are not questions of the para-mechanical form 'How do we see robins?', but questions of the form, 'How do we use such descriptions as "he saw a robin"?'

When we describe someone as having detected a mosquito in the room, what more are we saying than that there was a certain sort of singing in his ears? We begin by answering that he not only had a singing in his ears but also recognised or identified what he heard as the noise of a fairly adjacent mosquito; and we are inclined to go on to say in more generic terms that he was not only having a singing in his ears, but was also thinking certain thoughts; perhaps that he was subsuming the singing under a concept, or that he was coupling an intellectual process with his sensitive state. But in saying this sort of thing, though we have one foot on the right track, we also have one foot on the wrong track. We are beginning to go on the wrong track, when we say that there must have taken place such and such conceptual or discursive processes; since this is in effect, if not in intention, to say that detecting a mosquito could not happen, unless some special but unobserved ghostly wheels had gone round, wheels whose existence and functions only epistemologists are clever enough to diagnose. On the other hand, in saying this sort of thing we are also on the right track. It is certainly true that a man could not detect a mosquito if he did not know what mosquitoes were and what they sounded like; or if, through absent-mindedness, panic or stupidity, he failed to apply this knowledge to the present situation; for this is part of what 'detecting' means.

We do not, that is, want tidings or hypotheses about any other things which the listener may have privily done or undergone. Even if there had taken place three, or seventeen, such *entr'actes,* news about them would not explain how detecting a mosquito differs from having a shrill singing in the ears. What we want to know is how the logical behaviour of 'he detected a mosquito' differs from that of 'there was a singing in his ears,' from that of 'he tried in vain to make out what was making the noise,' and from that of 'he mistook it for the noise of the wind in the telephone wires.'

Let us consider a slightly different situation in which a person would be described as not merely hearing something, and not merely listening to something, and not merely trying to make out what he was hearing, but as identifying or recognising what he heard, namely the case of a person who recognises a tune. For this situation to obtain, there must be notes played in his hearing, so he must not be deaf, or anaesthetised, or fast asleep. Recognising what he hears entails hearing. It also entails heeding; the absent-minded or distracted man is not following the tune. But more than this, he must have met this tune before; and he must not only have met it, but also have learned it and not forgotten it. If he did not in this sense already know the tune, he could not be said to recognise it on listening to it now.

What then is it for a person to know a tune, that is to have learned and not forgotten it? It certainly does not entail his being able to tell its name, for it may have no name; and even if he gave it the wrong name, he might still be said to know the tune. Nor does it entail his being able to describe the tune in words, or write it out in musical notation, for few of us could do that, though most of us can recognise tunes. He need not even be able to hum or whistle the tune, though if he can do so, he certainly knows the tune; and if he can hum or whistle plenty of other tunes, but cannot produce this one, even when prompted, we suspect that he does not know this tune. To describe him as knowing the tune is at the least to say that he is capable of recognising it, when he hears it; and he will be said to recognise it, when he hears it, if he does any, some or all of the following things: if, after hearing a bar or two, he expects those bars to follow which do follow; if he does not erroneously expect the previous bars to be repeated; if he detects omissions or errors in the performance; if, after the music has been switched off for a few moments, he expects it to resume about where it does resume; if, when several people are whistling different tunes, he can pick out who is whistling this tune; if he can beat time correctly; if he can accompany it by whistling or humming it in time and tune, and so on indefinitely. And when we speak of him expecting the notes which are due to follow and not expecting notes or bars which are not due to follow, we do not require that he be actually thinking ahead. Given that he is surprised, scornful or amused, if the due notes and bars do not come at their due times, then it is true to say that he was expecting them, even though it is false to say that he went through any processes of anticipating them.

In short, he is now recognising or following the tune, if, knowing how it goes, he is now using that knowledge; and he uses that knowledge not just by hearing the tune, but by hearing it in a special frame of mind, the frame of mind of being ready to hear both what he is now hearing and what he will hear, or would be about to hear, if the pianist continues playing it and is playing it correctly. He knows how it goes and he now hears the notes as the progress of that tune. He hears them according to the recipe of the tune, in the sense that what he hears is what he is listening for. Yet the complexity of this description of him as both hearing the notes, as they come, and listening for, or being ready for, the notes that do, and the notes that should, come does not imply that he is going through a complex of operations. He need not, for example, be coupling with his hearing of the notes any silent or murmured prose-moves, or 'subsuming' what he hears 'under the concept of the tune.' Indeed, if he were told to think the thought of 'Lillibullero,' without producing, imagining or actually listening to the tune itself, he would say that there was nothing left for him to think; and if he were told that the fact that he could recognise the tune, even though played in various ways in various situations, meant that he had a Concept, or Abstract Idea, of the tune, he would properly object that he could not think what it would be like to be considering or applying the Abstract Idea of 'Lillibullero,' unless this meant merely that he could recognise the tune, when he heard it, detect mistakes and omissions in it, hum snatches from it and so on.

This enables us to reconsider what was said earlier, namely, that a person who recognises what he hears is not only having auditory sensations, but is also thinking. It is not true that a person following a familiar tune need be thinking thoughts such that there must be an answer to the question, 'What thoughts has he been thinking?' or even 'What general concepts has he been applying?' It is not true that he must have been pondering or declaring propositions to himself, or to the company, in English or French; and it is not true that he must have been marshalling any visual or auditory images. What is true is that he must have been in some degree vigilant, and the notes that he heard must have fallen as he expected them to fall, or shocked him by not doing so. He was neither merely listening, as one might listen to an unfamiliar air, nor yet was he necessarily coupling his listening with some other process; he was just listening according to the recipe.

To clarify further the senses in which following a known tune is and is not 'thinking,' let us consider the case of a person hearing a waltz for the first time. He does not know how this tune goes, but since he knows how some other waltz tunes go, he knows what sorts of rhythms to expect. He is partially but not fully prepared for the succeeding bars, and he can partially but not completely place the notes already heard and now being heard. He is wondering just how the tune goes, and in wondering he is trying to piece out the arrangement of the notes. At no moment is he quite ready for the note that is due next. That is, he is thinking in the special sense of trying to puzzle something out.

But, in contrast with him, the person who already knows the tune follows the tune without any business of puzzling or trying to make out how the tune goes. It is completely obvious to him all the time. There need be no activity, not even a very swift and very easy activity, of trying to resolve uncertainties, for there are no uncertainties. He is not listening in a worrying-out way; he is just listening. Yet he is not merely hearing notes, for he is hearing 'Lillibullero.' Not only are the notes clearly audible to him (perhaps they are not), but the tune is quite obvious to him; and the obviousness of the tune is not a fact about his auditory sensitiveness, it is a fact about what he has learned and not forgotten and his present application of those lessons.

Finally, though following a familiar tune entails having become familiarised with it, it does not require going through any operations of reminiscence. Memories of past hearings of the tune need not well up, or be called up. The sense of 'thinking' in which a person following a familiar tune can be said to be thinking what he is hearing, is not that thoughts of past auditions are occurring to him. He has not forgotten how it goes, but he is not recalling how it formerly went.

Roughly, to know how a tune goes is to have acquired a set of auditory expectation propensities, and to recognise or follow a tune is to be hearing expected note after expected note. And this does not entail the occurrence of any other exercises of expectation than listening for what is being heard and what is due to be heard. The description of a person hearing expected notes is indeed different from that of a person hearing unexpected notes and from that of a person who hears notes without any expectations at all, (like a person who is hearing but not listening); but this does not mean that there is something extra going on in the first person which is not going on in the second or the third. It means that the hearing is going on in a different way, the description of which difference involves, not a report of extra occurrences, but only the characterisation of his hearing as specially schooled hearing. That a person is following a tune is, if you like, a fact both about his ears and about his mind; but it is not a conjunction of one fact about his ears and another fact about his mind, or a conjoint report of one incident in his sensitive life and another incident in his intellectual life. It is what I have called a 'semi-hypothetical,' or 'mongrel-categorical,' statement.[4]

We can now turn to consider some of the kinds of perceptual episodes which are ordinarily taken as the standard models of perceptual recognition. We shall see that they are in many important respects of a piece with the recognition of a tune. I chose to start with the example of someone following a familiar tune, because

4 *Loc cit.*, p. 141.

this is a protracted occupation. We can see a gate-post in a flash, but we cannot hear 'Lillibullero' in a flash. There is here, consequently, no temptation to postulate the occurrence of lightning intellectual processes, processes too rapid to be noticed, but intellectual enough to execute all the Herculean labours demanded by epistemologists.

When a person is described as having seen the thimble, part of what is said is that he has had at least one visual sensation, but a good deal more is said as well. Theorists commonly construe this as meaning that a description of a person as having seen the thimble both says that he had at least one visual sensation and says that he did or underwent something else as well; and they ask accordingly, 'What else did the finder of the thimble do or undergo, such that he would not have found the thimble if he had not done or undergone these extra things?' Their queries are then answered by stories about some very swift and unnoticed inferences, or some sudden and unrememberable intellectual leaps, or some fetching up of concepts and clapping them upon the heads of the visual data. They assume, that is, that because the proposition 'he espied the thimble' has a considerable logical complexity, it therefore reports a considerable complication of processes. And as these processes are not witnessed going on, it is postulated that they must be going on in a place where they cannot be witnessed, namely, in the finder's stream of consciousness.

Our analysis of what we have in mind, when we say that someone recognises a tune, can be applied to the new case. Certainly a person who espies the thimble is recognising what he sees, and this certainly entails not only that he has a visual sensation, but also that he has already learned and not forgotten what thimbles look like. He has learned enough of the recipe for the looks of thimbles to recognise thimbles when he sees them in ordinary lights and positions at ordinary distances and from ordinary angles. When he espies the thimble on this occasion, he is applying his lesson; he is actually doing what he has learned to do. Knowing how thimbles look, he is ready to anticipate, though he need not actually anticipate, how it will look, if he approaches it, or moves away from it; and when, without having executed any such anticipations, he does approach it, or move away from it, it looks as he was prepared for it to look. When the actual glimpses of it that he gets are got according to the thimble recipe, they satisfy his acquired expectation-propensities; and this is his espying the thimble.

As with the tune, so with the thimble; if the recognition is impeded by no difficulties, if, that is, the thimble is obvious to the observer from the first glance, then no extra thinking or pondering, no puzzlings or reminiscences need be performed. He need not say anything in English or in French, to himself or to the world; he need not marshal memory images or fancy images; he need not wonder, make conjectures, or take precautions; he need not recall past episodes; he need do nothing that would be described as the thinking of thoughts, though, if linguistically equipped, he can be expected to be ready to do some of these things, if there arises any call to do so. The sense in which he is thinking and not merely having a visual sensation, is that he is having a visual sensation in a thimble-seeing frame of mind. Just as a person who recognises a tune from the first few bars is prepared both retrospectively for those already heard and those now being heard and prospectively for the bars that are to follow, though he goes through no additional operations of preparing for them, so a person who recognises a cow at sight is prepared for a multifarious variety of sights, sounds and smells, of none of which need the thought actually occur to him.

The difficulty will probably be felt that even if this sort of account of the visual obviousness of thimbles and the auditory obviousness of tunes is true, the real question remains unanswered. How do we learn that there are thimbles in the first place? How can a person who starts with mere sensations reach the stage of finding out that there are physical objects? But this is a queer sort of how-question, since, construing it in one way, we all know the answer perfectly well. We know how infants come to learn that some noises do, and others do not, belong to tunes; that some tuneless sequences of noises, like nursery rhymes, have recognisable rhythms; others, like clock-noises, have recognisable monotonies; while yet others, like rattle-noises, are random and disorderly. We know, too, the sorts of games and exercises by which mothers and nurses teach their infants lessons of these sorts. There is no more of an epistemological puzzle involved in describing how infants learn perception recipes than there is in describing how boys learn to bicycle. They learn by practice, and we can specify the sorts of practice that expedite this learning.

Now clearly stories about learning by practice will not be felt to give the solution of the how-question asked above. This question was not intended as a question about the stages through which capacities and interests develop, or about the aids and impediments to their development. What then was intended? Perhaps its poser might say something like this. 'There is, perhaps, no philosophical puzzle about how children learn tunes, or recognise them, when they have once learned them. Nor perhaps is there a puzzle about analogous learning of recipes in respect of sights, tastes and smells. But there is a big difference between learning a tune and finding out that there are such things as violins, thimbles, cows and gate-posts. Finding out that there are material objects requires, as learning tunes does not, getting beyond noises, sights, tastes and smells to public existents other than, and independent of, our personal sensations. And by the metaphorical expression "getting beyond" is meant getting to know that such objects exist on the basis of originally knowing only that these sensations exist. Our puzzle is, therefore, in accordance with what principles, and from what premisses, can a person validly conclude that cows and gate-posts exist? Or, if by some lucky instinct he correctly believes such things without inferences, by what inferences can he justify these instinctive beliefs?' That is, the how-question is to be construed as a Sherlock Holmes question of the type 'what evidence had the detective ascertained which enabled him to confirm his suspicion that the gamekeeper was the murderer?' And construing the question in this way, we can swiftly see that it is an improper question. When we speak of the evidence ascertained by the detective, we are thinking of things which he or his informants had observed or witnessed, such as fingerprints found on glasses and conversations overheard by eavesdroppers. But a sensation is not something which its owner observes or witnesses. It is not a clue. Listening to a conversation entails having auditory sensations, for listening is heedful hearing, and hearing entails getting auditory sensations. But having sensations is not discovering clues. We discover clues by listening to conversations and looking at fingerprints. If we could not observe some things, we should not have clues for other things, and conversations are just the sorts of things to which we do listen, as fingerprints and gate-posts are just the sorts of things at which we do look.

This improper how-question is tempting, partly because there is a tendency mistakenly to suppose that all learning is discovery by inference from previously ascertained evidence; and then a process of sensing sense data is cast for the role of ascertaining the initial evidence. In fact, of course, we learn how to make inferences from previously ascertained facts just as we learn how to play chess, ride bicycles, or recognise gate-posts, namely by practice, reinforced, maybe, by some schooling. The application of rules of inference is not a condition of learning by practice; it is just one of the countless things learned by practice.

As has been shown, listening and looking are not merely having sensations; nor, however, are they joint processes of observing sensations and inferring to common objects. A person listening or looking is doing something which he would not do, if he were deaf or blind; or, what is quite different, if he were absent-minded, distracted or quite uninterested; or, what is quite different again, if he had not learned to use his ears and eyes. Observing is using one's ears and eyes. But using one's ears and eyes does not entail using, in a different sense, one's visual and auditory sensations as clues. It makes no sense to speak of 'using' sensations. It will not even do to say that in watching a cow, I am finding out about the cow 'by means of' visual sensations, since this too would suggest that sensations are tools, objects which can be handled in the same sorts of ways as the things seen and heard can be handled. And this would be even more misleading than it would be to say that manipulating a hammer involves first manipulating my fingers, or that I control the hammer by dint of controlling my fingers.

There is another favourite model for the description of sensations. As flour, sugar, milk, eggs and currants are among the raw materials out of which the confectioner concocts cakes, or as bricks and timber are among the raw materials of the builder, so sensations are often spoken of as the raw materials out of which we construct the world we know. As a counterblast to even more misleading stories this story had some important merits. But the notions of collecting, storing, sorting, unpacking, treating, assembling and arranging, which apply to the ingredients of cakes and the materials of houses do not apply to sensations. We can ask what a cake is made of, but not what knowledge is made of; we can ask what those ingredients are to be made into, but not what is going to be concocted or constructed out of the visual and auditory sensations which the child has recently been having.

We can conclude, then, that there is no difference of principle, though there are plenty of differences in detail, between recognising tunes and recognising gate-posts. One such difference may be mentioned, before we leave the subject. At a fairly early stage of infancy, the child learns to co-ordinate, for example, the sight recipes, the sound recipes and feel recipes of things like rattles and kittens; and having begun to learn how things of particular sorts can be expected to look, sound and feel, he then begins to learn how they behave; when, for example, the rattle or the kitten makes a noise and when it makes none. He now observes things in an experimental way. But the relatively contemplative business of learning tunes does not, by itself, involve much co-ordination of looks with sounds, or give much room for experimentation. But this is a difference of degree, not one of kind.

*Sensation and Observation*     155

One or two residual points should receive brief notice. First, in talking of a person learning a perception recipe, I am not talking of his discovering any causal laws, such as those of physiology, optics or mechanics. The observation of common objects is prior to the discovery of general correlations between special kinds of common objects. Next, in talking of a person knowing a perception recipe, e.g., knowing how common objects are due to look, sound and feel, I am not crediting him with the ability to formulate or impart this recipe. Somewhat as most people know how to tie a few different sorts of knots, but are quite incapable of describing those knots, or following spoken or printed descriptions of them, so we all know how to identify a cow at sight a very long time before we can tell the world anything about the visible marks by which we recognise it, and quite an appreciable time before we can draw, paint or even recognise pictures of cows. Indeed, if we did not learn to recognise things on sight or hearing, before we had learnt to talk about them, we could never start at all. Talking and understanding talk themselves involve recognising words on saying and hearing them.

Though I have drawn most of my instances of seeing according to perception recipes from cases of non-mistaken observation, such as espying a gate-post, where there is a gate-post, the same general account holds for mistaken observations such as 'espying" a huntsman, where there is really a pillar box, 'discerning' a stick, where there is really a shadow, or 'seeing' a snake on the eiderdown, when there is really nothing on the eiderdown. Getting a thing wrong entails what getting it right entails, namely, the use of a technique. A person is not careless, if he has not learned a method, but only if he has learned it and does not apply it properly. Only a person who can balance can lose his balance; only a person who can reason can commit fallacies; only a person who can discriminate huntsmen from pillar boxes can mistake a pillar box for a huntsman; and only a person who knows what snakes look like can fancy he sees a snake without realising that he is only fancying.

# CHAPTER 8

# Human and Mechanical Recognition

KENNETH SAYRE

Development of pattern-recognition mechanisms is motivated by both practical and theoretical interests. An audible pattern recognizer coupled with an automatic encoder could provide an efficient means of communicating with electronic computers, and a reliable recognizer of imperfectly formed visual patterns could be developed into a reader for the blind. Similar practical applications could be found in business, industry, and government.

Theoretical interest in mechanical pattern recognition centers around the hope that a self-organizing electronic network which responds as we do to repeated stimulation by similar patterns would suggest promising directions of research into the nature of some of man's mental processes.

Moderate success has been achieved in constructing mechanisms which recognize standard patterns such as printed letters and spoken vowels. However, attempts to design machines which approximate human behavior in recognizing variously formed patterns, like letters in script or spoken words, have been at best exploratory. There is a feeling among technologists concerned with the problem that a "breakthrough" is needed.

One difficulty in the endeavor to match mechanical to human behavior in this regard is that it is far from clear what sort of activity counts as recognition of a pattern by a human being. It is not clear consequently what sort of behavior is to be duplicated or approximated by mechanical devices. Although some investigators seem aware of this problem, there is little evidence of any sustained attempt to sharpen our understanding of human pattern recognition. The deficiency at point is not the admitted lack of a comprehensive psychological theory of recognition, but rather the lack of a clear description of what humans do in various situations which normally would be taken as instances of pattern recognition. In this paper I wish to discuss briefly several typical instances of human pattern recognition, to describe available techniques of mechanical recognition, and then to indicate which aspects of human performance can and which probably cannot be duplicated by mechanical means. Such a comparison, if even partially successful, would provide the considerable assistance of indicating what sort of deficiencies count most in our inability to construct mechanical recognizers with a versatility approaching that of human beings.

'Recognition' is a relational term, in the typical use of which there is reference to a recognizer or group of recognizers, to an object of which the recognizer is aware, and to a class of which the object is identified as a member. The suggestion that some reference to each of these is necessary in a satisfactory definition of 'recognition' is fortified by the following observations: (1) it would be senseless to say that an object was recognized or recognizable, but that it was recognized or recognizable by no one; (2) we would not say under any ordinary circumstances that we recognize an apple, or some other object, but were aware of no such object; and (3) it seems to follow in common use of the terms that it would be inconsistent to say we recognize an apple but that the object recognized could not be identified as a member of the class of apples. Thus for our purposes, to say that an observer O recognizes an object $x$ may be understood to mean that there is a class of objects of which $x$ is a member, and that O in being aware of $x$ has identified $x$ as a member of that class.

It is not a consequence of this definition that O be able to specify the characteristics with reference to which he is able to identify $x$ as a member of its class. Although it may seem paradoxical to suggest that we identify an object without being able to specify the characteristics by which we identify it, in fact there are common situations in which this happens. Consider case 1) below, in which a human typically is able to recognize a written letter but unable to say how he does so.

*Case* 1). A human observer is presented with a series of written symbols, some but not all of which are instances of the letter $A$. No two instances of $A$ have exactly the same shape, nor have they any other obvious features in common. Some have crossbars (A), others none ( *a* ), some contain closed loops ( *a* ), others not ( A ), some are squared off on top ( A ), others not (A), etc. None of the letters, however, is radically distorted. A set of symbols meeting these conditions could be provided which is such that a large majority of subjects would identify the same symbols as instances of the letter $A$ and reject all others. Yet few of the subjects, if any, would be able to specify exactly what characteristics of the chosen symbols furnished the criteria by which they made their choices. If, in fact, it were a routine matter to specify the characteristics by which ordinary instances of the written letter $A$ could be identified, it would be a relatively routine matter to construct a machine which could perform this identification.

It is not part of this case to suggest that it is in principle impossible to find a set of characteristics which would uniquely identify all or almost all symbols which normally would be taken as instances of A. Let us assume to the contrary that such a set of characteristics can be provided. This case, then, illustrates situations in which we are able to recognize objects as being of a certain type without being able to specify characteristics which all objects of that type possess, although there is a set of such characteristics which are specifiable in principle.

*Case* 2). There are some objects we often recognize without reference to their identifying characteristics, even though these characteristics would be relatively easy to specify. For example, we are able to recognize square figures as squares without counting sides and without any conscious reference to a definition of the square which makes explicit its property of having four straight sides. And a five-pointed star often can be recognized as such without explicit counting of the points. In such cases it is always possible to apply specific criteria in identifying the object, but usually we are able to perform successful identifications without bringing the criteria to mind.

*Case* 3). Recognition of objects whose relevant characteristics cannot be taken in at a glance requires explicit application of identifying criteria. Recognition of a 1000-sided figure, or of a correct proof in logic, requires deliberate reference to the defining properties of the object to be recognized. If one cannot assess the specific features required of a proper logical proof, he cannot recognize a proper proof when confronted with one; if one cannot count, he cannot recognize a 1000-sided figure.

*Case* 4). There are some objects which we recognize with high reliability, but for which no identifying characteristics can be specified. One type of example concerns unanalyzable qualities such as red, sweetness, or pleasure. By 'red' or 'sweetness', etc., in this respect, I mean the quality directly presented to the percipient, and not the physical occurrences which may have occasioned the presentation of the quality to us. The *light* normally associated with the experience of red can be characterized in terms of measurements by spectrometers, or by a range of frequencies within the visible spectrum. But *red as experienced* is not a complex property, and hence cannot be defined in terms of other properties. Thus our recognition of red must proceed without involvement of a set of identifying criteria.

In a sense, however, red is not a pattern, and our main concern is with the recognition of patterns. An alternative example is provided by configurations of radar returns on a display scope which represent moving aircraft. An experienced radar operator can usually discriminate configurations which correspond to aircraft, from those caused by anomalous radar returns, without difficulty in instances where an inexperienced observer would be unable to see any difference between them. Yet it seems impossible in fact if not in principle to formulate any set of characteristics which are shared by all aircraft returns and which are at least in part missing in all anomalous configurations.

Another suggestive example is the maze of lines and shadows which conceals the visual image of an ordinary object. Once the object is "seen" in the scramble, it stands out clearly and can be easily recognized in subsequent viewings of the maze. A description of the lines and shadows within the maze after the object had been identified would not differ from a similar description of these properties as they appeared previous to identification of the object. That is, a description of the geometrical properties of the picture in which the object is recognizable will not differ from a geometrical description of the picture in which the object does not appear. Criteria for identification of the object thus cannot be given in terms of the geometrical constituents of the image of the object as it appears in the maze.

Cases 1), 2), and 4) have in common that no explicit set of criteria figures in recognition of the concerned objects. Only in case 3) does ability to recognize depend upon ability to enumerate specific properties which an object must have in order to qualify as a member of its class.

In cases where criteria for recognition operate, there is a further distinction to be made between ways of acquiring the criteria prior to recognition. Recognition requires precognition. It is clear that becoming aware of criteria is part of the process of learning to recognize objects of certain types. In such cases we would not normally speak of recognizing objects of a given class if we had no previous information regarding properties of objects of that class. Frequently the criteria can be expressed in terms of properties which we have already learned to discriminate. In other instances a *novel* discrimination is necessary before we can grasp all the properties entering into the criteria for identification. The following examples illustrate this distinction.

*Case* a). A regular tetrahedron may be defined in terms already familiar to a student who has the concepts of a solid and an equilateral triangle. Thus in learning what characteristics are relevant to the identification of a tetrahedron the student need not learn to discriminate properties with which he was previously unfamiliar. Learning to recognize under such circumstances requires no new descriptive categories, but consists merely in ordering familiar descriptive categories in a new way. Ability to recognize objects which can be described in familiar terms can be acquired by a merely verbal learning transaction without recourse to physical illustrations.

*Case* b). Ability to recognize objects of a novel type sometimes can be acquired by being presented with a single object of that type, along with information concerning what the object is. A person familiar with various sorts of wine glasses, for example, might learn to recognize a brandy glass merely by being shown one and by being told what the glass is for. This information would alert someone that the configuration of the stem and base, the shape and size of the bowl, and the contour of the cross-section, all are significant factors in the identity of the object. Someone already accustomed to distinguishing these characteristics in wine glasses of other sorts very likely would be able to tell at a glance what is unique about brandy glasses.

*Case* c). Learning to recognize an object whose identifying properties are different from any the learner previously had been able to discriminate involves the acquisition of novel descriptive categories. A person who could not distinguish between the sides and other features of a polygon could not be taught to recognize a 1000-sided figure. Neither could he be taught to recognize a hexagon. At some stage in the development of a person learning to recognize increasingly complex geometrical configurations, he must become able to focus his attention on features of geometrical patterns which previously had always escaped his notice. Similarly, a person who did not possess the concept of an electronic element in a vacuum tube would be unable to recognize a rectifier as distinct from an amplifier without first acquiring the concept of an electronic element.

In cases a) and b) the subject is able to learn the identifying criteria of a novel sort of object without having first to acquire the ability to distinguish characteristics of which previously he was unaware. In cases like c), it is part of his learning to recognize a novel sort of object that he learn to distinguish novel characteristics as well.

Learning to focus attention upon novel characteristics is not simply a matter of instruction or of behavioral conditioning. A child may be presented with several objects which have only the color red in common in an effort to teach him the use of the term 'red', but unless he has the ability to consider the color of an object apart from its shape or size no learning will occur. A pigeon can be taught to discriminate basic colors and shapes, but this is only possible because pigeons have the ability before conditioning to concentrate upon color in some of its responses and shapes in others. Responses which involve isolation of features of his environment perhaps can be reinforced in a pigeon; but the unlearned ability to isolate characteristics is a precondition of our being able to reinforce *any* of his responses, or to change the structure of his behavior in any way. Similarly, when a person attempts to learn how to recognize an object some of whose identifying characteristics are novel to him, he can do so only if he is able to focus his attention on instances of those characteristics and to consider them as distinct from other characteristics which may be present in the object he is observing.

The ability illustrated in case c) which is different from anything present in cases a) and b) is that of acquiring new descriptive categories, which cannot be defined or taught in terms of other categories with which the subject previously was familiar.

In this section we discuss briefly various mechanical recognition techniques which have shown moderate promise, and propose that it is inherent in these techniques (a) that no patterns can be recognized by them whose identifying characteristics cannot be specified completely in terms of categories provided to the recognizing system (as in cases 1), 2), and 3) above), and (b) that no refinement conceived at present will make these systems capable of arriving at novel identifying characteristics (as in case c) above). Use of an electronic computer is involved in all promising systems for mechanical recognition. Thus we begin by indicating various features of computers which suggest the propositions (a) and (b) above.

Our current electronic computers share the ancestry of the mechanical desk calculators common in business offices. This ancestry traces directly back to the difference engines of Charles Babbage (about 1820), and indirectly to calculating mechanisms built by Pascal and Leibniz. Yet the major developments which separate the electronic computer from the desk calculator have taken place within the past 25 years.

In Babbage's engine, as well as in the desk calculator, each number entered into the machine is represented by the position or orientation of one or several mechanical components. In a simple machine two adjacent wheels with numerical two's displayed on top might indicate the number twenty-two; yet it would be the position of the wheels rather than what happened to be marked on them that would represent the number in the machine. Calculations in such a machine would occur in motions of interconnected physical parts. Thus the operating speed of such a machine is limited by the speed with which its components can be moved, and its information-handling capacity is limited by the physical constraints involved in the efficient mechanical connection of a large number of distinct physical parts.

Computer technology in the contemporary sense was made possible by the substitution of electronic storage and switching devices for the cogs and levers of calculating machines. Previously an item of information could be represented within a machine only by mechanical states of its components. Now it is possible to represent information in terms of the momentary electromagnetic states of vacuum tubes. Since vacuum tube states can be altered very rapidly, the operating speed of these machines was greatly increased. But the information-handling capacity of the early electronic computers was severely limited by the technical problem of dissipating the heat energy resulting from the simultaneous operation of the large number of vacuum tubes needed to represent a large number of separate information bits. This particular restriction was overcome only recently by the development of electronic storage devices other than vacuum tubes, and by the invention of small solid-state electronic switching and amplifying devices which perform most of the functions of vacuum tubes more quickly and with less energy dissipation. With these devices incorporated into contemporary computers, both storage and speed capabilities have been extended by several orders of magnitude over corresponding capabilities of the older machines.

The point to be retained in this cursory survey is one regarding the way information is stored and handled by computing machinery generally. Any item of information, whether a number, an instruction, or a rule of procedure, must be represented within the machine in a form which will enable it to have the desired effect upon the machine's operation. Since the representation of information within an electronic computer is in the form of electromagnetic states of its components, the user of the machine must communicate with it in terms of a specially devised language. Various equipments, such as card and tape punches, have been developed to help the user communicate with the machine, but the result of the communication in each case is the representation within the computer of each item of information by electromagnetic states of one or more of the computer's components. In this sense, what we can instruct the machine to do is limited by the capabilities of the machine. We cannot instruct it to perform a function which cannot be expressed entirely in terms of the computer's special language of electromagnetic states.

Another restriction upon what the computer can do lies with the user of the machine. Lady Lovelace, discussing one of Babbage's machines, remarked that "the Analytical Engine has no pretensions whatever to originate anything. It can do whatever we know how to order it to perform."[1] From the context it is clear that Lady Lovelace intended to say that the Engine can do *only* what we know how to instruct it to do. There is a sense in which this is true of contemporary computers, but also a sense in which it is false.

To illustrate the sense in which computers can do more than we can tell them how to do, consider the hypothetical case of the communication system interconnecting all major cities of a nation at war. The system automatically transmits messages between any two points along optimal routes which involve the least over-all communication delay at a given time. Since optimal routings will vary with number and distribution of messages at a given time, the task of finding optimal routings is assigned to a computer. Normally, adjacent cities would communicate directly, and non-adjacent cities would be linked indirectly through one of several possible intermediate points. When both the number of messages to be transmitted and the number of promising routes for any message are small, routing instructions could be given the computer for selecting a few likely combinations of routings and calculating which one of these few actually involve the least over-all communication delay. When several of these communication routes are broken by enemy action, however, the computer no longer can rely upon routine procedures. It has the dual problem of routing immediately an increased number of messages through a decreased number of channels, and of determining new procedures for the future routine transmission of messages. Immediately after the attack it passes messages randomly through any route available at the moment. By recording and continually re-examining the average delays involved in each randomly selected route, it seeks to develop a processing routine which incorporates more and more regularly those routings which turn out to be most expeditious. Soon after the attack, the computer has devised a new set of routings which enable it to route most messages through the altered communication system with minimum delay.

[1] Quoted on p. 398 in *Faster Than Thought*, B. V. Bowden (ed.), (London, Sir Isaac Pitman and Sons, Ltd., 1953).

In this example, the computer is given a specific task to do, and a specific criterion by which to judge the success of its performance. But it is not told specifically how to perform the task. Instead it is given general instructions covering many possible ways in which the task might be done. It is programmed to try these alternatives in random order, and then to begin to bias its instructions for selecting alternatives towards those which begin to appear more advantageous relative to the others. The computer would continue to alter its own operating instructions in this fashion until an optimal or near-optimal routine has been determined.

Although there are well-known difficulties involved in this sort of computer application, they do not seem insurmountable. Computers can do more than we tell them how to do, in the sense of selecting by trial and error optimal processing routines which we could not predict in advance. In such cases, however, it is necessary that we provide the computer with instructions for undertaking its process of selection, and with criteria for determining when the process has been completed.

A more obviously fictitious example will illustrate a sense in which computers cannot do more than we instruct them to do. Consider that astrophysicists perfect a radio-telescope capable of receiving a broad spectrum of wave lengths. While experimenting with the instrument they detect wave patterns analogous to music save for their higher frequency range. All attempts to analyze these patterns in terms of distinct frequencies, with harmonics and rhythmic intervals, however, fail to yield an intelligible hypothesis as to the origin of the waves. The scientists then decide to connect the radio-telescope to the most versatile computer available and to give the computer free rein in interpreting the patterns. To this end, they refrain from instructing the computer how to organize the data fed into it from the radio-telescope. The computer is given the job of finding its own categories in terms of which to process the data, and in terms of which to detect regularities which the scientists hope will enable them to find some connection with previously understood phenomena.

To understand better the plight of this computer, recall that all information is processed by a computer in the form of a series of electromagnetic charges. Different items of information are represented by different formations of these series. For the computer to accept a bit of information, it must be presented in a way which admits unique translation into one or another of these serial formations. Since many different items of information will be supplied to a computer in a typical problem, the person supplying the information must share with the computer a set of well-defined conventions regarding how much data in a given series of charges is relevant to a particular item of information, and regarding the order in which information of different kinds will be presented over a given period of time. These conventions are the only means the computer has of organizing the discrete electromagnetic signals presented to it in a way enabling them to be construed as representing information. Without these conventions, the input signals could represent nothing but themselves; they could not be taken as part of an information-laden pattern. Since no such conventions govern the imagined input to the computer in our example, it would be incapable of construing data from the telescope as information and consequently could produce no intelligible output.

These two hypothetical examples are helpful in illustrating techniques of pattern recognition, employing electronic computers, discussed in the section below.

As proposed above, to recognize an object $x$ is to identify $x$ as member of a class. An object is identifiable as member of a class with reference to the characteristics by virtue of which it is a member of that class. The term 'invariant' will be used to refer to that characteristic which distinguishes a given class of individuals from all other classes, and the possession of which qualifies an individual for membership in that class. The characteristic will be said to be *invariant over* the class of individuals. One basic problem of preparing a machine to recognize a given pattern is to find what characteristics are invariant over the class of individual instances of that pattern.

It might seem natural, in order to find the invariants of a pattern, to determine what characteristics are involved in human recognition of the pattern. But this is not an easy task, even with such a simple pattern as the letter $A$. Normally we encounter little difficulty in *applying* whatever criteria we in fact use in distinguishing $A$ from other letters, but it has proven difficult to *describe* these criteria explicitly in terms which can be entered into a computer. A more promising approach is to discover sets of characteristics which are easily expressible in computer language and which, when taken as invariant over a certain class, enable the computer to select approximately the same inscriptions which a human typically would recognize as members of that class. It might be the computer cannot be made to employ precisely the same criteria we employ in recognizing inscriptions of the letter $A$; but if it could be provided criteria by which it would identify all and only those inscriptions which we unhesitantly would recognize as $A$, we would be satisfied that we had produced a machine capable of recognizing $A$.

Three general approaches to the problem of providing invariants for the mechanical recognition of patterns have been explored by computer technologists. Listed in order of relative sophistication, they are (1) the template method, (2) the property list method, and (3) the adaptive programming method.

The *template method* provides a workable technique for recognizing inscriptions of patterns which are uniform in size, shape, and orientation. Each inscription to be recognized is positioned in a photo-electric scanner which is capable of discriminating small light and dark areas, and which is connected to a computer in such a way that a unique location in the computer's storage corresponds to each small area discriminated by the scanner. Each dark area may be represented in the computer by an electromagnetic charge interpretable as 'yes', and each light area by a charge interpretable as 'no.' In preparation for its recognition task, the computer has been provided with a standard figure with which to compare the presented inscription. This standard figure also is represented in the computer by an ordered series of yes's and no's, enabling it to be directly compared with the inscription to be tested. If all yes's and no's of the standard figure correspond respectively to yes's and no's of the presented inscription, the computer indicates that the inscription has been determined to be one of the same type as the standard. If there are few correspondences, a response occurs signifying no recognition. As a rule, however, neither of these extreme cases will occur. Since even carefully formed inscriptions often deviate considerably from any chosen standard, each inscription tested will correspond less than perfectly with the standard figure. The human director of the recognition program thus must decide in advance what degree of correspondence is necessary for an affirmative response by the computer.

The template method works well where the inscriptions to be recognized admit little variation in shape, but is generally inapplicable in cases where complete standardization is not achieved. In most cases successful recognition requires invariants more subtle than the actual shape of a configuration. In these cases it may be better to *describe* the relevant invariants rather than to attempt to represent them by particular standard configurations stored within a computer.

In the *property list method,* any feature or set of features of a pattern which can be described in computer language can be taken as an invariant feature of that pattern. Among features of letters which have been exploited in actual research with this method are closure, concavity, curvature of side, and various other edge characteristics. One researcher lists 32 features which in some combination figure as invariants in his recognition program.[2] But the great latitude of choice of invariants provided by this approach introduces its own problems. Since any consistent combination of features can serve as an invariant, the number of invariants the researcher would want to examine in order to ascertain the combination which gives the best results in recognizing a particular pattern might be excessive. For some applications, like programming a computer to play tic-tac-toe with actual circles and crosses, the relevant invariants are obvious. In some other applications, an arbitrary choice of invariants might be acceptable. But when the researcher's hope is to produce a machine which performs as human beings perform in recognizing poorly formed inscriptions, his proper choice of invariants is neither obvious nor arbitrary. Rather than undertake the endless task of trying all possible combinations of features, it is natural that the researcher enlist the aid of a computer in finding which combination will work best. This is the point of the adaptive programming method.

The *adaptive programming method* is an application of the principle of the self-optimizing system. Any system, natural or artificial, which has a specific function to perform, is capable of qualitative improvement or degradation in its performance. A system the performance of which cannot be further improved within a given set of circumstances has been optimized within those circumstances. When a system moves from an inoptimal to an optimal state, without any direct external control over the way it responds to its circumstances, it is said to have optimized itself. Now the function of a mechanical pattern recognizing system is to classify inscriptions in its environment according to some explicit criterion of correctness. If the system can increase its tendency to identify inscriptions of a pattern correctly on the basis of the results of its past performance, without further external alteration of its programs, it is a self-optimizing, or adaptive, system.

The programmer's part in such a process is to supply the machine with a list of features in terms of which inscriptions presented to it can be characterized, and to prepare a routine for the computer which initially makes equally probable the use of any promising combination of these features to describe a given pattern. Thus the invariants with which the machine begins its recognition attempts will be randomly generated, and generally unsuccessful. Individual features which enter into partially successful combinations as learning progresses are given higher probabilities of recurring in future combinations. When the learning phase is completed, the computer

[2] S. H. Unger, "Pattern Detection and Recognition." *Proceedings of the IRE,* Vol. 47, Oct. 1959, pp. 1737-52.

should have adapted its recognition criteria to achieve the highest percentage of correct identifications within its capability. The programmer's main contribution to this end is merely to provide a set of operating instructions which insures that any change the computer makes in its set of invariants will tend towards the optimal combination of features.

Adaptive pattern recognition systems are still in the research stage, although their feasibility has been determined.[3] Among major problems remaining are how to bring the program to an optimal combination in a relatively brief time, and how to insure that the program does not develop towards a good but not optimal combination and in the process lose its path towards the one optimal combination.

Two limitations of any method which has been proposed for the mechanical recognition of patterns appear significant in comparison with human recognition capabilities. The first is best exhibited by the adaptive programming method. In this method, the computer program itself tests various combinations of features, initially supplied by the programmer, in order to determine what combination provides the best invariant for identification of a given pattern. Great versatility is possible here, since the number of combinations available as invariants increases geometrically with the number of features initially provided to the machine. Yet the machine is incapable of generating an invariant which is not a combination of these initially provided features. The machine is not capable of discriminating features to which it has not been explicitly programmed to respond. Thus human ingenuity in discerning and defining promising features of patterns to be recognized remains a limiting factor in the recognition power the machine can develop, regardless of the facility it shows in moving towards an optimal set of identification criteria.

In a word, there is no analogue in the computer's repertoire to the human's ability to learn to recognize an object whose identifying characteristics are not reducible to other characteristics he previously had been able to discriminate. Thus the example of the computer which was set the task of interpreting the radio-telescope's message in terms of novel categories is fated to remain fictional, regardless of future developments in the astronomer's art.

[3] See: a) O. G. Selfridge, "Pandemonium: a Paradigm for Learning." *Proceedings of a Symposium on Mechanization of Thought Processes,* Vol. II (Her Majesty's Stationery Office. London, 1959). b) D. M. MacKay, "The Epistemological Problem for Automata." *Automata Studies,* Shannon and McCarthy (eds.) (Princeton, N.J.: Princeton University Press, 1956). c) T. Marill and D. M. Green, "Statistical Recognition Functions and the Design of Pattern Recognitions." *IRE Transactions on Electronic Computers.* (Dec. 1960).

The second limitation of any mechanical recognition system lies in its dependency upon distinct features of a pattern to provide identifying criteria for inscriptions of that pattern. If a pattern for some reason cannot be analyzed in terms of some set of its features, there is no way to prepare a machine to recognize it. The only configurations which a computer can discriminate directly are series of electromagnetic charges. All other configurations must be described in terms of their characteristics, and can only be recognized indirectly by testing for the presence of these characteristics in particular instances. As a consequence, any pattern which cannot be *analyzed* cannot be recognized by mechanical means. Human recognition, on the other hand, usually seems to occur without reference to specific identifying criteria, even in such cases where criteria would be easy to ascertain. Only with fairly involved configurations, like the 1000-sided figure, does human recognition normally involve reference to specific features of the configuration. Machine recognition, by contrast, invariably involves reference to specific features in even the simplest patterns.

The human typically is able to recognize certain patterns without reference to constituent characteristics, and is capable of discriminating novel characteristics when need arises. Mechanical recognition systems at present possess neither of these capabilities. This suggests that the significant difference between human and mechanical recognition systems lies not so much in the area of data processing as in the area of data acquisition or discrimination. It is in this latter area that a technological "breakthrough" is needed if machines are to approximate human recognition behavior.

# CHAPTER 9

# Stimulus Analysing Mechanisms

NORMAN SUTHERLAND

## SUMMARY

Two distinct approaches to the problem of stimulus analysing mechanisms in organisms are outlined. The first, often adopted by engineers, is to assume that there is a very general analysing system at work for each modality which in principle is capable of categorising stimuli in all possible ways. The second approach is to assume that specific analysing mechanisms are at work and that stimuli can only be categorised in a limited number of ways by these specific mechanisms.

If the first sort of system were correct it would be impossible to make predictions about how stimuli would be categorised based merely on the system: such predictions could only be made from a knowledge of previous inputs to the system. Evidence is produced to show that it is highly probable that some stimulus analysis is performed by specific mechanisms, at least in sub-mammalian organisms where many categorisations seem to be innate. The evidence for mammals is inconclusive, but suggestions are made for how it would be possible to test for the existence of the general type of analysing mechanisms in mammals. The existence of specific analysing mechanisms would not only be economical in terms of the number of nerve cells required, but it would account for many facts of animal and human behaviour, particularly if we envisage the possibility that the same specific analysing mechanisms may actually be used in different ways of categorising stimuli in one sensory modality and that some of the analysing mechanisms may be common to more than one modality. Thus competition for specific analysing mechanisms would explain why the human being seems to function as a single information channel, it would give a rationale for recent neurological findings on the peripheral blocking of incoming stimuli, and it would account for findings on animals which suggest that animals learn not merely to attach a response to a stimulus but also learn which analysing mechanims to switch in on a given occasion. Some of the difficulties in using behavioural evidence to set up hypotheses about specific analysing mechanisms are discussed, and the difficulty of deciding what sorts of coding mechanisms are at work in the central nervous system is discussed with reference to a particular example of a simple discrimination. It is suggested that engineers might profitably turn their attention to the design of specific analysing mechanisms intended to account for some of the ways in which animals are known to classify stimuli.

## INTRODUCTION

This paper will be concerned with the problem of how ideas based on engineering concepts can best be applied to help solve some of the problems which arise when we consider how patterned stimuli are classified by organisms. The paper will deal mainly with visually presented patterns.

There are two different kinds of theoretical mechanism which have been proposed to explain what organisms do. The first kind is one which attempts to give a very general explanation of what organisms do by postulating a broad model or type of connectivity, and then pointing to some very general features of the model's behaviour which are said to be shared by animals. Examples of this type of theory are those of Hebb (20), Uttley (63, 64), Taylor (61), Ashby (1).[1] The second kind of theory is of a more specific sort and is designed to explain a limited range of behaviour by putting forward a model whose parts are highly differentiated: examples of this kind of model are those put forward by Deutsch (10), Dodwell (11), and Sutherland (55) to explain certain features of shape recognition, or by Tinbergen (62), to explain certain features of instinctive behaviour. In the specific type of mechanism, the parts are arranged in a highly systematic way. In this sort of mechanism, information contained in the input can be selectively lost so that this sort of system is potentially more economical than general analysing mechanisms. This gain in economy is offset by a loss in flexibility. Wherever the classification of stimuli can be shown to be innate, the existence of a specific analysing mechanism is implied. Specific analysing mechanisms could, however, arise out of an initially randomly connected network as a result of learning: a small initial bias in part of the

[1] Numbers in parentheses refer to the list at the end of this article, ordered alphabetically by author (editors' note).

system could in theory lead to a highly specific system being developed out of an initially randomly connected network. For example, Sutherland (55), has suggested that the tendency of the octopus to move its head up and down while viewing shapes could lead through a learning process to the development of a visual analysing system in which the vertical extents of shapes are counted at different points on the horizontal axis, while other information is lost.

In what follows the two types of theory will be discussed in detail, and an attempt made to specify their characteristics. The rather general type of system will be considered first, and it ought to be said at the outset that I am perhaps prejudiced against this type of system. The rationale of this prejudice will be made clear later. In general it is typical of the first sort of system that it is put forward by engineers who know little about psychology, it is typical of the second sort that it is put forward by psychologists who know little engineering: Hebb is an exception to this rule.

### Characteristics of General Analysing Systems

If the neural mechanisms mediating stimulus classification are highly unspecific, this sets a severe limitation on the possibility of discovering what the neural mechanisms are and working from knowledge of the mechanisms to predictions about what animals will actually do. This can be illustrated with reference to Hebb's theory of shape recognition. According to Hebb the connections from the primary visual projection area in the brain are initially random: thresholds at synapses will presumably vary in a random way from moment to moment according to such factors as how recently the post-synaptic nerve cell has fired. This means that when a given shape is first projected onto the retina, it is impossible to predict what output the system will give: initially any shape is as likely to produce a given output as any other. However, once a shape has given a certain output the chance of its giving the same output on the next occasion of presentation will be increased (provided it stimulates the same retinal cells), since it is postulated that the probability of a given synaptic connection being used increases every time it is in fact used. Moreover, given that a given shape falling on a given part of the retina excites a given cell assembly as a result of an increase in the probability of transmission at specific synapses, any shape projected onto the retina in close temporal contiguity with the initial shape should come to excite the same cell assembly through the mechanism of spatial summation in the nervous system: of the random connections which the new shape might excite the ones it will be most likely to excite are those already excited by the initial shape. Thus the two shapes will come to have a cell assembly in common—they will tend to give a common output. Since the same shape will be constantly being shifted across the retina from moment to moment, this means that the same shape projected to different parts of the retina should come to give the same output.

An interesting paradox arises. When Hebb's theory was first put forward it was hailed as showing how it might be possible to account for behaviour in terms of plausible neurophysiological mechanisms: it was thought that Hebb had demonstrated the possibility of explaining the findings of psychology in physiological terms. However, a moment's reflection shows that, if he is right, what he has really succeeded in doing is to demonstrate the utter impossibility of giving detailed neurophysiological mechanisms for explaining psychological or behavioural findings. According to Hebb the precise circuits used in the brain for the classification of a particular shape will vary from individual to individual with chance variation in nerve connectivity determined by genetic and maturational factors, they will vary within the individual with chance variations in the threshold at synapses at times when a given shape is first seen and during the succeeding presentations, and they will vary according to the frequency and temporal order of shapes projected onto the retina when learning is occurring. This means that even if we knew the precise sequence of shapes an animal has been subjected to in its previous history, it would be impossible to translate the effects of that sequence into actual brain circuitry and then work from the brain circuitry to predictions about subsequent behaviour: the circuits will be so complex, so scattered over different parts of the brain and, above all, they will vary so much from individual to individual that trying to take the intermediate steps for translating the effects of early experience of shapes into actual brain circuitry becomes an impossibility. Different individuals will achieve the same end result in behaviour by very different neurological circuits. If we wish to make predictions about individuals we must concentrate on correlating differences in early environment with differences in later behaviour, and translating these differences in early environment into differences in brain circuitry and then working from there to predictions about subsequent behaviour becomes impossible. If Hebb's general system is right, it precludes the possibility of ever making detailed predictions about behaviour from a detailed model of the system underlying the behaviour. This seems to me a most unfortunate consequence since the explanation of complex phenomena in terms of a simpler system is something which is intellectually satisfying, and which is in some ways more exciting than the working out of statistical correlations between early stimulus sequences and subsequent behaviour. This is clearly not a reason for rejecting the account given by Hebb, but it is certainly a good reason for looking to see whether it is possible that the initial system is less randomly organised than Hebb supposes.

The same sort of consideration would apply if Taylor's model for classification were correct or if Uttley's were. Taylor is in fact trying to discover whether a system of the general sort Hebb proposes would have the properties Hebb attributes to it, by actually building a model of it. This is one of the cases in which building a physical model of a system is useful, because it is impossible to predict whether or not Hebb's system will have the properties he attributes to it, and it would be impossible even if some of the variables in the system were precisely specified because the equations necessary for a solution would be too complex to solve. Thus as more and more shapes occur together on the retina it seems possible on Hebb's system that all cells will ultimately be connected up with all other cells so that any shapes will eventually fire all cell-assemblies: Milner (*34*) has recently proposed a most ingenious solution to this problem, but in order to do so he has to assume considerably more specificity in the arrangement of cortical cells than Hebb envisaged.

In the discussion of Hebb's theory so far, no account has been taken of the specific mechanisms which he alleges may be present from birth. The most important of these is the alleged tendency of animals to fixate successively the corners of figures, which in the case of rectilinear figures would result in the scanning of the contours. This mechanism would result in the equivalence of figures of different sizes since if corners are successively fixated the successive patterns at the fovea will be identical for the same shape irrespective of size and also eye movements will occur in the same directions though they will be of different lengths. Unfortunately Hebb never bridges the gap between recognition occurring in this way and recognition occurring without eye movements and when shapes are projected to different parts of the retina, although it is quite certain that human beings are capable of recognition under both these conditions (*7*). It should be noticed that in order for the eye movements to occur at all there must be a specific mechanism in the brain for reading off the position of a point relative to another in order to send the appropriate message to the eye muscles, and this is already a considerable limitation on the randomness of further connections from the primary projection area. If such a specific mechanism exists then logically it might play a part in shape recognition without the eye movements occurring. Since this is a limitation on the operation of a general mechanism which could according to training discriminate any shape from any other shape, and since evidence about the role of eye movements in shape recognition is almost entirely lacking, it will not be further discussed here. The possibility of using the way information is coded to determine some primitive response (such as fixation) to throw light on possible coding mechanisms in use to perform more complex functions (such as shape discrimination) will, however, be further discussed below.

Uttley (63 & 64) has proposed a system of classification based on the principles of set theory. Input units are connected to output units in such a way that each possible combination of input units is connected to one output unit: whether or not a given combination of input units is firing can then be detected by reading off whether the appropriate output unit is firing. With some limitations, the same result can be achieved with an initially random connection of input and output units. Such a system will not mediate generalisation where the generalisation involved is not from a given input pattern to a pattern of which it is a subset. Uttley postulates a further system which works out conditional probabilities of one unit firing given that another unit has fired: connections between units are altered in such a way as to represent conditional probabilities. Such a system could account for generalisation occurring between patterns one of which was not a subset of the other. Once again, the detailed model would be of little use in prediction: we could predict only by knowing the details of the previous inputs to the system, and our predictions would not involve following transformations of an input through a mechanism to arrive at an output, but merely considering previous inputs in terms of their class relationships of inclusion and exclusion and the working out of conditional probability relationships between different sets.

It should be noticed that all three theories make the assumption that the actual classificatory mechanism used by animals arises wholly as a result of learning. This is not accidental: in any general system of this kind where initial connections are random or are arranged in all possible ways, it would be very hard to account for any innate classification. For example on Hebb's system it cannot be determined at birth what cell assembly will be used for what classification: thus it would be impossible genetically to specify any connections which would lead to a given response being given to a given stimulus. Even if some such system as Hebb, Taylor and Uttley suggest is at work in parts of the brain—and from the degree of perceptual relearning that can occur in human beings as evidenced by studies with distorting lenses (24), it seems likely that a system of this sort may operate

—it would be extremely interesting to discover what its limitations are: these limitations indicate non-randomness of connections and therefore suggest analysing mechanisms of the specific kind at work which will explain and predict behaviour and which do not vary from individual to individual in a given species. It is important therefore to examine the evidence for stimuli innately producing specific reactions since any examples of this must severely limit the applicability of the general systems I have been describing, and open the way to the postulation of more specific systems.

## EXPERIMENTAL TESTS FOR GENERAL ANALYSING SYSTEMS

### INNATE STIMULUS-RESPONSE CONNECTIONS

Evidence has been accumulating that at least in many sub-mammalian organisms there is a considerable degree of specificity in the classificatory mechanisms at work. The studies cited by Tinbergen (62) on innate fright reactions of gallinaceous birds to a ⌐+ figure moving in the direction of the short arm, and on other innate releasing stimuli often of a complex configurational kind are well known. Unfortunately, there is still some doubt about their validity because often these reactions were not studied under strict laboratory conditions and in only a few cases were precautions taken to exclude the possibility of the reaction coming into being as a result of early learning. However, more recent studies are not open to these objections and have confirmed that some classification can occur without learning. Thus Fantz (15) has shown unequivocally that dark reared chicks exhibit a preference in their pecking behaviour for round objects as opposed to square or triangular ones, under conditions where the preference could not have been influenced by rewards and punishments. Wells (66) has shown that newly hatched Sepia have a very specific preference for attacking Mysis, a small crustacean with a complex and specific form: although unrewarded for their attacks, the latency of attacks decreased with the number of attacks made, and it was difficult to persuade them to attack any other shape. Rhiengold and Hess (43) have shown that chicks' preference for water is determined by its visual properties, and that chicks rely upon the same visual properties before and after experience with water.

By fitting chicks with prisms, Hess (21) has demonstrated that the direction and distance at which a chick will peck to a stimulus are both innately determined. Some years ago Sperry (51, 52, & 53) demonstrated that fly catching behaviour in the newt was determined by a highly specific neural organisation: if the eye ball was rotated through 180° and the optic nerve severed and allowed to regenerate, reactions to objects moving in the visual field were made to a position 180° from the position of the stimulus in the visual field. If the severed optic nerve can re-establish connections with such precision despite their biological uselessness to the animal, this suggests that the original connections may have had the same degree of specificity. Thus there can no longer be any question but in many submammalian species there is a degree of specificity present in the arrangement of the connections in classificatory mechanisms which means that theories of the general type cannot satisfactorily account for stimulus classification in these animals.

### PERCEPTUAL DEPRIVATION

The situation with regard to mammals is still not resolved. Several investigators—Riesen (44, 45 & 46), Riesen, Kurke and Mellinger (47), Riesen and Mellinger (48), Chow and Nissen (6) have demonstrated that some mammals (cats and chimpanzees) discriminate less well between visually presented shapes if they have been brought up without prior experience of patterned light. Although this is sometimes taken to mean that these animals have to learn to classify stimuli or more specifically to build up specific connections out of initially random ones, this conclusion is far from forced upon us by the evidence. Thus there are at least four alternative explanations for why animals brought up without pattern vision should learn a given visual discrimination less readily than a normally reared animal. These are: (1) Possible degeneration in the system due to lack of use: it is impossible to know whether this has been eliminated even where animals have been brought up in diffuse light rather than total darkness. (2) The disruptive effects on learning of emotional responses given to completely novel stimuli: Miller (33) found that rats brought up in the dark and trained on a maze habit in the dark actually performed worse when run in the light. (3) The possibility that there are specific connections present initially, but that they become more specific only with use, and irrespective of how they are used. This possibility is underlined by the experiments of Wells (66) and Hess (21): Hess found that the pecking response increased in accuracy with use, even in the case where because of distortion introduced by a prism in front of the eye the increase in accuracy merely led to the chick pecking consistently in the wrong spot. It is also suggested by an experiment of Chow and Nissen (6): they found incomplete interocular transfer where chimpanzees had been brought up with one eye receiving pattern vision, the other diffuse light: this suggests that the anatomical overlap of fibres from opposite eyes is at first incomplete, but that it

*Perceptual Acts*    178

becomes complete with use. The conditions necessary for its completion, however, do not include knowledge of results since it is completed if patterned light is given alternately to either eye. Riesen and Mellinger (*48*) obtained a similar result with cats. (4) The possibility that increased learning time for a visual discrimination is brought about because animals have learned to switch in analysing mechanisms for other sensory modalities through previous experience: animals might switch off the input from vision when it first appeared because it could not initially be useful in solving a problem and would only interfere with a solution achieved through some other sensory modality. Recent results on the peripheral blocking of sensory input from a modality to which the animal is not attending (e.g., Sharpless and Jasper, *50*) underline this possibility. These results will be referred to in more detail below.

The upshot of this is that at the moment there is no reliable evidence on the extent to which the classificatory system is of the extremely general sort suggested by Hebb and others in mammals, and on how far the actual classificatory system used in later life develops only as the result of learning. If mammals have few innate responses to stimuli and if the type of experiment which has been performed on perceptual learning to date is inconclusive, it must be asked whether it would be possible to obtain evidence which would help to decide how far the classificatory mechanisms at work in mammals were of the very general sort proposed by Hebb, how far they were more specific.

## FURTHER TESTS FOR GENERAL ANALYSING SYSTEMS

It seems to me that it is possible to perform experiments designed to test this.[2] A number of different possible approaches to this problem are outlined below:

(1) If the classes of shapes which will be categorised together are determined as a result of learning, we might expect that animals brought up without visual experience will either exhibit very different kinds of transfer from adult animals or will exhibit no transfer to new shapes at all. For example if the equivalence between rectangles in different orientations is determined through learning, we would expect that an animal brought up without pattern vision and then trained to discriminate between a square and a horizontal rectangle would show no transfer to a vertical rectangle. Similarly we would

[2] The author wrote in the original article: "We are planning such experiments as part of a programme on stimulus-analysing mechanisms at Oxford financed by the Nuffield Foundation." (Editors' note).

expect no transfer from a triangle in one orientation to a triangle in another orientation. Such experiments must, of course, be very carefully controlled: in particular if an approach-avoidance habit is being learned it is necessary in transfer to prevent the animal performing correctly by avoiding or approaching the figure which remains constant (i.e. the square in the first example). The method of successive discrimination avoids this difficulty since only one shape is shown on one trial and the animal learns either to approach or avoid it. Again it is necessary to be certain that what is transferred is a method of classifying the shapes and not the habit of attending to the shapes: this possibility can again be eliminated by proper controls (e.g. comparing transfer to a series of different shapes only some of which bear any resemblance to the original: the degree of transfer to shapes bearing no resemblance to the original then gives a base line for measuring genuine transfer due to a method of classifying the shapes). If the order of ease of transfer to different shapes were markedly different from that found in an adult animal, this would provide very good evidence for the importance of learning in determining the ways in which shapes are classified and hence for the more general type of mechanism: it would be impossible to explain such changes in order of transfer by means of any of the four possible alternative explanations listed above, because although they might reduce all transfer there is no reason to suppose that they would reduce transfer to different shapes differentially. Although many experiments involving bringing animals up without pattern vision have been performed, there has been no attempt made to investigate how such animals transfer to new shapes.

(2) If a very general mechanism is at work, it should be possible to alter drastically the discriminability of shapes and the ways in which transfer will occur by giving animals unusual perceptual environments. Gibson and Walk (17) performed an experiment of this kind in which they showed that rats which have been kept in cages in which black circles and triangles were exposed were subsequently better able to discriminate these shapes than a control group brought up in cages without these forms being exposed. Unfortunately, the experimental animals may have learned to orient themselves in their cages by means of the exposed forms so that in the discrimination learning situation they may have transferred a habit of attending rather than a method of classifying. This could be controlled against to some extent by keeping the shapes exposed in constant movement round the cage, and also by finding out whether the superiority of the experimental group on shape discrimination was confined just to

the pair of shapes to which they had been exposed by testing both groups on other shape discriminations.

It might be worth trying a different method of producing perceptual learning. If equivalence relationships are determined by the time sequence of shapes on the retina then it should be possible to build into animals very unusual equivalences. Thus animals could be brought up in a cage with a shape in view which was constantly distorting to another shape: for example if animals were allowed to view a triangle distorting into a circle during the early part of their life, it would be predicted that the triangle and circle would thereafter be equivalent figures for them. Discrimination between these figures would presumably be more difficult for such animals on a general mechanism and much more transfer from one to another should be exhibited than in normally reared animals.

(3) A third possible way of discovering how far specific mechanisms are involved in shape discrimination is by testing for interocular transfer under conditions where the animal has never experienced the same shape simultaneously on the two eyes. In a mammal because there are both crossed and uncrossed fibres in the optic pathways corresponding parts of both eyes project to the same hemisphere: because of this, results of experiments using this technique are inconclusive since the interocular transfer found may be due to the same excitation being set up in the primary projection area irrespective of which eye is stimulated. For what it is worth, Chow and Nissen (6) and Riesen and Mellinger (48) have found almost complete interocular transfer in animals which had had alternating pattern vision on both eyes, but had never had pattern vision with both eyes simultaneously. It would be possible to overcome the difficulty in interpreting these experiments by cutting the optic chiasma before any pattern vision was given: this would mean that the left eye projected only to the left hemisphere and the right eye only to the right hemisphere. If under these conditions interocular transfer were found with previous experience limited to pattern vision alternating on the two eyes, then it would be established that further connections from area 17 were highly specific and that classification of shapes was not effected by growth processes in initially random connections. Myers (36) in fact has found that interocular transfer occurs after severing the optic chiasma, but his animals had had normal pattern vision and hence the chance to establish equivalence between the same pattern projected to the two hemispheres since during the animals' previous binocular experience the same patterns had been being transmitted simultaneously to the two hemispheres.

*Stimulus Analysing Mechanisms*     *181*

Before leaving general systems it is perhaps worth making two further points. Firstly, it is sometimes supposed that because classifying systems seem to reflect the probability of environmental events, therefore they must have come into existence as a result of learning in the individual. For example a variety of animals—monkeys (19), rats (27), octopuses (59)—have been found to classify right-left mirror images together more readily than updown mirror images. This might arise because in an animal's normal environment if the animal goes behind a given shape it will receive a right-left mirror image of the same shape, whereas it would have to stand on its head to receive an up-down mirror image of a shape: clearly the former happens more frequently so we might expect animals to classify right-left mirror images together more frequently than up-down mirror images. This cannot be used as an argument for a general type of system in which equivalences develop as a result of learning on the part of the individual organism because we would expect a specific system to exhibit the same features since it will have come into being as a result of an evolutionary process. A specific system which treated right-left mirror images as the same would clearly be useful to an animal since they often are given by the same object whereas a system which treated up-down mirror images as the same would be less useful to an animal because in general they will emanate from different objects. Thus it might be expected that specific mechanisms built in as a result of evolution would be adaptive in much the same way as the actual classifications that come to be made in a general mechanism as a result of learning.

Secondly it is sometimes supposed that it might be possible to work out the number of discriminations an animal can make and to correlate this with the total number of possible connections in the brain or in some part of the brain. In this way it might be possible to work out what were the neural elements involved in a general system, and to make a correlation between some form of neural connectivity and the number of things an animal can discriminate. Unfortunately it is completely impossible to set any upper limit to the number of discriminations an animal can make by means of behavioural experiments. The literature of the subject is strewn with assertions that a particular animal could not perform this or that discrimination when all that was justified by the data was that the animal could not perform a particular discrimination within the limits of the particular experimental situation used. Thus in 1930 Munn (35) wrote "The inability to learn the discriminations was due not to the characteristics of the apparatuses per se, but to a deficiency in the rat's ability to discriminate visual detail": Lashley was shortly to demonstrate that the discrimination between the shapes Munn used with his rats (that between a cross and a square) was in fact one of the easiest pattern discriminations for the rat in the jumping stand situation (27). Yet there is no guarantee that the jumping stand is itself the optimal learning situation for shape discrimination in the rat, and it would be as misguided to claim that the limits of the rat's capacity for shape discrimination found with the jumping stand represented the upper limit of the rat's capacity as it was to claim that the rat has no capacity for detail vision on the basis of experiments with a modified Yerkes apparatus as used by Munn. Apart from variations in the experimental situation used to train animals in visual shape discrimination, a second factor may contribute largely to what limits are found for their discriminatory capabilities. This factor is the extent to which animals are pretrained on shapes exhibiting gross differences along the same dimensions as the shapes they will ultimately be required to discriminate. Thus Lawrence (30) found a group of rats trained to discriminate black and white cards and then transferred gradually to more and more similar shades of grey reached a much better criterion of learning on the two closest shades of grey used than a group given the same total number of trials on the two closest shades of grey from the outset of training. Saldhana and Bitterman (49) found that whether or not rats learned a given series of discriminations depended on the order in which they were presented. Thus the approach of arriving at the number of switches in the brain by analysing the total number of discriminations an animal can make is one which it is not possible to follow, though it is an approach which might suggest itself to the engineer interested in applying information theory to organisms.

## EVIDENCE FOR SPECIFIC ANALYSING MECHANISMS

### ECONOMY OF SPECIFIC ANALYSING SYSTEMS

Some of the evidence which has already been presented suggests that specific analysing systems must be at work at least in the case of certain submammalian organisms which exhibit innate responses to some classes of stimuli. Although the crucial experiments have not been performed on mammals there is evidence from other directions that some specific classifying mechanisms must be at work even here. Both behavioural and physiological evidence indicate that part of what is involved in discriminating shape is the switching in of an appropriate analysing mechanism. In what follows, I shall argue that within any sensory modality, there are probably different specific ways of processing incoming information: these different methods correspond to different ways of classifying incoming information. Probably part of what an animal faced with a discrimination task learns is to switch in the correct analysing mechanism: a second part is to attach a response according to which output the mechanism switched in is giving. This general idea has some plausibility on the grounds of economy. Presumably many of the operations to be conducted on incoming data will be the same from one sense to another and also for different ways of classifying information from any one sense, though here the sequence of operations may differ from one method of classifying to another. If this is the case it would presumably be most economical to use the same actual analysing mechanisms in a variety of different classifications rather than to have a separate analysing mechanism for each classification (the latter is implicit in the general type of theory put forward by Uttley). Thus in the use of computers it is most economical to have one computer capable of carrying out operations on different kinds of data and of varying the sequence of the operations it carries out according to the way in which it is programmed, rather than to have different computers for every variety of information which is to be fed in and for every variation in the sequence of operations to be carried out. To summarise this crudely, in the model envisaged the brain is being viewed as containing at least three different boxes: (1) A number of different analysing mechanisms. (2) A control centre which determines which of these mechanisms shall be switched in on any given occasion and in what sequence they shall be switched in. (3) A further box which is responsible for selecting the response to be attached to the output from the analysing mechanisms. This is obviously a gross oversimplification and in practice the boxes may turn out to be not so very discrete, but it is worth seeing how far available evidence supports this conception.

EVIDENCE FOR SPECIFIC ANALYSING MECHANISMS

One consequence of this crude model is that the nervous system would not be able to process information in two different ways at once, since there would then be competition for the common analysing mechanisms. There is plenty of evidence to suggest that this is in fact the case. Thus Mowbray (37, 38) found that when the eye and ear are presented with complex stimuli at the same time, the information presented to one or the other is made effective in the response but not the information presented to both: Mowbray points out that this finding is against the type of theory put forward by Hebb. Broadbent (2) shows that digits simultaneously presented to the two ears are not accepted by the analysing mechanisms in their temporal order of presentation but all digits presented to one ear are accepted and then all presented to the other ear; he has extended this finding to digits presented simultaneously to ear and eye (3). To explain the finding that information presented simultaneously on two channels can be accepted although it is accepted successively not simultaneously, he postulates a short term memory store in which information can be stored until the central analysing mechanisms are ready to receive it. The idea that the same central analysing mechanisms may be used in processing information from different modalities gives a rationale for the finding that it is not possible to accept information from two channels at once. Davis (8, 9) has shown that where two stimuli requiring different but peripherally compatible responses are presented with intervals of less than about 200 milli-seconds, the response to the second one is delayed: in an ingenious series of experiments involving different modalities, he has shown that the amount of delay is approximately the same as the amount of overlap between the time the first stimulus occupies central pathways and the time the second stimulus would have occupied central pathways if it could have been accepted immediately: this suggests that the second stimulus cannot get access to central analysing mechanisms until the first one is cleared.

A second line of evidence suggesting the same general conception of the working of the central nervous system is that provided by recent studies on the recticular formation and on the peripheral blocking of input on sensory pathways. Since there have been a number of recent reviews of this evidence (e.g. 31), it is unnecessary to go into it in detail here. Hernandes-Peon, Scherrer, and Jouvet (23) found that a click given to a cat's ear evokes a markedly reduced potential at the cochlear nucleus if the cat is simultaneously shown a mouse or given a whiff of fish. This suggests that stimuli unimportant for the animal can be blocked at a peripheral level if more important stimuli are being received: the blocking is itself under central control possibly mediated by the reticular formation (22). Once again the rationale behind this can only be that central analysing mechanisms can only be set in one way at a time, and if different stimuli were given access to them simultaneously their efficiency in dealing with any one stimulus would be impaired. In addition to giving support for the existence of specific analysing mechanisms used for a variety of stimuli, such experiments suggest in themselves a considerable degree of specificity in the innate organisation of the central nervous system and thus constitute evidence against the very general systems proposed to carry out stimulus analysis. It should further be noted that the existence of analysing mechanisms which although specific could be used for a variety of purposes is in line with the findings on mass action, i.e. the failure of lesions outside the primary sensory and motor areas of the cortex to produce loss of some specific functions only. In addition the idea that the same analysing mechanisms might be used in processing information from different sensory modalities may account for some examples of synaesthesia.

LEARNING TO SWITCH IN ANALYSING MECHANISMS

The degree to which the same analysing mechanisms actually function when incoming information is being processed in different ways is of course extremely speculative, and is almost impossible to test at the moment: it would only become possible to test the idea when we had begun to work out in detail for the different senses what the specific analysing mechanisms at work were. The main point of importance for our present purpose is that it is likely that there are specific analysing mechanisms at work irrespective of the degree to which these are used in common when stimuli are being categorised in different ways. There is excellent evidence to support this more general point drawn from another realm of experimentation. This evidence indicates that in learning to make a discriminatory response animals both learn how to analyse the stimuli and also learn to attach a given response to differential outputs from the analysing mechanism once found. This is one explanation for results which support non-continuity theory as opposed to continuity theory of discrimination learning. Non-continuity theorists as represented by Lashley (28) and Krechevsky (25) maintained that animals only learn to attach a response to cues to which they are attending, continuity theorists (e.g. Spence, 54) that they learn to attach a response to any differential cues impinging upon the organism.

Early attempts to test between these two possibilities were not very successful since the experiments yielded conflicting results (26, 32, 54, 13, etc.): these experiments sought to discover whether animals learned anything about the relevant cues during the first few trials of training in a discrimination during which they tend to react more in terms of spatial position than in terms of the differential shapes. Since the results of these experiments are ambiguous they will not be further discussed here, though it should be noticed that the finding that some learning does occur in early trials is only against an extreme non-continuity theory position, because even in a sequence of trials where animals are attending on most trials to spatial position, they might on some trials be attending to shape (or on the model here proposed, be switching in the appropriate analysing mechanism) and therefore some effect of early training on later learning would be demonstrable.

Lashley (28) tried to solve the problem by giving animals a set to solve discrimination problems in terms of one sort of categorisation (size) and then demonstrating that they learned little or nothing about other aspects of the stimuli to be discriminated provided they could continue to solve the problem in terms of the original way of categorising. Unfortunately, Lashley used an insensitive test of the amount of learning of other aspects of the stimuli—he used transfer tests rather than relearning, and the results of his own experiment can be disputed.

Lawrence (29) in an extremely well controlled experiment tried a different approach to the problem: he gave animals a set to respond in terms of one cue, subsequently another cue was made relevant to the discrimination. When tested with the cues in isolation animals performed better when the original cue was relevant than when the additional cue was relevant. More important however, was the finding that when the original positive stimulus was made negative and the original negative was made positive animals learned to reverse their responses quicker than when they had to learn to reverse their responses to the additional cue. Unless some other learning had occurred than learning to attach a given response to all cues present it is impossible to explain this finding. It can, however, readily be explained if the group reversed on the preferred cue had learned to switch in the appropriate analysing mechanism and merely had to learn to attach responses differently to the outputs from that mechanism, whereas the group reversed on the less preferred cue would be more likely to switch in the wrong analysing mechanism and so take longer to switch in the less preferred one and also learn to reverse responses to that one.

A number of experiments have recently confirmed this type of finding. Thus Reid (42), Pubols (40), and Capaldi and Stevenson (5) have all shown that the more training is given on a given discrimination the more readily rats learn to reverse their responses on the same discrimination. This finding is unintelligible if we assume animals are merely learning to attach a response to a given output from stimulus analysing mechanisms since we are faced with the paradox that the better the response is attached the easier it is to reverse it. It becomes intelligible, however, if we suppose animals have learned to switch in a given analysing mechanism: animals which have learned this most thoroughly will presumably continue to switch this mechanism in when their responses begin to give the wrong results and so will have a chance to learn to reverse their responses to the outputs of that mechanism. Animals which have not learned so thoroughly may switch in other analysing mechanisms and hence take longer to relearn since they will meanwhile not learn anything about the relationship of correct response to the outputs from the original analysing mechanism.

Bruner, Matter and Papanek (4) demonstrated that the obverse of this is true: rats were given different amounts of training on one cue. They were then given 20 trials training with a second cue added to the first. They then had to learn to respond in terms of the second cue only (i.e. the first was removed). The more training they had had on the initial cue, the less they learned about the new cue during the training with both cues present. This again suggests that the more thoroughly they had learned to switch in the analysing mechanism which would detect the original cue, the less they switched in different analysing mechanisms when both cues were present and therefore the less they learned during this period about the second cue.

It has been known for some time that if an animal is repeatedly conditioned and extinguished on the same habit, the length of time necessary for successive conditioning and extinction becomes less and less. More recently it has been shown by Harlow (18) that if monkeys are trained on a discrimination and then the correct response is reversed successively they will eventually come to reverse their response in one trial: Pubols (41) has demonstrated that rats also are capable of learning to do this. Again this suggests that animals do not learn simply to attach a response to a stimulus, though in order to explain these findings it is necessary to suppose an extra complication in the crude model here put forward. Not only must there be a control mechanism for switching in analysing mechanisms which mediates the learning of which analysing mechanism to switch in, but there must be a further control mechanism which can switch the relationship between the outputs from the stimulus analysing mechanism and the response.

## The Problem of Specific Analysing Mechanisms

I have now reviewed some of the evidence for supposing that there are specific analysing mechanisms at work and that on different occasions different analysing mechanisms may be switched in. This raises a serious obstacle to working out in detail what the analysing mechanisms used for any stimulus modality are. The technique which I have used with octopuses (56, 57, 58) is to try to discover by experiments which shapes they can most readily discriminate and also what are the properties of the shapes they are analysing when they do discriminate between them by running transfer tests with new shapes in which the properties of the original shape are systematically altered. For example (57) if an octopus is trained on a circle and a square of equal area, discrimination is unimpaired by altering the size of the original figures and this establishes that octopuses were not discriminating originally in terms of absolute length of outline or absolute breadth or height; on the other hand they will not transfer from the square to a diamond (i.e. a square rotated through 45°) and this establishes that they were not originally discriminating the properties of having straight lines and corners as against the properties of not having straight lines and not having corners. On the basis of this sort of work it is possible to suggest hypothetical analysing mechanisms which would account for one's results, and to draw predictions from such analysing mechanisms about the discriminability of further pairs of shapes. Unfortunately, though, in the case where animals succeed in discriminating shapes which on the original analysing mechanism should not be discriminable one does not know whether this is because one's original guess at the analysing mechanism at work was wrong or whether it is because a second analysing mechanism is at work which is switched in where the original one does not give differential outputs for different pairs of shapes (for an example of this, see 60). This means that where one predicts that an animal cannot distinguish shapes the finding that it cannot distinguish them is some confirmation for the existence of the original analysing mechanism, while the finding that it can discriminate them is not complete disconfirmation. On the other hand where one predicts that a pair of shapes should be readily discriminable the finding that they are is only partial confirmation of the theory, whereas the finding that they are not would be a complete refutation of the theory. However, possibly because of the existence of different possible analysing mechanisms it is difficult to discover pairs of shapes which are not discriminable. Although the existence of independent analysing mechanisms makes investigation of the specific analysing mechanisms at work difficult, it does not make it impossible: one approach to this problem which has not been tried would be to preset the analysing mechanisms in a given way by training on shapes whose discrimination involves this or that type of analysing mechanism, and then to test for whether when animals are trained on further shapes the ways in which they transfer to new shapes are altered by the way in which the analysing mechanisms have been preset.

A further problem which confronts investigators who are trying to make hypotheses about the specific analysing mechanisms at work is to decide in what ways the nervous system is most likely to code information. Thus coding in terms of intensity of firing (i.e. rate of firing) and position of firing certainly occurs in the peripheral nervous system: it is difficult to know how far the nervous system may operate at more central levels on a coding in terms of time. Since peripheral response mechanisms would appear to work only in terms of the position of impulses and their intensity of firing decoding into these methods of carrying information would be necessary before the effector system was reached. A concrete example may help both to make this clear, and also to illustrate how far our ignorance of specific mechanisms goes.

Suppose we tell a human being that we are going to present two lights to his eye, one of which will be brighter than the other and he is to respond by pressing one of two keys to his right and left: if the bright light is to the left of the dim light he is to press the left hand key, if it is to the right of the dim light he is to press the right hand key. If we now control the subject's fixation and flash the lights on different parts of the retina, one would expect him to press the correct key for any retinal position occupied by the two lights provided their separation is greater than the minimum separable for the part of the retina on which they are projected. If we take the minimum separable to be 3 minutes or better out to a peripheral angle of 60° (39) this means that each light can occupy over 1,000,000 discriminably different positions on the eye and the two lights could occupy over $10^{12}$ different positions. We give the left hand response for half of these possible input states, and the right hand response for the other half. Now, on Uttley's theory of how the equivalence for each group of $10^{12}/2$ input states has arisen, there would be one unit to represent each of these $10^{12}/2$ states and all these units would be connected to one further unit which is common to all of the $10^{12}/2$. We would in fact require more units than there are neurons in the central nervous system to cope with this one very simple discrimination. This in itself suggests that some specific mechanism of a more economical kind is operating, and it is the purpose of the example to throw light on the difficulties which arise in specifying the more specific mechanisms.

Despite the simplicity of the problem, there are as far as I know no discussions in print of what sort of analysing mechanism could mediate this generalisation or even this type of generalisation. The problem is to get rid of the information about the actual spatial positions occupied by the two lights and preserve only the information about their relationship to one another along the horizontal axis. One way of doing this would be to convert spatial positions into a time series: for example points on the cortex representing retinal points from left to right might fire successively into the same channel: the two lights will now be represented by a small excitation and a large excitation and a detector mechanism could sort out whether the large light was on the right or on the left by whether a large excitation was succeeded or preceded by a small one. Both Deutsch (10) and Dodwell (11) have proposed mechanisms for shape recognition which get rid of spatial position occupied on the retina by coding position in terms of time. The trouble with this sort of system is that we have to assume some sort of pacing mechanism which must operate in a very regular way, and also that the central nervous system is capable of detecting very small differences in time. There is evidence that the nervous system can decode very small time differences produced by external stimuli (e.g. time differences of 30 microseconds can be detected in auditory localisation: (65), but here the time differences are produced by an external stimulus and this does not show that the nervous system can itself recode information in terms of time with such accuracy.

Another possible method of recoding the information would be to code position on the retina in terms of intensity: successive positions say to the right of the fovea would be represented by greater and greater intensities. We now need a second mechanism for associating the brightness of the light with the intensity of firing associated with it in the system representing its spatial position in intensity terms, and to respond merely to the spatial position of the light we have to detect whether the intensity associated with the bright one in the system representing horizontal retinal position is greater or less than the intensity associated with the dim one. This sort of recording at least for visual discrimination is possibly more plausible than recording in terms of time, since it does not involve any sort of regular pacing mechansm. Moreover, it is already known that at one stage the nervous system does recode spatial information on the retina in terms of intensities. Thus one primitive response we make to objects stimulating the retina is that of fixation movements: one pair of muscles (lateral and medial recti) are mainly responsible for the horizontal components of eye movements, while two further pairs (superior and inferior recti and superior and inferior oblique) are mainly responsible for the vertical components of eye-movements. The immediate efferent control of these muscles must be in terms of intensity of firing in efferent nerves. Moreover there is some evidence that there are separate efferent tracts for the vertical and horizontal components of eye muscles: thus it seems likely that the efferent tract for lateral eye movements runs through the pons, whereas that for vertical eye movements runs through the superior colliculus (*12*). If information about the position on the retina of a point to be fixated has to be divided into the two coordinates vertical and horizontal in order to be fed over efferent pathways onto the eye muscles, it might represent some economy if the same system were used for analysing the position of stimulated points on the retina relative to one another. Such a system could be developed to account for shape recognition irrespective of retinal position, and would make many predictions in common with the theory put forward by the present writer (*55*) for recognition of shape and orientation in the octopus. The approach of discovering how information from a given modality must be coded in order to govern some primitive response in order to gain suggestions for analysing mechanisms which govern more complex responses is one which might be used more than it has been in the past.

There is one further point which may be worth making about specific systems of shape recognition. It seems likely that any such system must operate by comparing relative quantities somewhere in the nervous system rather than by taking into account any absolute quantity at any given stage. This is indicated not only by the fact that in all species tested it has been found that having learned to discriminate between shapes of a given size they will transfer the discrimination readily to shapes of different sizes, but by more general considerations about the operation of the nervous system. Any discrimination task which necessarily involves the storage of information about absolute quantities is in fact very poorly performed in terms of the information which can be extracted on any one presentation of the stimulus. Thus Garner (*16*) showed that where human beings were asked to make judgments of absolute loudness, judgments were most accurate as measured by the amount of information transmitted per judgment where only five categories were used: increasing the number of categories led to a decrease in accuracy which was not compensated for in terms of extra information transmitted by means of the additional number of categories used. Similarly Ericksen and Hake (*14*) found that where subjects were asked to judge the size of squares, increasing the number of categories used above five did not lead to any increase in the amount of information transmitted per judgment: it led to a decrease in the accuracy of judgments which was partially compensated for by the increase in number of categories used. In both studies about 2.1 bits of information per stimulus were transmitted. It is obvious that in human beings and many animals very much more information per stimulus can be transmitted where visual patterns are being classified, particularly if there are no severe limitations on the length of time the stimulus is exposed or the length of time within which a response must be made. This can only mean that the nervous system performs more efficiently in terms of information transmitted where it is analysing relationships between quantities simultaneously present in it, than where it is analysing one absolute quantity. The explanation of this feature of the nervous system may have to do with changes in states of adaptation: it may be impossible to analyse accurately absolute quantities due to changes in states of adaptation of parts of the nervous system, but the changes in states of adaptation might be such that the relation between different quantities of excitation is preserved provided they are transmitted over the same parts of the nervous system. A mechanism for distinguishing shapes which depends upon an analysis of relative quantities is therefore more plausible than one which depends upon an analysis of absolute quantities.

CONCLUSION

It has not been the purpose of this paper to examine in detail any specific theories of how the nervous system classifies shapes. I have tried to show that the very general type of analysing system which engineers have tended to propose for pattern recognition may not correspond to the way in which the nervous system works, and to give reasons for supposing that there are in fact more specific and more economical analysing systems at work. I have also tried to suggest ways of testing between the two alternatives, and ways of working out what the more specific analysing mechanisms are. The engineer could obviously be of enormous help to the physiologist and the psychologist in setting up hypotheses about specific analysing mechanisms, but to do so he would have to start by taking into account the known facts about which shapes are classified together and which are classified apart, and to develop theories about analysing mechanisms in collaboration with experimentalists who could test the specific predictions made from this type of theory.

REFERENCES

1. Ashby, R. C. *Design for a Brain.* London: Chapman & Hall (1952).
2. Broadbent, D. E. "The Role of Auditory Localisation in Attention and Memory Span." *J. exp. Psychol.* (1954), 47, 191.
3. Broadbent, D. E. "Successive Responses to Simultaneous Stimuli." *Quart. J. exp. Psychol.* (1956), 8, 145.
4. Bruner, J. S., Matter, J. & Papanek, M. L. "Breadth of Learning as a Function of Drive Level and Mechanization." *Psychol. Rev.* (1955), 62, 1.

5. Capaldi, E. J. & Stevenson, H. W. "Response Reversal Following Different Amounts of Training." *J. comp. physiol. Psychol.* (1957), 50, 195.

6. Chow, K. L. & Nissen, H. W. "Interocular Transfer of Learning in Visually Naive and Experienced Infant Chimpanzees. *J. comp. physiol. Psychol.* (1955), 48, 229.

7. Collier, R. M. "An Experimental Study of Form Perception in Indirect Vision." *J. comp. Psychol.* (1931), 11, 281.

8. Davis, R. "The Limits of the 'Psychological Refractory Period'." *Quart. J. exp. Psychol.* (1956), 8, 24.

9. Davis, R. "The Human Operator as a Single Channel Information System." *Quart. J. exp. Psychol.* (1957) 9, 119.

10. Deutsch, J. A. "A Theory of Shape Recognition." *Brit. J. Psychol.* (1955), 46, 30.

11. Dodwell, P. C. "Shape Recognition in Rats." *Brit. J. Psychol.* (1957), 43, 221.

12. Duke-Elder, W. S. *Textbook of Ophthalmology.* Vol. IV. *The Neurology of Vision. Motor and Optical Anomalies.* London: Henry Kimpton (1949).

13. Ehrenfreund, D. "An Experimental Test of the Continuity Theory of Discrimination Learning with Pattern Vision." *J. comp. physiol. Psychol.* (1948), 41, 408.

14. Ericksen, C. W. & Hake, H. W. "Absolute Judgments as a Function of the Stimulus Range and the Number of Stimulus and Response Categories." *J. exp. Psychol.* (1955), 49, 323.

15. Fantz, R. L. "Form Preferences in Newly Hatched Chicks. *J. comp. physiol. Psychol.* (1957), 50, 422.

16. Garner, W. R. "An Informational Analysis of Absolute Judgments of Loudness." *J. exp. Psychol.* (1953), 46, 373.

17. Gibson, E. J. & Walk, R. D. "The Effect of Prolonged Exposure to Visually Presented Patterns on Learning to Discriminate Them." *J. comp. physiol. Psychol.* (1956), 49, 239.

18. Harlow, H. F. "Studies in Discrimination Learning by Monkeys: I." *J. gen. Psychol.* (1944), 30, 3.

19. Harlow, H. F. "Studies in Discrimination Learning by Monkeys: III. Factors Influencing Solution of Discrimination Problems by Rhesus Monkeys." *J. gen. Psychol.* (1945), 32, 213.

20. Hebb, D. O. *The Organisation of Behaviour.* New York: Wiley (1949).

21. Hess, E. H. "Space Perception in the Chick." *Scientific American* (1956), 195, 71.

22. Hernandos-Peon, R. & Scherrer, H. *Federation Proc.* (1955), 14, 71.

23. Hernandos-Peon, R. & Scherrer, H. & Jouvet, M. "Modification of Electric Activity in the Cochlear Nucleus During 'Attention' in Unanaesthetised Cats." *Science* (1956), 123, 331.

24. Kohler, I. "Uber Aufbau and Wandlugen der Wahrnehmungswelt." *Oesterr. Akad. Wiss. Philos—Histor. Kl. Sitz—Ber.* (1951), 227, 1.

25. Krechevsky, I." 'Hypotheses' versus 'Choice' in the Pre-Solution Period in Sensory Discrimination Learning." *Calif. Univ. Publ. Psychol.* (1932), 6, 27.

26. Krechevsky, I. "The Genesis of 'Hypotheses' in Rats." *Calif. Univ. Publ. Psychol.* (1932), 6, 45.

27. Lashley, K. S. "The Mechanism of Vision: XV. Preliminary Studies of the Rat's Capacity for Detail Vision." *J. gen. Psychol.* (1938), 18, 123.

28. Lashley, K. S. "An Examination of the 'Continuity Theory' as Applied to Discriminative Learning." *J. gen. Psychol.* (1942), 26, 241.

29. Lawrence, D. H. "Acquired Distinctiveness of Cues. II. Selective Association in a Constant Stimulus Situation." *J. exp. Psychol.* (1950), 40, 175.

30. Lawrence, D. H. "The Transfer of a Discrimination along a Continuum." *J. comp. physiol. Psychol.* (1952), 45, 511.

31. Lindsley, O. R. "Psychophysiology and Motivation." In Jones (Ed): *Nebraska Symposium on Motivation. V* (1957), pp. 44-105.

32. McCullogh, T. L. & Pratt, J. G. "A Study of the Pre-Solution Period in Weight Discrimination by White Rats." *J. comp. Psychol.* (1934), 18, 271.

33. Miller, M. "Observation of Initial Visual Experience in Rats." *J. Psychol.* (1948), 26, 223.

34. Milner, P. M. "The Cell Assembly: Mark II." *Psychol. Rev.* (1957), 64, 242.

35. Munn, N. L. "Visual Pattern Discrimination in the White Rat." *J. comp. Psychol.* (1930), 10, 145.

36. Myers, R. E. "Interocular Transfer of Pattern Discrimination in Cats Following Section of Crossed Optic Fibres." *J. comp. physiol. Psychol.* (1955), 43, 470.

37. Mowbray, S. H. "Simultaneous Vision and Audition: the Comprehension of Prose Passages with Varying Levels of Difficulty." *J. exp. Psychol.* (1953), 46, 365.

38. Mowbray, S. H. "The Perception of Short Phrases Presented Simultaneously for Visual and Auditory Reception." *Quart. J. exp. Psychol.* (1954), 6, 86.

39. Polyak, S. L. *The Retina.* Chicago: Univ. of Chicago Press (1941).

40. Pubols, B. H. "The Facilitation of Visual and Spatial Discrimination Reversal by Overlearning." *J. comp. physiol. Psychol.* (1956), 49, 243.

41. Pubols, B. H. "Successive Discrimination Reversal Learning in the White Rat: A Comparison of Two Procedures." *J. comp. physiol. Psychol.* (1957), 50, 319.

42. Reid, L. S. "The Development of Noncontinuity Behaviour through Continuity Learning." *J. exp. Psychol.* (1953), 46, 107.

43. Rhiengold, H. I. & Hess, E. H. "The Chick's Preference for Some Visual Properties of Water." *J. comp. physiol. Psychol.* (1957), 50, 417.

44. Riesen, A. H. "The Development of Visual Perception in Man and Chimpanzee." *Science* (1949), 106, 107.

45. Riesen, A. H. "Arrested Vision." *Scientific American.* (1950), 183, 16.

46. Riesen, A. H. "Post and Partum Development of Behaviour." *Chicago Med. School. Quart.* (1951), 13, 17.

47. Riesen, A. H., Kurke, M. I., & Mellinger, J. C. "Interocular Transfer of Habits Learned Monocularly in Visually Naive and Visually Experienced Cats." *J. comp. physiol. Psychol.* (1953), 46, 166.

48. Riesen, A. H. & Mellinger, J. C. "Interocular Transfer of Habits in Cats after Alternating Monocular Visual Experience." *J. comp. physiol. Psychol.* (1956), 49, 516.

49. Saldana, E. L. & Bitterman, M. E. "Relational Learning in the Rat." *Amer. J. Psychol.* (1951), 64, 37.

50. Sharpless, S. & Jasper, H. "Habituation of the Arousal Reaction." *Brain* (1956), 79, 655.

51. Sperry, R. W. "Reestablishment of Visuomotor Coordination by Optic Nerve Regeneration." *Anat. Rec.* (1942), 84, 470.

52. Sperry, R. W. "Visiomotor Coordination in the Newt *(Triturus vividesceus)* after Regeneration of the Optic Nerve." *J. comp. Neurol.* (1943), 79, 33.

53. Sperry, R. W. "Optic Nerve Regeneration with Return of Vision in Anurans." *J. Neurophysiol.* (1944), 7, 57.

54. Spence, K. W. "An Experimental Test of the Continuity and Non-Continuity Theories of Discrimination Learning." *J. exp. Psychol.* (1945), 35, 253.

55. Sutherland, N. S. "Visual Discrimination of Orientation and Shape by the Octopus." *Nature* (1957), 179, 11.

56. Sutherland, N. S. "Visual Discrimination of Orientation by Octopus." *Brit. J. Psychol.* (1957), 48, 55.

57. Sutherland, N. S. "Visual Discrimination of Shape by Octopus. Circles and Squares, and Circles and Triangles." *Quart. J. exp. Psychol.* (1958), (in press).

58. Sutherland, N. S. "Visual Discrimination of the Orientation of Rectangles by *Octopus vulgaris* Lamarck." *J. comp. physiol. Psychol.* (1958), (in press).

59. Sutherland, N. S. "Visual Discrimination of Orientation by Octopus: Mirror Images." *Brit. J. Psychol.* (1959), (in press).

60. Sutherland, N. S. "A Test of a Theory of Shape Discrimination in Octopus." *J. comp. physiol. Psychol.* (1959), (in press).

61. Taylor, W. K. "Electrical Simulation of Some Nervous System Functional Activities." In Cherry, C. (Ed.): *Information Theory.* Third London Symposium, 314-327. London: Butterworths Publications (1956).

62. Tinbergen, N. *The Study of Instinct.* Oxford: Clarendon Press (1951).

63. Uttley, A. M. "Conditioned Probability Machines and Conditioned Reflexes." In Shannon, C. E. & McCarthy, J. *Automata Studies,* 253-75. Princeton: Princeton Univ. Press (1956).

64. Uttley, A. M. "Temporal and Spatial Patterns in a Conditioned Probability Machine." In Shannon, C. E. & McCarthy, J. *Automata Studies,* 277-85. Princeton: Princeton Univ. Press (1956).

65. Wallach, H., Newman, E. B. & Rosenzweig, M. R. "The Precedence Effect in Sound Localization." *Amer. J. Psychol.* (1949), 62, 315.

66. Well, M. J. "Factors Affecting Reactions to MYSIS by Newly Hatched SEPIA." *Behaviour* (1958), 8, 96.

# CHAPTER 10

## On The Conceptual Consciousness

ARON GURWITSCH

Many contemporary logicians seek to account for the notion of class in terms of propositional function. Let $f$ signify, for example, "is red" or "is a dog." Then one has the propositional function f (x) which, $x$ being a variable, has the signification "$x$ is red" or "$x$ is a dog." Through the substitution of individual terms for the variable, the propositional function gives rise to propositions which, according to the substitutions which are made, are true or false. One then defines the class as the set of individual terms which, substituted for the variable, confer a value of truth upon the propositions which are derived from the original propositional function by means of these substitutions.[1]

By proceeding in this way, one not only defines the concept in extension, because in terms of class (which appears opportune from the operational point of view), but it also seems possible to avoid all "Platonism" and to exempt oneself from having recourse to those "metaphysical" entities such as the Idea or the concept taken in comprehension. In fact, the procedure which has just been sketched does not seem to rely on any presupposition. All that is required, is the verification of propositions such as "this book is red." The very notion of concept being thus avoided, no ontological problem can consequently be posed in its regard.

It is certainly legitimate to make a propositional function correspond to every class and to define the latter as the ensemble of individual terms which satisfy the condition mentioned. From the formal point of view, this presentation certainly offers advantages. How-

---

[1] Cf. Ch. Serrus, *Traité de logique*, pp. 176-177, and J. Piaget, *Traité de logique*, p. 53.

ever, it remains to be seen whether, by proceeding in this fashion, one can succeed in accounting for the notion of class and of conceptual thought in general. In particular it must be asked whether the process itself by which propositions of the type in question are verified, does not contain hidden presuppositions.

In this regard the pathology of language has some significant findings. Gelb and Goldstein have drawn attention to patients suffering from amnesic aphasia who, when one presents them very familiar objects, for example a pencil, an umbrella, a knife, etc., are not capable of saying what these objects are called.[2] It is not that the patients no longer recognize them: on the contrary, by using circumlocutions, the patients describe adequately the use for which these objects are intended. Nor is it they have forgotten the words. When they are presented with a series of words, they almost never make an incorrect choice, indeed they seize upon the proper word for the object presented.[3] Moreover, the patients readily use words such as "handkerchief," "fountain pen," etc., but they do so only when these words have a function other than that of serving as *names which designate a certain class or category of objects*. It is only when the words fulfill this function of designation that the patients are no longer capable of finding them.

Gelb and Goldstein explain these phenomena as the result of a weakening or even a total loss of the "categorial attitude." According to these authors, the patients are reduced to the "concrete attitude." Of these rather complex notions, let us retain only the following characteristics.[4] To be reduced to the "concrete attitude" means to be absorbed by the present concrete situation before one, to be dominated by the given reality in all its massiveness, to the point where it becomes impossible to establish any distance between oneself and the present situation of the moment; it means still to know how to act and to manipulate things, but without being able to render an account of what one does. The objects with which the patient has to

[2] For what follows, we refer to the articles of A. Gelb, "Remarques générales sur l'utilisation des données pathologiques pour la psychologie et la philosophie du language" and of K. Goldstein, "L'analyse de l'aphasie et l'étude de l'essence du language," pp. 471-91. The two articles appeared in the *Journal de Psychologie Normale et Pathologique* (1933) and have been reprinted in the collection of articles *Psychologie du language* (Paris, 1933). We refer also to the book of Goldstein, *Language and Language Disturbances* (New York, 1948) IV A, V B, and VIII.

[3] We leave aside the case of amnesia of the names of colors, where the difficulties which the patients experience increase further because of the very nature of color names; cf. Goldstein, L'analyse de l'aphasie . . ." *loc. cit.* pp. 487-89.

[4] For a general characterization of "concrete" and "categorial" attitudes, cf. Gelb. *op. cit.* pp. 415-17, Goldstein, "L'analyse de l'aphasie . . ." *loc. cit.* p. 456; *Language and Language Disturbances* pp. 6-8; and also *The Organism* (New York, 1939), p. 30.

do present themselves to him as linked and bound to the situation of practical action. The objects appear to him in the light of the role which they play within a concrete situation, and appear to him only under that light. As they exist for the patients, the objects are completely determined by the function which they fulfill within a concrete situation. On the basis of the particular periphrases employed by the patients,[5] it may even be said that in their eyes the objects are defined by the usage to which they lend themselves, that they are as it were impregnated by the significance which they draw from their practical role, and that their significance is exhausted by that role. Thus, the patients are not capable of detaching an object which is presented to them from the situation of action in which that object is meant to function, in order to relate it to a context other than that of concrete action. In particular, the patients are no longer capable of regarding an object under the aspect of its similitude with other objects, of taking a given object as representative of other similar objects, which by reason of their similarity, can be considered as belonging to the same class. The patients can no longer perceive in the object presented to them an example or a particular case of a type or of a concept. To envisage an object in that manner it is in fact necessary to extract it from the context of concrete action and to set it in relation to a conceptual order. This is precisely what the patients can no longer do. Consequently, words, to the extent to which they express a conceptual classifying of things, and hence, for their comprehension, the adoption of the "categorial" attitude, have lost all meaning for the patients.

The theory which has just been summarized, perhaps too succinctly, allows us to make explicit a presupposition which, without being formulated or recognized, lies at the base of the explanation mentioned above of the notion of class in terms of propositional function and verified proposition. In reality, in order for a proposition such as "this book is red" or "this is a pencil" to be verified, it is not enough that a red book or a pencil be present and perceived. The book must be perceived *as red,* the pencil *as pencil.*[6] These objects thus would not appear so much in the light of a context of con-

---

[5] Cf. Goldstein, "L'analyse de l'aphasie . . ." *loc cit.* pp. 472 and 490, and *Language and Language Disturbances* pp. 248-50, 254, 287-88 for some representative examples of these periphrases.

[6] With respect to a patient suffering from amnesia of color names, and who was no longer even able to arrange skeins of wool according to a principle of classification such as fundamental hue, brightness, etc., Gelb, *op. cit.,* p. 411, writes: "To group . . . equally bright colors, because they agree in fact . . . is something wholly different than recognizing those colors *as analogous* by brightness, and then choosing this property as a principle of classification." This remark expresses clearly the presupposition we have in mind.

crete action as in the role which they play in relation to the propositional function and the proposition to be verified. More precisely, the object in question must be envisaged in reference to the propositional function, within which it is substituted for the variable, and in reference also to the proposition which, resulting from that substitution, acquires a value of truth from the fact of being related to that object. It is not enough that the object possess in fact the attributes and the qualities which make a pencil or a red book; it is necessary that it be regarded as presenting these qualities which, in their turn, must be seized as corresponding to the meanings which figure in the proposition in question. Nor must the verification of the latter be taken for granted. The object must be conceived as conferring a value of truth on the proposition which is related to it. Further it must be the case that the object in question, by the very fact that it is substituted for a variable, refers to other objects which can equally be substituted, and which will also confer a value of truth on the resulting proposition, and thereby enter into the same class with it.

Obviously all this is possible only in the "categorial attitude" which is revealed as the indispensable condition of conceptual thought. The Platonic problem thus persists, transferred, it is true, from the ontological plane to that of consciousness. What is in question, at least at first, is not the existence of Universals, nor their mode of being, but the conceptual consciousness itself whose specific and irreducible nature must be recognized.

If we have referred to the pathology of language, it is because the study of the patients who have lost the faculty of adopting the "categorial" attitude makes clear a precondition of conceptual thought, which, just because it is always fulfilled in normal persons, can easily be passed over and thus escape attention. It should be noted that the observations of Gelb and Goldstein fully confirm the views and the distinctions on which Husserl insisted from the time of the *Logische Untersuchungen*.[7] Moreover, it should be added that in order to manifest the full philosophical significance of the theory of Gelb and Goldstein, it seems to us that it must be placed in the perspective of Husserlian phenomenology.

While insisting on the specific character of the conceptual consciousness, we are far from contesting its link with perceptual consciousness. Following the general direction in which Husserl was oriented in the last period of his life, we maintain that in order to

[7] In this regard, *vide* our article "Gelb-Goldstein's concept of 'concrete' and 'categorial' attitude and the phenomenology of ideation," *Philosophy and Phenomenological Research*, X (1949).

account for conceptual thought it is necessary to resort to prepredicative experience. Let us sharpen the terms in which this problem poses itself.

In prepredicative experience, we do not find ourselves, at least as a general rule, before beings and objects wholly unique and particularized down to the last details. Except for a few beings and things which have for us the significance of unique individuals, we perceive in the vast majority of cases *objects and beings of a certain kind.* We perceive trees, automobiles, dogs, human beings, etc. In our practical life, we handle the objects which we encounter in the way in which objects of such and such a kind are treated. Perceived objects appear to us with generic determinations and as of a certain type.[8] But—and this is the decisive point—*to perceive an object of a certain kind is not at all the same thing as grasping that object as representative or as a particular case of a type.*[9] In other words, the prepredicative perceptual consciousness is indeed pervaded by the generic and typical; but the latter is enveloped in the perceived objects, inherent in them, incorporated in them. The words which we use in ordinary language seem to us to express that typicality in which things present themselves. In reality, as some logicians have long since noted, if one speaks of a blue fabric, this is not inevitably to place that fabric in the same class as the sky, the Mediterranean, some inks, certain person's eyes, etc.[10] We would rather say that the word "blue" here renders a typical chromatic quality, that manner of being blue which fabrics have in distinction, for example, from inks.[11] Moreover it seems to us that if patients suffering from amnesic aphasia sometimes use words which they cannot find when these words have a categorial meaning, i.e., when they designate objects as belonging to a certain class, this is because these words, in the eyes of the patients, express generic traits linked to the objects and inscribed in them. Goldstein characterizes these words as "proper names," or again as sonorous complexes which, properly speaking,

[8] This characteristic, very essential to perceptual experience, had been brought out by Husserl in *Erfahrung and Urteil* §8. It was explored and deepened by A. Schutz in several of his works, of which in particular we mention the articles "Language, language disturbances and the texture of consciousness," pp. 386-94 (written *à propos* of the book of Goldstein), *Social Research,* XVII (1950) and "Common-sense and the scientific interpretation of human action" (II l) *Philosophy and Phenomenological Research,* XIV 1953). We have spoken of the characteristic in question in connection with the phenomenological theory of perception, which we have developed in our book, *Théorie du champ de la conscience,* Partie IV, chap. II, e.

[9] Gelb, *op. cit.,* p. 411.

[10] Cf. Serrus, *op. cit.,* p. 213.

[11] See also M. Merleau-Ponty, *Phenomenology of Perception* (New York, 1962), p. 313: "A color is never merely a color, but color of a certain object, and the blue of a rug would never be the same blue if it were not a woolly blue."

are not meanings at all, but belong to the object as one quality among others. However, we believe that the expression "proper name" must not be taken strictly. In reality, if in the eyes of the patients a word is appropriate to a certain object, for example to a knife, it is not that the word is appropriate only to this individual knife to the exclusion of every other. We would say that the word is appropriate to the use which can be made of the knife, hence to its generic typicality which—let it be emphasized—remains inherent in it.[12] The same explanation can be given of the fact already mentioned that patients in the presence of an object whose name they cannot find, almost always choose the correct word among those proposed to them.

The first step in the constituting of conceptual consciousness consists in effecting a dissociation within the object perceived in its typicality. The generic traits which until then were immanent and inherent in the perceived thing are detached and disengaged from it. Rendered explicit, these traits can be seized in themselves and crystallize themselves into a new and specific object of consciousness. This object is the concept taken in comprehension. Consequent upon this dissociation, *the generic becomes the general*. From this aspect it opposes itself to the thing perceived from which it has just been disengaged, and which now is transformed into an example, a particular instance, and, in this sense, into a representative of the concept. At the same time, one can conceive the idea of a set of particular instances of the concept in question, which can be represented by each and every one of them, so that, with respect to the concept, they are all equivalent.[13] This is the notion of the concept in extension, or as modern logicians say, the notion of class.[14] The disengagement of the generic and its transformation into the order of the general can found a second operation by which ideal concepts are constituted, normative in some way, that is, ideas in the Platonic sense. They must be understood, at least in the initial phases of the analysis, purely as objects of consciousness, as seized by the conceptual consciousness, and without any ontological preoccupation.

The dissociation or disengagement just referred to seems to us to be a particular form of a very general function for which we propose the name of thematization. It consists in unfolding and articulating a noesis or a noema into its components. The latter, which before thematization were enclosed in the initial noesis or noema and had

---

[12] Goldstein, "L'analyse de l'aphasie . . ." *loc. cit.*, p. 476, and *Language and Language Disturbances*, pp. 61-63, 257-58 and 269.

[13] For a confirmation of this interpretation, cf. Goldstein, "L'analyse de l'aphasie . . ." *loc. cit.*, pp. 471-73 and 488-89.

[14] Cf. Piaget, *op. cit.*, p. 213.

an implicit efficacity—but nonetheless an efficacity—are now sorted out and unravelled. Consequently, they can be grasped and become themes themselves, whereas previously they only contributed to the constitution of another theme within which they played only a mute role. The result to which thematization tends evidently depends on the nature of the components in question. Since, in the case which interests us here, thematization is effected on generic traits and characteristics, it yields the general and the conceptual. It is to the operation of thematization that our attention has been directed; because of its universal scope, this operation of consciousness seems to us to merit more intensive study.

# CHAPTER 11

## Experience and the Perception of Pattern

### MICHAEL POLANYI

I hope that it will become clear in the course of this paper what I mean by calling some elements of science unaccountable.* Let me now say only that I shall speak of the contributions made to scientific thought by acts of personal judgment which cannot be replaced by the operation of explicit reasoning. I shall try to show that such tacit operations play a decisive part not only in the discovery, but in the very holding of scientific knowledge. I shall outline the structure of these acts and indicate to what extent this structure offers a justification for relying on such acts.

Let me start by recalling that even a writer like Kant, so powerfully bent on strictly determining the rules of pure reason, occasionally admitted that into all acts of judgment there enters, and must enter, a personal decision which cannot be accounted for by any rules. Kant says that no system of rules can prescribe the procedure by which the rules themselves are to be applied. There is an ultimate agency which, unfettered by any explicit rules, decides on the subsumption of a particular instance under any general rule or a general concept. And of this agency Kant says only that it 'is what constitutes our so-called mother-wit.' (*Critique of Pure Reason*, A.133.) Indeed, at another point he declares that this faculty, indispensable to the exercise of any judgment, is quite inscrutable. He says that the way our intelligence forms and applies the schema of a class to particulars 'is a skill so deeply hidden in the human soul that we shall hardly guess the secret trick that Nature here employs.' (*Critique of Pure Reason*, A.141.) We are told, in effect, that every time we

*Editor's note: this essay was originally titled "The Unaccountable Element in Science."

speak of dogs, trees or tables in general, or else identify something as a dog, a tree or a table, we are performing a secret trick which is unlikely ever to be revealed to our understanding.

One may wonder how a critique of pure reason could accept the operations of such a powerful mental agency, exempt from any analysis, and make no more than a few scattered references to it. And one may wonder too that generations of scholars have left such an ultimate submission of reason to unaccountable decisions unchallenged. Perhaps both Kant and his successors instinctively preferred to let such sleeping monsters lie, for fear that, once awakened, they might destroy their fundamental conception of knowledge. For, once you face up to the ubiquitous controlling position of unformalisable mental skills, you do meet difficulties for the justification of knowledge that cannot be disposed of within the framework of rationalism.

I shall deal here only with the most attenuated traces of unformalisable mental skills which we meet even in that citadel of exact science, that show-piece of strict objectivity, the classical theory of mechanics. Mechanics are the mathematical formulae by which the motions of the planets are governed. The theory is perfectly strict, and is usually said to predict strictly the observed positions and velocities of the planets. But such is not the case. For the observed readings will never coincide with theoretically predicted values, and the disparities will not only necessarily lie beyond the scope of the theory, but according to Kant's argument about the application of rules to individual instances of experience, can ultimately be interpreted only by unformalisable mental activities. Let us see what happens in practice.

When comparing observations with theoretical predictions, the first thing to decide is whether the deviations are wholly random or else show some significant trend. I shall place this question into a broader context. The picking out of significant shapes from a multitude of disorderly impressions is a task we perform unceasingly by looking at things in front of us. Usually this process of making sense of what we see goes on automatically and correctly. But there is evidence (of which I shall give examples later) that the capacity to see objects has to be acquired during infancy by a process of learning; and of course it is common knowledge that students of science have to learn laboriously to see things through a telescope, a microscope, or in the vague shadows of a radiogram. Indeed, occasionally, we all have to strain our eyes in order to pick out a vaguely visible object. Remember also that camouflage may conceal normally visible objects from the eye by breaking up their contours. And that, of course, our eyes may be misguided into seeing objects which apparently hang firmly together but actually don't exist. For many centuries people have regarded heavenly constellations as highly significant objects, though they are in fact purely accidental, illusory aggregates.

In general therefore, to perceive an object is to solve a problem; it is to answer the question whether there is anything there, and if so, what. We first stare at something we cannot quite make out. We strain our attention trying to make a guess, but as we gradually begin to feel sure of our guess, we may actually have been deceived by a shape which happens to simulate a real object. Such is also the way the astronomer has to decide whether the observed deviations from the theoretical path of a planet show any regularity. He must try to perceive the presence, or else make sure of the absence, of a significant shape in these deviations.

Decisions thus arrived at can of course be subject to further tests, and I shall come back to this. But ulterior tests cannot produce a discovery. The astronomer would spend his whole life in futile checkings, unless he had the faculty for picking out regularities which are quite likely to prove significant. This gift of seeing things where others see nothing is indeed the mark of scientific genius, a faculty guided by vague criteria, just as are the feats of keen eyesight. This is what the members of the first scientific society boasted of by calling themselves the Academia dei Lincei.

It is true that in certain cases you can apply a statistical analysis to decide between regularity and randomness. This method does work by strict mathematical rules. But actually its application depends both at the start and at its conclusion on decisions that cannot be prescribed by strict rules. We must start off by suggesting some regularity which the deviations seem to possess—for example, that they are all in one direction or that they show a definite periodicity— and there exist no rules for reasonably picking out such regularities. When a suspected pattern has been fixed upon, we can compute the chances that it might have arisen accidentally, and this will yield a numerical value (for example 1 in 10 or 1 in 100) for the probability that the pattern was formed by mere chance and is therefore illusory. But having got this result, we have still to make up our minds informally whether the numerical value of the probability that the suspected regularity was formed by chance warrants us in accepting as real or else in rejecting it as accidental.

Admittedly, rules for setting a limit to the improbability of the chances which a scientist might properly assume to have occurred, have been widely accepted among scientists. But these rules have no other foundation than a vague feeling for what a scientist may regard as unreasonable chances. The late Enrico Fermi is reported to have said that a miracle is an event the chances of which are less than one in ten. The rule which Sir Ronald Fisher has made widely current in his book, *The Design of Experiments,* is a little more cautious; it rejects as illusory only patterns for which the odds of having been formed by chance is less than one in twenty. But if anyone were to suggest that the limit should be set at one in five or at one in two hundred, nothing more could be said against this than that it does not seem reasonable. So the mathematical analysis of observed deviations from a theoretical equation can do no more than partially to formalise the process of identifying significant shapes—the process that perception carries out for us informally whenever we look at things. Mathematics only inserts a formalised link in a procedure which starts with the intuitive surmise of a significant shape, and ends with an equally informal decision to reject or accept it as truly significant by considering the computed numerical probability of its being accidental.

There is one field where we can take formalisation one step further. If we call the numerical improbability that a surmised pattern had arisen by chance its distinctiveness, we find that it is this quality that communication theory defines as the amount of information conveyed by a set of signals. We note, for example, that a series of twenty dots and dashes can present $2^{20}$ different configurations, each of which may convey a distinctive message. And this is the same as to say that the distinctiveness of any single configuration of twenty consecutive dots and dashes is $2^{20}$—in view of the fact that the probability of the sequence having turned up by chance is $2^{-20}$. So now both the distinctiveness of the pattern (if true), and the probability of its occurrence by chance (if specious) have a numerical value attached to them. But the physical fact of twenty consecutive dots and dashes does not reveal whether it is distinctive or else means nothing. It is only by our interpretation of the sequence as a coded message that it acquires its distinctive character; it is endowed with its distinctiveness of $2^{20}$ by our effective use of it as a set of symbols. Only when we have thus attributed a meaning to a sequence, can we assess the probability of the sequence having occurred by chance, and find that the odds against this are 1 to $2^{20}$.

So we see that while communication theory does make the distinctiveness of certain patterns vividly explicit, it brings out also clearly that this quality is the result of an informal act of our own. And this can be seen to exemplify also once more that randomness can be conceived only in relation to a potential order, so that both randomness and order express the outcome of an informal act of personal interpretation. For if the twenty signals had in fact flowed through the channel at random, we could attribute no probability to their particular arrangement. The sequence would then be described technically as a mere 'noise,' within which any particular configuration of signals will have to be identified with any other of its $2^{20}-1$ alternatives. In fact, any ordinary noise is a noise only by virtue of the fact that we indiscriminately identify any particular configuration of its elements with any other configuration of them and thus interpret them all as the same noise. This is the philosophy of noise.

It brings out a new aspect of the task facing the astronomer in pondering on any particular set of deviations from the theoretical path of a planet. All channels of communication are affected by a certain amount of noise and we have to read the signals against the disturbing background of this noise. If the noise level is high and the true signals scanty, we must strain our attention to pick out the significant sequence while indiscriminately lumping together, as mere background, the signals which form the noise. And this is precisely what the astronomer must try to do if he wants to distinguish a slight but significant perturbation in the path of a planet from a background of random observational errors.

Moreover, to equate noise with background offers an illuminating transition to a more general principle entering into the recognition of significant shapes. A communication distinguished from the accompanying noise may be looked upon as a particular instance of the contrast between figure and background, a relation extensively explored by gestalt psychology. Remember the famous ambiguous pictures, such as Rubin's 'vase or faces.' You may look at this picture in one way and see two faces in profile with an empty space between them, and then look at it in another way and see a vase in the middle, with an empty background on either side where you saw the faces before. This experience shows that when an area is seen as a figure, it acquires significance and solidity, which it instantly loses when it is made to function as background—while at the same time the area which a moment ago was mere background now becomes a significant and substantial figure. We may generalise this by saying that the figure is something distinctive seen against a background that is indeterminate. Let me elaborate this.

Mimicry renders an insect invisible against its background by repeating on its wings the pattern of the leaves or blades of grass among which it lives. Camouflage acts in a similar way. In both instances, patterns will be particularly effective if they divert attention from the object's outlines. The opposite result, of rendering an object conspicuous, is achieved by covering it with a distinctive pattern which emphasises its contours. And of course, this clear pattern will be most effective when set against a background of blurred, randomly scattered features. Indeed, an object cannot be strictly distinguished from its background unless its particulars lack any definite correlation with those of the background, and this condition is necessarily fulfilled if the particulars of the background are themselves random. Once more then, randomness is shown to safeguard the indeterminacy of a background. Insufficient randomness of background is represented in science by systematic errors which, by simulating a real effect, obscure the outline of any real effect actually present. Systematic observational errors obscure, for example, any real deviation of a planet's course from its theoretical orbit, by introducing a specious regularity from which the real deviation cannot be readily distinguished. A figure can also be concealed, as in puzzles, by covering it with random scribblings; this corresponds to a message being drowned by noise, as mentioned above.

But I must leave for a moment the subject of observational errors in order to enlarge the whole conception of a background as distinct from an object. I have said before that we see the ambiguous figure of Rubin quite differently, depending on 'how we look at it.' I must explore a little further our curious capacity of looking at a thing so effectively in two different ways, and shall pass on for this purpose to an object rendered distinctive by moving against its background. We see a cow strolling in a field. The field, and indeed the whole landscape, with the entire universe as far as the eye can reach and even beyond it to infinity—are seen, or thought as, being at rest, with the cow trotting along in the midst of it all. The background extending indefinitely and comprising an infinite range of unknown or at least unheeded particulars is seen to be at absolute rest, while certain circumscribed objects may be seen to move—as we too may feel ourselves moving—against this background.

This relation holds in fact also in reverse. An area which fills our field of vision up to the horizon will in general be seen at rest. If you look down from a bridge on the waters of a broad river like the Danube, you see the water fixed rigidly at rest while you feel yourself and the parapet over which you are leaning, flying over it. If you are looking upstream you fly forward, if downstream, backward. But the moment you lift your eyes so that your vision includes the borders of the river, the motion of the bridge stops and the water starts once more streaming below it. So each time the area which extends indefinitely beyond the horizon functions as a background—even when as a result of it we are compelled to see a racing river stand still and the bridge on which we stand fly through the air above it.

This shows how very effective can be the act of looking at an area one way rather than another; to see it as a background to a neighbouring area which we look upon as an object—or to see the two areas the other way round. It is becoming clear also that the different ways of looking at neighbouring areas are correlated. An object is seen as such *by virtue* of our seeing its surroundings as its background —and vice versa. This has come out now strikingly in the fact that the perception of an object *in motion* appears functionally related to seeing around it an indefinitely extended background at absolute rest. It suggests that we are performing one single mental act in jointly seeing an object against its background and that this seeing may be right or illusory; indeed, that *we are aware of the background in terms of the object's appearance*—e.g., of its being in motion— and that this view of the object *may be true or false*.

This gives us the first inkling of the structure of that mother-wit to which Kant surrenders the application of rules to experience and of that inscrutable power hidden in the bosom of Nature, by which he accounts for our capacity to form and apply universal conceptions—the tacit power which I shall try to identify and justify as the unaccountable element in science.

Our next step towards this aim leads us to the beautiful experiments of Ames in which figures were seen against the background of a room—a room of a very special kind. Opposite each other in two corners of this room stood a grown man and a young boy and the boy looked taller than the man. This was due to the fact that the shape of the room was distorted so that at the two corners where the figures stood, the height of the ceiling and the distances from the opposite wall differed greatly. The boy standing at the corner with the lower ceiling and closer to the observer was seen taller than the grown man seen further away at the opposite corner, where the ceiling was higher.

This result is due to an illusion in two stages, both of which are relevant to us. (1) Viewed (with one eye) from the position prescribed for the experiment, the irregularly shaped room appears normal. (2) Against the background of this apparently normal but actually skew-angled room we see the sizes of persons standing in two opposite corners mistakenly as if they were standing in the opposite corners of a normal room. The illusory appearance of the room serves as a background to the illusory appearance of the figures; and the room itself is seen illusorily against another background, namely our lifelong experience that rooms have regular rectangular shapes.

Both illusions are compelling when the room is seen, as prescribed, with one eye placed at a point from which the angles subtended by the edges of the skew-shaped room are the same as those of a normal room. The impression made by the room is then determined—in the absence of any striking clues to the contrary—by the past experience of normal rooms; and once the room is seen as normal, it functions as the background to the figures and thus determines their apparent size in the way a normal room would.

But the flow of this account conceals a decisive gap. It describes a sequence of two stages in which clues operate to make us see two figures at absurd sizes. But why do clues not operate in the opposite direction? The fact that young boys are smaller than adults could form a clue to correct our illusory perception of the room and controvert thereby the rule that all rooms are right-angled parallelipepedes.

We must admit that clues *might* in fact operate in this way. This does happen when you look at the experimental arrangement from a forbidden angle. Other 'give-away' clues have the same effect, for example clues collected by tapping the walls of the irregular room with a long stick. Such a scrutiny may destroy the illusion and make us see the two figures once more at their proper size. But the effort needed to achieve this shows how great is the power that operates in the opposite direction. This power resides in the area which tends to function as a background because it extends indeterminately around the central object of our attention. Seen thus from the corner of our eyes, or remembered at the back of our minds, this area compellingly affects the way we see the object on which we are focusing. We may indeed go so far as to say that we are aware of this subsidiarily noticed area mainly in the appearance of the object to which we are attending.

This interplay of background and figure illustrates a general principle: the principle that whenever we are focusing our attention on a particular object, we are relying for doing so on our awareness of many things to which we are not attending directly at the moment, but which are yet functioning as compelling clues for the way the object of our attention will appear to our senses. An obvious and often commented instance of this is our tendency to overlook things that are unprecedented. Having no clue to them, we do not see them. Charles Darwin has described how the Fuegians crowded wonderingly around the rowing boat which took his party on shore from the *Beagle,* but failed to notice the ship itself lying at anchor in front of them. Scientists are of course as subject to this failing as these Fuegians were: even astronomers observing planets, to whom I have so far restricted myself. When Neptune was discovered by Galle in 1846 by following up the predictions of Leverrier, the past positions of the new planet were computed and their identity established with a star recorded by Lalande in Paris in May 1795. This being communicated to the Paris observatory, an examination of Lalande's notebook showed that he made two observations of the planet, on the 8th and 10th of May, and finding them discordant (since the planet had moved) had rejected one as probably in error and marked the other as questionable. The Cambridge astronomer Challis who undertook to test the predictions of Leverrier and Adams sighted the planet four times during the summer 1846 and once even noticed that it had a disc, but these facts made no impression on him since he doubted the hypothesis he was testing. Before its discovery as a planet by Sir William Herschel in 1781, Uranus had been recorded as a fixed star at least seventeen times: seventeen times its motion had gone unnoticed. What is more, it would be idle to reproach these astronomers for succumbing to this Fuegian attitude to the unprecedented. For the craving to find strands of permanence in the tumult of changing appearances is the supreme organon for bringing our experience under intellectual control. In fact if astronomers had gone on testing every new star on the possibility of its being a very slowly moving planet, they might well have wasted all their time in obtaining an immense mass of meaningless observations.

Yes, the principle which misguided the Fuegians is of inestimable value. The boundless variety of raw experiences is devoid of all meaning and our perceptive powers can render it intelligible only by identifying very different appearances as the same objects and qualities. How do our eyes do this? Snow at dusk sends less light into our eyes than a dinner jacket in sunshine, and if you look at the surface of these objects through a blackened tube, snow may appear dark and the black cloth light. But when we look at them in the usual way, snow will always be seen to be white, and a dinner jacket to be black. It is the supreme achievement of our eyes to show us objects as having a constant colour, size and shape, irrespective of their distance, position and illumination. The experiment with the blackened tube shows that this is done by taking in clues from the whole field of vision, coming from the utmost corners of our eyes, and relying on our awareness of these peripheral clues for the way we see the object which occupies the centre of our attention.

Such is the function of peripheral impressions when used as clues, and it is our powers of comprehension that bring them into action by looking at them with a bearing on the object of our attention. It is this art, the art of seeing infinite varieties of clues in terms of relatively few and enduring objects, by which we make sense of the world. It is this process of skilful integration that a monkey brought up in darkness has to learn slowly when faced with the task of recognising his feeding bottle by the help of its eyes, and which the human baby has probably to learn likewise when acquiring the skill of looking at things. It is the same kind of learning which students have laboriously to pursue on a higher level in the practical classes of anatomy and microscopy, of radiology and clinical observation, the kind of study by which the zoologist and botanist acquires his expert capacity for identifying individual specimens of different species.

The main clues on which perception relies are in fact deeply hidden *inside the body* and cannot be experienced in themselves by the perceiver. Though we may notice the strain in our eyes and are aware of the posture of our head, the intricate pattern of internal stimuli arising from the adjustment of the lenses in our eyes, from the muscles controlling the convergence of the eyeballs, from the inner ear, etc., and the elaborate system by which our perception makes us aware of these data in the appearance of the objects we are looking at, these can hardly be experienced in themselves at all. Moreover, gestalt psychology has shown how much ingenuity is required to track down even the clues within sight of the eyes, since they are seen only incidentally and their effect on the appearance of the object perceived can be revealed only by elaborate experimental investigations. Most of the clues used in seeing objects may therefore never be identified, and besides, if identified and seen in themselves would lose their suggestive power as clues and bereft of this function would tend to be lost among other meaningless details. Yet all these hidden evaluations of not identifiable clues are conducted, particularly when perception is strained, by the full powers of our intelligence, relying on operations which, as experiments have proved, must be acquired by efforts which in certain cases may prove so strenuous that their persistent pursuit leads to mental breakdown.

We are at last facing here fully that secret power of our nature which Kant despaired of elucidating. We see that a great deal can be known about the way it works, but we realise also that the better we know it, the less it appears capable of definition by precise objective rules. On the contrary, it is ever more clearly seen to be an intrinsically personal effort, guided by unspecifiable clues towards the achievement of a coherence sensed by ourselves in pursuing it.

Let me return with this in mind to the astronomer making up his mind whether the observed deviations from the theoretical path of a planet show any real regularity against the background of random —or perhaps somewhat systematic—observational errors. We have left him having to realise that in his enquiry he must rely on a personal interpretation of the evidence since neither order nor randomness can be measured or otherwise strictly ascertained, so that he must recognise order by his own sense of orderliness and identify randomness by his sense of randomness. The astronomer might find support for acquiescing in this situation by reflecting on the system of crystallography, a thoroughly respectable part of the exact sciences, which can be controverted by no experimental facts, since it only sets up a system of perfect order to which solids might conform; so that observed deviations from crystallography are not seen as failures of crystallography but as imperfections of the specimens in question. And as to the assessment of random chances, he might have found consolation in the fact that the laws of quantum mechanics, as well as those of thermodynamics, being statements of probabilities, are controvertible only by using some arbitrary rejection rule for denying the possibility of very odd chances.

But now the astronomer pondering on his observed data has to face further methodological worries. He must realise that the intellectual framework acquired in his scientific training will induce him to see what conforms to this framework and to ignore what does not; and he will be aware also of the dilemma that this evident menace to his originality is also the indispensable guide of all scientific thinking, the very safeguard of true scientific discipline. Yet he wants to get on with his enquiry. Looking at his data, he must try to make out whether they show any significant shape, perhaps a deviation from existing theory as important as Kepler found in Tycho's data of the path of Mars, or Leverrier found in the perturbations of the planet Uranus—a new feature that, if rightly interpreted, would bring him immortal fame, but if claimed mistakenly, would stamp him as a fool forever. Judging by the structure of perception, there is no explicit rule by which he can proceed to solve his problem. He must strain his attention towards any signs of regularity, but his effort must be based on an awareness of peripheral data, noticed only from the corner of his eye or remembered only at the back of his mind— while it may also require the appreciation of novel kinds of order, never met before.

But I had now better leave the astronomer to deal with his particular worries and try to widen the question facing him to include other lines of scientific research. Remember that the efforts of perception are evoked by scattered features of raw experience suggesting the presence of a hidden pattern which will make sense of the experience. Such a suggestion, if true, is itself knowledge, the kind of foreknowledge we call a good problem. Problems are the goad and guide of all intellectual effort, which harass and beguile us into the search for an ever deeper understanding of things. The knowledge of a true problem is indeed a paradigm of all knowing. For knowing is always a tension alerted by largely unspecifiable clues and directed by them towards a focus at which we sense the presence of a thing—a thing that, like a problem, embodies the clues on which we rely for attending to it. This is the lesson derived from perception, which we have now to apply generally to the pursuit of knowledge by scientific enquiry. We shall see that it covers the unaccountable elements of science from the dawn of discovery to the holding of established scientific knowledge.

All research starts by a process of collecting clues that intrigue the enquiring mind, clues that will largely be like the peripheric clues of perception, not noticed or not even noticeable in themselves. And a good problem is half a discovery. In the case of the diffraction of X-rays by crystals, Laue's discovery followed almost immediately on the stating of the problem. Lee and Yang recently earned the Nobel prize by merely pointing out in practical terms the question whether the two directions of helicity are equivalent in nature. It took over forty-eight hours of experimental work to discover that they were not. But the elucidation of some problems may take years or even centuries. The question raised by Aristarchus of Samos whether, contrary to appearance, it was perhaps the earth that moves around the sun, was not finally settled till Newton's discovery of general gravitation.

A problem is something that is puzzling and promising and research carries this excitement into action, which in discovery culminates in triumphant satisfaction. A scientist must have the gift of seeing a problem where others see none, of sensing the direction towards a solution where others find no bearings, and of eventually revealing a solution that is a surprise to all. By contrast, persons engaged in mere surveying enlarge knowledge without being beset by problems or excited by dawning solutions, without experiencing triumph or causing surprise by completing their task. Surveying is dull because its performance is closely prescribed by rules, while science is and must be exciting, since it relies on largely unspecifiable clues which can be sensed, mobilised and integrated only by a passionate response to their hidden meaning. We have noted and analysed how perception is performed by straining our attention towards a problematic centre, while relying on hidden clues which are eventually embodied in the appearance of the object recognised by perception. This, I suggest, is also how the pursuit of science proceeds; this is the unaccountable element which enters into science at its source and vitally participates throughout even in its final result. In science this element has been called intuition. The purpose of this paper is to indicate that the structure of scientific intuition is the same as that of perception. Intuition, thus defined, is not more mysterious than perception—but not less mysterious either. Thus defined, it is as fallible as perception, and as surprisingly tending to be true. Intuition is a skill, rooted in our natural sensibility to hidden patterns and developed to effectiveness by a process of learning. Scientific intuition is one of the higher skills, like music, politics or boxing, all of which require special gifts, gifts in which a few exceptional people greatly exceed all others. Great powers of scientific intuition are called originality, for they discover things that are most surprising and make men see the world in a new way.

It is customary today to represent the process of scientific enquiry as the setting up of a hypothesis followed by its subsequent testing. I cannot accept these terms. All true scientific research starts with hitting on a deep and promising problem, and this is half the discovery. Is a problem a hypothesis? It is something much vaguer. Besides, supposing the discovery of a problem were replaced by the setting up of a hypothesis, such a hypothesis would have to be either one formulated at random or so chosen that it has a fair initial chance to be true. If the former, its chances of proving true would be negligible; if the latter, we are left with the question how it is arrived at. Why are exceptional scientific gifts required to find it? How do these operate? Such questions reveal instantly that the powers of intuition are indispensable, at all stages of establishing new scientific knowledge, and that any scheme which misses them out, or tacitly takes them for granted, or else includes them merely by the vagueness of its terms, is irrelevant to the subject of scientific enquiry and of the holding of scientific knowledge. Almost every paragraph of this paper presents an unsurmountable obstacle to any theory of knowledge which does not accord a decisive function to the intuitive powers of the mind as defined here.

But even the highest degree of intuitive originality can operate only by relying to a considerable extent on the hitherto accepted interpretative framework of science. This will supply the scientist with general clues for his enquiries, just as the experience stored at the back of our minds supplies us with general clues for the perception of novel objects. Such general clues are the premisses of science and include the current methods of scientific enquiry. It is said that the constitution of the United States is what the Supreme Court says it is. The premisses of science are likewise what current discoveries prove them to be. Strictly speaking, the premisses of science are today what the discoveries of tomorrow will reveal them to be.

Even so, these premisses are rooted in the body of science as accepted today, and we must yet explain how the holding of our scientific knowledge today can guide scientists to discover further knowledge, unknown and indeed inconceivable today. This is recognised today by saying that the greatness of a discovery lies in its fruitfulness. But this description conceals what it would explain. It still leaves us with the paradox that we can know the presence of hidden knowledge, and can pursue its discovery guided by a sense of its growing proximity.

My own answer to this paradox is to restate an ancient metaphysical conception in new terms guided by gestalt psychology. We make sense of experience by relying on clues of which we are often aware only as pointers to their hidden meaning; this meaning is an aspect of a reality which as such can yet reveal itself in an indeterminate range of future discoveries. This is in fact my definition of external reality: reality is something that attracts our attention by clues which harass and beguile our minds into getting ever closer to it, and that, since it owes this attractive power to its independent existence, can always manifest itself in still unexpected ways. If we have grasped a true and deep-seated aspect of reality, then its future manifestations will be unexpected confirmations of our present knowledge of it. It is because of our anticipation of such hidden truths, that scientific knowledge is accepted and it is their presence in the body of accepted science that keeps it alive and at work in our minds. This is how accepted science serves as the premiss of all further pursuit of scientific enquiry.

The efforts of perception are induced by a craving to make out what it is that we are seeing before us. They respond to the conviction that we can make sense of experience, because it hangs together in itself. Scientific enquiry is motivated likewise by the craving to understand things. Such an endeavour can go on only if sustained by hope, the hope of making contact with the hidden pattern of things. By speaking of science as a reasonable and successful enterprise, I confirm and share this hope. This is about as much as I can say here in justification of a pursuit of knowledge based largely on hidden clues and arrived at and ultimately accredited, on grounds of personal judgment. I believe that this commitment makes sense in view of man's position in the universe.

# Selected Bibliography for Part III

1. Adrian, E. D., *The Physical Background of Perception*. Oxford: The Clarendon Press, 1947.
2. Barnes, W. H. F., "Talking about Sensations," *Proceedings of the Aristotelian Society*, Vol. 54 (1953-54), pp. 261-278.
3. Bledsoe, W. W., and Browning, I., "Pattern Recognition and Reading by Machine," *Proceedings of the Eastern Joint Computer Conference*, 1959, pp. 225-232.
4. Block, H. D., "Analysis of Perceptrons," *Proceedings of the Western Joint Computer Conference*, 1961, pp. 281-289.
5. Bruner, J. S., Goodnow, J. J., and Austin, G. A., *A Study of Thinking*. New York: John Wiley and Sons, Inc., 1956.
6. Cherry, C. (ed.), *Information Theory*. New York: Academic Press, Inc., 1961.
7. Clark, W. A., and Farley, B. G., "Generalization of Pattern Recognition in a Self-Organizing System," *Proceedings of the Western Joint Computer Conference*, 1955, pp. 86-91.
8. Farrell, B. A., "Experience," *Mind*, Vol. 59 (1950), pp. 170-198.
9. Frishkopf, L. S., and Harmon, L. D., "Machine Reading of Cursive Script," *Information Theory*, C. Cherry (ed.), pp. 300-315.
10. Geach, P., *Mental Acts*. London: Routledge and Kegan Paul, Ltd., 1957.
11. Hamlyn, D. W., "The Visual Field and Perception," *Aristotelian Society Supplementary Volume 31* (1957), pp. 107-124.
12. Hanson, N. R., *Patterns of Discovery*. Cambridge, at the University Press, 1958.
13. Hirst, R. J., "The Difference between Sensing and Observing," *Aristotelian Society Supplementary Volume 28* (1954), pp. 197-218.
14. Hirst, R. J., *The Problems of Perception*. London: George Allen and Unwin, Ltd., 1959.
15. Hovland, C. I., and Hunt, E. B., "The Computer Simulation of Concept Attainment," *Behavioral Science*, Vol. 5 (July 1960), pp. 265-267.
16. Hunt, E., *Concept Learning*. New York: John Wiley and Sons, Inc., forthcoming 1963.
17. Köhler, W., *Gestalt Psychology*. New York: Mentor paperback, 1959.
18. Lettvin, J. Y., Maturana, H. R., McCulloch, W. S., and Pitts, W. H., "What the Frog's Eye Tells the Frog's Brain," *Proceedings of the Institute of Radio Engineers*, Vol. 47 (November 1959), pp. 1940-51.
19. Lloyd, A. C., "The Visual Field and Perception," *Aristotelian Society Supplementary Volume 31* (1957), pp. 125-144.
20. Marill, T., and Green, D. M., "Statistical Recognition Functions and the Design of Pattern Recognizers," *The Institute of Radio Engineers Transactions on Electronic Computers*, EC-9 (December 1960), pp. 472-477.
21. Merleau-Ponty, M., *Phenomenology of Perception* (trans. C. Smith). New York: Humanities Press, 1962.
22. Pitts, W., and McCulloch, W. S., "How We Know Universals," *Bulletin of Mathematical Biophysics*, Vol. 9 (1947), pp. 127-147.
23. Reichenbach, Hans, "On Observing and Perceiving," *Philosophical Studies*, Vol. 2 (1951), pp. 92-93.
24. Rosenblatt, F., "Perceptron Simulation Experiments," *Proceedings of the Institute of Radio Engineers*, Vol. 48 (March 1960), pp. 301-309.
25. Selfridge, O. G., "Pandemonium: A Paradigm for Learning," *Mechanisation of Thought Processes*, Blake and Uttley (eds.). London: Her Majesty's Stationery Office, 1959, Vol. 1, pp. 513-526.
26. Selfridge, O. G., and Neisser, U., "Pattern Recognition by Machine," *Scientific American*, Vol. 203 (August 1960), pp. 60-68. Reprinted in *Computers and Thought*, Feldman and Feigenbaum (eds.).
27. Shaffer, J., "Could Mental States Be Brain Processes?", *Journal of Philosophy*, Vol. 58 (1961), pp. 813-822.

28. Uhr, L., and Vossler, C., "A Pattern Recognition Program that Generates, Evaluates and Adjusts its own Operators," *Proceedings of the Western Joint Computer Conference,* Vol. 19 (1961), pp. 555-569. Reprinted in *Computers and Thought,* Feldman and Feigenbaum (eds.).
29. Urmson, J. O., "Recognition," *Proceedings of the Aristotelian Society,* 1955-56, pp. 259-280.

## Part IV

The  Modeling  of  Mind

# CHAPTER 12

## Mindlike Behaviour in Artefacts*

DONALD MACKAY

### INTRODUCTION

In popular usage the term *machine* has come to stand for something which is essentially servile. The commonly-heard expostulation that 'a machine only does what you tell it to do' thus becomes virtually a tautology. The term *artefact* in the sense of 'artificial construct' has been used in the title of this paper in order to minimise misunderstanding from this cause, for the mechanisms with which we shall be concerned will differ radically from the common notion of a slave-machine.

Equally important is the fact that we shall not be concerned with existing *digital computing machines*. For certain functions the artefacts we consider may make use of digital techniques; but present-day digital computers are deliberately designed to show as few as possible of the more human characteristics. Originality, independence in opinion, and the display of preferences and prejudices are not favoured by the mathematician in his computing tool. The comparison of *contemporary* calculating machines with human brains appears to have little merit, and has done much to befog the real issue, as to how far an artefact *could* in principle be made to show behaviour of the type which we normally regard as characteristic of a human mind.

Our enquiry might be roughly framed in the form of three questions marking progressive stages:

(i) Can an artefact be made to show the behavioural characteristics of an *organism?*

---

*Reprinted from *The British Journal for the Philosophy of Science*, 1951-52. More recent writings of the author on this topic are listed on p. 241.

(ii) How closely in principle could the behaviour of such an artificial organism parallel that of a human mind?

(iii) On what philosophical issues, if any, do these possibilities have a bearing?

GOAL-DIRECTED ACTIVITY

One of the most distinctive features of an organism is that of *goal-directed activity*. Associated with this feature are a group of concepts such as *purpose, control,* and the like, which cease to have meaning in its absence. To avoid committing anthropomorphism— one of the two currently unforgivable sins—we may define the statement 'A seeks the goal X' as follows:

Let the current state of A (plus its environment) be defined as Y. Let X define that state of A-plus-environment which we term the *goal of A*. Then the statement above implies that the activity of A in a defined group of circumstances is such as *inter alia* to minimise the discrepancy between X and Y.

In a still more formal sense we may consider the two states X and Y to be representable by two points $X$ and $Y$ in an abstract space, the coordinates of each point being given by some set of parameters defining the corresponding state. We may then say that A functions in such a way as to minimise the interval $XY$, or some time-average of the magnitude of this interval. The situation may then be depicted in the manner of Fig. I, which indicates the essential requirements for such goal-directed activity to be possible.

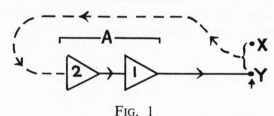

FIG. 1

(i) There must be an effector (1) capable of altering the state $Y$. This perhaps would qualify for the title of 'machine' in the usual sense.

(ii) The activity of this effector must be controllable by an element (2) capable of receiving information.

(iii) Information as to the magnitude of $XY$ must be *fed back from the field of activity* to the controlling element (2), there to give rise (after analysis) to activity in (1) leading to the minimisation of some measure of $XY$.

*The Modeling of Mind* 226

There are many familiar examples of devices satisfying these requirements, ranging in complexity from the simple thermostat, in which the effector is a heating unit and the space of $XY$ is a one-dimensional scale of temperature, to the self-directing missiles and automatic processing plants with multi-dimensional fields of activity which are now emerging from the blue-print stage. They are all characterised by the *circulation of information* indicated in Fig. 1— by the presence, in other words, of *feedback*. Perhaps the simplest form of control is one in which the frequency or intensity of activity is proportional to the discrepancy $XY$. This evidently has a state of equilibrium only when the discrepancy is zero. (Such 'error-operated' fedback systems may, however, easily become unstable in the presence of delays or inertia in the information loop, so that the control element (2) must normally include quite complex computing operators if the information is to be used to optimum effect.)

The impression seems to be current that fedback systems form a class by themselves, subject to different laws from those of 'straight' systems. It is perhaps worth pointing out here that from the physical standpoint a fedback system is only a particular case of the general non-fedback type. If an input $x$ to the control point of a normal mechanism causes an output $y$ which is some function $F(x)$, then the introduction of feedback amounts to setting $x$ equal to some function $G(y)$. The problem set by the system is thus the solution of the normal equation $z = G(F(x))$ for the special case wherein $z = x$. No exemption from ordinary laws accrues. The features of interest in its behaviour arise from the limitations on its behaviour-pattern set by this equation.

The systems we have considered can evidently be thought of from another standpoint. If we focus attention on the transformations of information which are usually necessary in (2), we can think of the latter as a type of computer, which makes logical deductions from data acquired from a field which is *affected by the results* of the deductions. This leads us to ask what types of field are open to the activity of such an artefact. Among the most interesting are the following:

(*a*) *The field of physical variables outside the artefact*. This we have already considered in the examples above.

(*b*) More interesting, the field of physical variables *widened to include the artefact itself*. In a primitive sense, an artefact capable of receiving and acting on information about the state of its own body can begin to parallel many of the modes of activity we associate with self-consciousness. At a lower but equally important level, as Ashby's

'Homeostat'[1] illustrates, it can adjust its internal modes of functioning so as to become in principle self-repairing.

(c) The field of *mathematical and other logical propositions*. The interest of this field from our viewpoint lies in the possibility of generating continuous and significant trains of reasoning, not dependent on the continuous supply of information by an operator. To a limited extent this mode of operation is realised in present-day computing machines; and the well-known discipline of Boolean algebra enables logical deduction also to be arithmetised for treatment, by the same method as numbers on the scale of (2).

(d) In any or all the above, a field *including a human interlocutor*. This is perhaps of greatest interest. An artefact can for example be designed to play a game of chess with a reasonable frequency of success against a human opponent.[2] In principle such an artefact may truly be said to engage in logical *dialogue,* and no barrier of principle prevents the field of dialogue from covering topics other than chess.

But we may cut short the enumeration of these possibilities, for they have already received much publicity. Among the more important functions of which we shall hereafter assume an artefact to be capable, we may list the following in summary:

(a) *Receiving, selecting, storing, and sending information.*

(b) *Reacting to changes in its 'universe,'* including *messages* and *data on its own state.*

(c) *Reasoning* deductively from premises which can include the results of previous deductions and data on the relative success of different courses.

(d) Observing and controlling its own activity, whether symbolic or otherwise, so as to further some *goal.* This may be only a very general objective, such as the maximisation of efficiency in some defined sense, or the attainment of equilibrium, leaving a wide scope for the development of subsidiary 'purposes' *ad hoc* by the artefact as the result of its experience.

(e) *Changing* its own pattern of behaviour as a result of experience so as to develop quite complex and superficially unpredictable characteristics capable of rational description in purposive terms.

The above enumeration has not been made in the belief that these possibilities are philosophically significant, except in so far as they remove confusion due to insufficient thought. For they are merely consequences of a principle which is generally accepted: any pattern of observable behaviour which can be specified in terms of unique

1 W. R. Ashby, *Electron. Eng.* (1948), **20,** 379.
2 C. E. Shannon, *Phil. Mag.* (1950), **41,** 256.

and precisely-definable reactions to precisely-definable situations can in principle be imitated mechanically. (As a last resort, the decomposition of the specification in terms of Boolean algebra can always in principle lead to a description of a relay system which satisfies it.)

It is suggested in other words that no new philosophical issues are raised by the possibilities so far considered. These artefacts are merely deterministic performers of functions which we ourselves would describe as 'mechanical' were we to carry them out. There seems no reason to deny, however, that in principle such artefacts could merit the title of organisms.

## A Probabilistic Reasoning-Mechanism

The type of artefact that we have just considered would meet many of the classical tests for mindlike behaviour. We have still, however, to meet the question implicit in our first paragraphs: Is it possible for an artefact to show originality, independence of opinion, and, for example, such illogical human characteristics as prejudice, and preference? Or can we find analogues of such impalpable processes as the weighing of evidence? In short, how closely in principle could the behaviour of an artefact parallel that of the human mind?

To answer this question we shall consider a rather different type of artefact, which is perhaps most easily introduced as a development of the first. We have been making an implicit assumption that all the data used are exact, and lead to deductions which are unique and certain. This follows from our assumption that decomposition into elementary 'yes-or-no' propositions is possible without distortion. But in human intercourse this is seldom the case. Data are only moderately certain, and the closest attainable approach to a unique conclusion is often an estimate of the relative probabilities of several. It appears likely that an artefact to imitate the more human thought-processes, should operate on a much less deterministic and inflexible basis. What is required in fact is a means of introducing the concept of *partial truth* or *probability*.

This is a twofold problem. First, we require means of handling, combining and computing probabilities—in effect, of making statistical analyses. Secondly, we should evidently design our artefact so that its actions based on such probabilistic data can parallel those of a rational mind in the same circumstances. This implies that the *statistical structure* of its behaviour pattern shall be that logically justified by the statistics of the data if it is to be described as reasonable and unprejudiced. It is possible to envisage a very simple mechanism which can meet these requirements admirably, and incidentally has a well-known neurological parallel. It is the mechanism of *threshold control*. Consider an element which changes from one to another of two states when a controlling input exceeds a certain threshold level. If the magnitude of signal and threshold are precisely specified, the consequent state of the element is uniquely determined (excluding the infinitely improbable case where the magnitudes are exactly equal). But if now we introduce an element of randomness —which is inevitable in any real case—we shall only be able to say that the probability of change of state is some known function of the signal and threshold magnitudes. For example, we might use electronically generated random noise-signals to perturb the threshold level, in such way that the individual actions of the element would become unpredictable *in principle*. At the same time its *statistical* behaviour pattern would reflect quite precisely the information-content of the threshold: signal configuration. In short, such an element would behave as if *uncertain* of the truth of the proposition represented by the stimulating signal.

It is not of course necessary to adhere literally to the notion of a determined threshold randomly perturbed. Any functional perturbation which can give meaning to the notion of *control of transition-probability* is sufficient to provide the kind of statistically-sensitive element we require. In an artefact constructed on this new principle, information would be represented not only by the current excitation-patterns, but also by the changing probabilities of excitation. In fact it could be thought of as two interlocked computing networks, one representing and handling information in the form of discrete symbols, the other handling information relative to the probabilities to be associated with them.[3]

At the risk of oversimplification, we might clarify the picture by describing our earlier reasoning-mechanism as a switchboard with rigidly-interlocked levers. We have now moved from this notion to the notion of a switchboard in interaction with an analogical network controlling the *probabilities* of throwing the switches.

We have in fact passed by easy stages to a new concept of a reasoning mechanism, in which the control of transition probabilities plays a dominant rôle. 'Thinking' in such a mechanism becomes a stochas-

[3] This complementary relationship is closely analogous to that between structural and metrical information in the formalism of information theory (D. M. MacKay, *Phil. Mag.* (1950), **41**, 289), which in fact was the stimulus leading to the ideas now presented. The connection will not be developed here, though it may be remarked that the representation of *meaning* by the orientation of an information vector suggests a direct interpretation of the concept in terms of the functioning of a statistical mechanism of this kind.

tic process, proceeding along paths determined only statistically. Guiding the statistical process is the network which computes and governs transition-probabilities, which may in many cases be more important than the excitation-pattern.

It is natural to ask what it is which prevents such activity from becoming nonsensical. In the first place, it must be remembered that only an increase in threshold is necessary to make the mechanism operate on the simple digital principle. It is thus capable of all the activities of the digital artefact considered earlier. Lowering of threshold need take place only where statistical 'thinking' is appropriate. But in the second place, the activity is always distinguished from nonsense by its statistical pattern—by the effects of the guiding transition-probabilities at each point of divergence. Individually its actions may be unpredictable; statistically (or collectively) they make sense. The behaviour pattern of a human being in many respects provides a parallel here; and there is no reason in principle why precisely the same degree of reasonableness should not be attained by the artefact, since its upper bound of performance is the perfection of rigid logic.

It is not difficult to see how such a flexible mechanism can manifest most of the 'typically human' characteristics. Continuously-variable (and irregularly excitable) *prejudices, preferences,* and other 'emotional' effects can obviously be shown if transition-probabilities are linked appropriately to the 'causes' of the prejudices. *Weighing* of evidence can be represented by subliminal manipulation of probability-amplitudes. *Originality* of a kind can be constantly in evidence because of the lack of a deterministic link between input and output; and on those occasions when a random excitation-pattern finds itself in logical equilibrium with the current data-pattern, quite significant contributions could be made to a train of thought, with full claim to be called original.[4] *Learning* in such artefact could take place in more than one way. Discrete representations similar to those used in digital computers could of course be used. But the most natural process would be one in which the frequency of past success or failure of a given action determined the transition-probability to that action in future. Such a self-guiding learning mechanism has been built by the author. It is readily envisaged both in electronic and physiological terms, and has the advantage that stored information is immediately available at the relevant point. It seems increasingly likely, in view of physiological evidence, that the human brain also may retain much of its information in this form rather than in localised 'stores.' In comparing the possibilities of such an artefact with the

---

[4] Normally, of course, the life of a sequence uncorrelated with the main stream of thought would be short, because of the improbability of the necessary transitions.

performance of a human mind, it is important to remember the part played in the development of the human mind by intercourse with other human beings. We must be prepared to imagine as much care and attention to be spent on the 'education' of our artefact as on that of a child. If we do so, it is difficult to deny that such an artefact could be made to develop statistically consistent modes of behaviour which in a human being we should describe as constituting a personality.

Our conclusion in fact may reasonably be expressed in a generalisation of our previous axiom, as follows: 'Any pattern of observable behaviour which can be defined *statistically*, in terms of *probable* reactions to given situations, can in principle be shown by an artefact.'

The implications of this conclusion are of greater interest.

## ABSTRACTION

It is not the purpose of this paper to enter into technical details of artificial mechanisms. The foregoing sketch has sought only to establish the width of the class of functions which can be realised in an artefact, so as to place the later discussion in proper perspective. There is, however, one central problem which deserves closer consideration because of its connection with longstanding philosophical issues. It is the problem of abstraction—the recognition of pattern or *Gestalt*. Related to it is the question whether an artefact could with reasonable frequency generate significant hypotheses.

We have indeed begged a thorny question in assuming implicitly that all incoming data were *intelligible* to our artefact. How is it possible to ensure that the significant invariant of a pattern of data is selected for propositional representation? Given a situation in which recognition of *triangularity* is required—to take a stock example— how can we ensure that the response of the artefact could remain invariant with respect to changes in size, shape and orientation of a triangle?

It is a fact which may perhaps be thought surprising, that contemporary artefacts can much more readily be made to perform elaborate calculations that would strain a human brain to the limit, than simple feats of recognition which children or some lower animals perform instinctively.

Two fundamentally distinct approaches to this problem are possible. The first may be called the passive or template-fitting method, which has been described by McCulloch[5] and Wiener[6] among others.

[5] W. S. McCulloch and W. Pitts. (1) *Bull. Math. Biophys.* (1943), **5**, 115-23; (2) *ibid*. 1947, **9**, 127-47.

[6] N. Wiener, *Cybernetics* (New York: Wiley, 1948).

A typical sample of the pattern to be recognised is stored in the arte-fact as a kind of template. Incoming signals are now subjected to a systematic series of transformations inverse to those under which the pattern is invariant. If the artefact is to recognise a triangle irrespec-tive of its size, shape or orientation, it must change all three aspects of the incoming signal systematically until it matches the stored sample-signal—the 'ideal triangle'—representing the concept 'triangu-larity.' At this stage the artefact can adopt a course of action indicative of its *recognition* that the pattern is triangular.

Such an artefact recognises in the act of *reception*—hence our use of the term 'passive' to describe the mechanism, which acts essentially as a filter. Some features of the structure of the visual cortex have been adduced as evidence in support of the hypothesis that cerebral pattern-perception functions in the same manner,[7] but the idea does not appear to have found universal favour; and for our purpose it is possible to envisage a mechanism on a different principle, which is not open to the same objections.

By way of introduction to this second notion, let us first consider the way in which a blindfold man might seek to recognise a solid triangular figure, by moving his finger around the outline.[8]

He requires essentially to perform two kinds of motion—recti-linear movement, and sudden changes of direction. As his finger moves round the outline, he finds it necessary to issue to them just two types of order, in a characteristic sequence. This sequence is in prin-ciple invariant with respect to the size, shape or orientation of the triangle. To the blindfold man, the concept of triangularity is in-variably related with and can be defined by the sequence of elemen-tary responses necessary in the act of replicating the outline of the triangle.

Let us generalise this approach to the problem of recognition, and consider now an artefact whose response to incoming stimuli of any kind is an *act of replication,* in some formal sense, of the stimuli re-ceived. In other words, disequilibrium signals are generated in the artefact and cause activity therein until there is a sufficient degree of resemblance between a synthetic replica and the incoming pattern. This situation is simply a particular case of the general scheme of

[7] W. S. McCulloch and W. Pitts, *Bull. Math. Biophys.* (1947), **9**, 134-36.

[8] The usefulness of defining the form of a geometrical figure by its 'natural equa-tion' (i.e., the equation specifying curvature as a function of distance along the periph-ery) has been noticed independently by a number of workers. Some development of the idea has been found in the writings of Craik (K. G. W. Craik, *The Nature of Explanation,* Cambridge, 1943); and Dr. O. Straus of Massachusetts Institute of Tech-nology in a personal communication (25/1/51) has described a method of identifying curvilinear figures on this principle by computing their natural equation.

Fig. I, wherein $X$ and $Y$ would now represent the incoming and imitative patterns respectively.

At this point we introduce a crucial feature. We suppose that our artefact possesses at any time a finite number of standard methods of replication—a finite number of commands and command-sequences to the replicating effectors. Evidently then, if recognition is a function of the act of replication, the total of recognised experience for the artefact is describable and identifiable in terms of this one set of commands. *The elementary acts of replication define the basic vocabulary in terms of which the artefact describes its own experience.*

The term 'experience' though anthropomorphic appears to have justifiable metaphorical use here, since it refers to that fraction of the total of received stimuli which has evoked the analogue of *conscious awareness* in the artefact—the fraction with which subsequent behaviour may show correlation.

Evidently the problem of recognising complex patterns now reduces to the problem of learning to make complex (formal) replicas, which is of the same class as other problems of coordination such as learning to walk or write. And since our artefact uses as its elementary symbols the elementary acts of replication, no problems of *identification* arise. Complex concepts are represented by complexes of symbolic (internal) acts of representation.[9] The significance or meaning of any concept to the artefact, is *described* in its language by the same complex of responses as that which makes up its name. This introduces a vast simplification into the kind of learning-mechanism which we may envisage. Transition-probabilities now require to be established, not between a stimulus and an action via an identification-link, but between one action and another—between the act of replication constituting recognition and the learned response which should follow recognition.

In the above discussion we have incurred two debts. We have omitted all mention of the statistical aspects of recognition; and we have tacitly assumed that our artefact has been taught to make the standard sets of responses which symbolise the universals of its world. It is almost time to leave technical discussion for more philosophical stock-taking, but a very brief indication of solvency may be given.

The first debt is readily discharged. All that has been said earlier about statistical thought-sequences can apply equally to the process of recognition. Replication is, of course, never perfect. A practical recog-

---

[9] It should be clear that the input dealt with by the replicatory mechanism is generally in quite a different physical form from the original input to the sensory receptors. An olfactory stimulus for example might be mapped electrically, and would not have to be replicated by generating odours!

nitive artefact need only have a finite resolving-power in its comparator, and could use parallel-operation to enable it to choose what it estimates to be the *most probable* replicatory command-sequence to 'describe' a given pattern. This has important implications for the concept of *meaning*. Evidently the meaning of a symbol can here be something more general than the specification of a unique combination of 'eigensymbols.' To our probabilistic artefact, a symbol means a probability-distribution over the set of eigensymbols; the selective operation performed by the symbol is a statistical one and may perhaps be validly followed by any one of several different responses. It may equally be impossible to give a unique verbal definition even in terms of responses, of some concepts appearing in the thought-process of the artefact, since these may be defined only in terms of the statistical conjunction of several responses.

Our second debt is a more important one. Could an artefact discover and recognise new invariants independently of prior instruction? Again a statistical mechanism makes it easy to envisage such a process. The only pre-requisite is a sufficiently frequent recurrence of the invariant in the patterns which are replicated. For in the absence of a 'recognised' pattern, the artefact could be made to try automatically in random fashion, various sequences of replicatory orders. The relative success of each could be caused to influence the probability of future trial. Thus if one of these happens to correspond to a recurrent pattern, it will rapidly grow in statistical status. If the recurrence of the response-pattern is persistent enough for it to become associated with actions, the pattern enters the vocabulary of the artefact as a new 'universal.'

In a final word we might examine the relation of this last mechanism to the making of hypotheses. A hypothesis in this context is a symbolisation not evoked as a direct replica of received stimuli. It is essentially a response-train prepared in advance of an expected pattern of stimuli. The simplest hypothesis—that past experience will recur—is thus made automatically by our artefact. But in the face of contradictory subsequent experience, it can be designed to adopt procedure identical in principle with the exploratory speculation which forms at least a large component of what *we* understand by making hypotheses. And because the transition-probabilities can be made to change automatically in accordance with the results of trials, there is no obvious reason in principle why the process should not converge as frequently and as fruitfully as in human speculative thought. Indeed it is a tenable hypothesis that the human cerebral mechanism may operate in just such a manner.

*Mindlike Behaviour in Artefacts*    235

We may generalise our concept in a further step. One way in which our artefact could respond, is to alter the order-pattern (or the relative probabilities of orders) in a standard group of orders. This is an important form of response, for it corresponds to the making of an *abstract* hypothesis—an hypothesis concerning an abstraction, as distinct from one concerning a pattern of stimuli. In other words, the response of an artefact may be to *alter the mechanism controlling response*. This is equivalent to recognising the pattern formed by the response-orders. Here we have the first step in a *hierarchy of abstraction,* in which the patterns formed by the responses of each level become the subject matter of the response-vocabulary of the next higher. This possibility may repay more detailed study on another occasion.

In summary we may note some of the more important features of the type of artefact we have been developing.

(*a*) We take for granted the ability to parallel the more mechanical aspects of human behaviour discussed in earlier sections.

(*b*) The distinction between *reception* and *perception* is fundamental to its operation, the latter being characterised by the element of *response.*

(*c*) The points (or regions) of *conscious attention* in a field of received data have their analogues in the regions under *active replication.*

(*d*) Many familiar psychological phenomena, such as optical illusions, find direct analogues in the normal functioning of the replicatory mechanism.

(*e*) The *basic symbols* of the vocabulary of the artefact are the *elementary acts of response.*

(*f*) The *universals* of its field of discourse are those *sequences of responses* which have found repeated application.

(*g*) Such an artefact is automatically adapted to concentrate on the *changing* features of its environment, since it is these which require the issue of new commands to the replicatory mechanism; and by (*e*) above this automatically amounts to *naming* the new features.

(*h*) It is possible to find an analogue for the activity of *making hypotheses,* which seems hard to distinguish in principle from the human parallel.

(*i*) The element of indeterminacy in the *modus operandi* is fundamental to its proper function in a statistically-fluctuating universe.

On what philosophical issues do these possibilities have a bearing? A systematic study of their implications would be lengthy; but they appear to illuminate a number of concepts from a new angle.

The interesting aspects of the behaviour of our artefact arise principally from the combination of two features—its goal-directed activity and its 'reasonable indeterminacy.' It has already been suggested that the first of these raises no new philosophical issue. It does, however, have some purgative influence on our thinking about the concept of *mind*. Mindlike behaviour is here conditional on the *circulation of information* in the sense referred to above, for the concepts of mindlike behaviour are defined only for closed-loop circulatory systems.

It now becomes easy to see the fallacy inherent equally in the analytical approach of the classical mechanist and in the Cartesian compromise. To claim that analysis of the nervous system into parts reveals 'no sign of the soul' is as indicative of a false approach as to suggest that any one organ might be the seat thereof. In terms of the information-diagram, the position is directly analogous to that of a man seeking the 'residence of triangularity' among the individual dots of a triangular dot-pattern.

We have in fact an ideal example of the destructive effect of abstracting a system from its environment, when the concepts of interest are essentially properties of the system-plus-environment.

A more subtle fallacy, however, lies in wait. The temptation is now to say that the mindlike features are 'nothing but' abstractions from the physical description. The question-begging phrase 'nothing but' appears to have no justification. The concepts relating to mindlike behaviour form a different logical group from those which appear in the analysis of elements of the artefact, so that it is true that the corresponding descriptions may be logically immiscible for some purposes of deduction. But for our recognitive artefact at least, the abstractions have as much logical respectability as the data in which they are recognised, since all are exemplified by replication-operations of one kind or another. All, in short, have operational status, at one level or another.

The false dualism which used to be expressed in the question 'how can matter produce mind' would now seem to have its origin in a genuine dualism of conceptual frames of reference, defined respectively for the viewpoint of actor and spectator. The situation is not a symmetrical one, but the concept of complementarity whose value we have been led to recognise in physics appears to have an analogue here that would repay development. The dualism of wave and particle in physics is resolved neither by arbitrary denials of 'reality' nor by 'explanations' of one as 'nothing but' an aspect of the other. The process of description is seen as a selective or projective operation; and it is not so much the validity but the appropriateness of a description which requires to be discussed in any given situation. Paradoxes arise when concepts defined for one logical background are mixed carelessly with those defined for another. Descriptions in terms only of one group or the other may both be valid. It is not the descriptions which are exclusive, but the logical backgrounds in terms of which they have meaning. The moral is obvious, and seems to admit of large-scale transfer to other fields of thought.

The artefact is also of interest in providing a direct analogue of the concept of *consciousness*. Consciousness, behaviourally speaking, is represented as we have seen by the region of the field of data evoking active response by (formal) replication. *Self*-consciousness appears to be shown if the field of replication includes a representation of the artefact itself, which of course introduces no special difficulty. The same situation could automatically ensure that the artefact would act as if aware that external events were located in a world external to its own body.

The application of a similar interpretation to the concept of human consciousness is of course purely hypothetical, but the parallel is at least suggestive. It would imply, if valid, that 'I' am the totality of currently reacting elements of my body, which are organised in terms of information-linkages so as to constitute an organism. The continuity which we predicate of our perceived experience despite the discontinuities of our received data, would find its origin in the persistency of the command-pattern by which experience is symbolically replicated and *ipso facto* perceived and described. Concepts such as responsibility are group-concepts defined for the totality, and define a valid calculus of behaviour at the level and in the language of *conscious* activity. Along such lines it seems possible that a consistent probabilistic theory of personality might be developed which could find a complementary place for some of the psychological dicta currently debated as antagonistic, particularly in relation to pathological conditions.

Another concept which now appears in a new light is the notion of randomness. Information theory enables us to give precise significance to a definition of randomness as "lack of information-content.' In particular, a completely random sequence *to a given receiver* is definable as one which exercises no selective operation on the information-space of the reciever. (*Absolute* randomness has probably as little meaning as other notions defined by prefixing the word 'absolute' to operationally defined concepts.)

We are accustomed to think of completely random activity as meaningless and dull. But our artefact shows randomness in the domain which in a human being is that of *free will;* and behaviourally there is no reason in principle why the two should be distinguishable. All *systematic* components of human behaviour-patterns can in principle be simulated. What remains is by definition devoid of systematic content for the observer, i.e. it exercises no selective action on the information-space of the observer. Equally by definition, it must then be classified as the 'completely random component' of the human behaviour pattern *from the observer's point of view.* Yet in the context of the systematic component it admits of a reasonable interpretation as the exercise of free choice; and by the actor himself the calculus of responsibility is normally acknowledged to be directly applicable to it as such.

The point cannot be pressed in detail here, but it may bear further consideration, since we are so often inclined to use 'mere randomness' as a term of dismissal or almost of explanation.

The connection between the apparent free will of our artefact and the determinate components of its behaviour-pattern inevitably suggests an analogy with the hoary problem of human free will. This is usually epitomised in the question, 'Is human free will genuine?' The question in this form is imprecise, but the parallel may be illuminating. The choices of a free man are seldom devoid of a statistically-predictable component; someone who knows him well can usually score a significant frequency of success in predicting his choices, though it is most unlikely that they form a stationary time-series. In the same way the choices of the artefact, given a knowledge of the various threshold levels defining transition-probabilities, are statistically predictable on a short term basis. The suggestion is that the choices of a free man may likewise be governed by statistical distribution-functions which have a physiological representation and are in principle determinate; but that individual choices can be unpredictable in principle, and it is probable that the distribution-functions are indeterminable in practice.*

To complete a sketchy stock-taking, it is suggested that these developments raise no new *theological* issues. This is, of course, a personal view; but the so-called 'theological objection' against which

---

*The notion of freedom here referred to is concerned with spontaneous rather than deliberate choice. The latter has been discussed more fully in the author's later papers cited at the end of this essay, where the view is expressed that no randomness of mechanism is *necessary* to validate human responsibility.

Turing[10] tilts in a recent paper appears to be a windmill without an owner among reputable contemporary theologians. Doubtless a full realisation of foregoing implications will have a purgative action on unwarranted speculative accretions in theology, but the central concern of Christian theology at least is framed in terms of the calculus of responsibility, whose categories in the author's view are unaffected by changes in the complementary categories of physical process used to describe brain function. No reputable theologian expects to find physical laws disobeyed in the human brain; and it is difficult to see how elucidation of the particular physical processes which happen to be used can in any way be relevant to the claims (whether admitted or not) which are made by Christianity on the personality whose thought is mediated by those processes.

CONCLUSIONS

Our principal conclusion is that we have failed to find any distinction in principle between the observable behaviour of a human brain and the behaviour possible in a suitably designed artefact. We would do well, however, to retain a sense of proportion; the human central nervous system is estimated to comprise some $10^{10}$ elements, each of considerable complexity. It is unnecessary to point out the practical difficulties of constructing, supplying and maintaining an artefact of comparable complexity, and the possibility need not be taken seriously. At the same time it must be realised that a much smaller number of elements would provide a complexity of behaviour comparable in most respects with that of human beings, so that no deductions in either direction need be made dogmatically at this stage.

We have seen that the designing of an artefact on statistical principles, using a combination of quantal and continuous processes, enables its statistical behaviour-pattern to be intelligible despite a controllable measure of freedom in individual choices. In such an artefact analogues of concepts such as emotion, judgment, originality, consciousness, and self-consciousness appear. It is capable of performing abstractions, and generating significant hypotheses with reasonable frequency—including hypotheses about its own mechanism for generating hypotheses.

Quite unintentionally, this paper appears to have provided an answer to some strictures of Professor Popper on the capabilities of 'machines.'[11] Professor Popper's emphasis on the limitations of Science (with a capital S) and on the dignity of human personality, we

10 A. M. Turing, *Mind* (1950), **59**, 433.
11 *The British Journal for the Philosophy of Science,* 1950, **I**, 194-5, especially footnote on p. 195.

should warmly endorse. His remarks that 'calculators' can have only 'senseless powers of producing truths,' and 'possess no method of picking out the interesting or important ones' are certainly true of contemporary computers, for good reasons. But when he says that 'It is only the human brain which can create interests, purposes, problems and ends'—then in face of the foregoing possibilities, he appears to shoulder a considerable *onus probandi* for no very clear reason.

This said, we might perhaps go even further than Professor Popper in insisting that the elucidation of the actual mechanisms mediating human thought, or the development of artificial organisms capable of a comparable function, affects neither the status of man's thought nor the extent to which he is answerable for the choices made on the level of moral and spiritual responsibility.

[Editor's note: more recent views of Professor MacKay on some of the topics of this essay may be found in:

1. Mentality in Machines; (Third paper in Symposium); *Supplement to the Proceedings of the Aristotelian Society,* 1952, XXVI, 61-86.

2. The epistemological problem for automata; *Automata Studies,* Princeton University Press, 1955, pp. 235-51.

3. Towards an information-flow model of human behaviour; *British Journal of Psychology,* 47, 30 (1956).

4. On the Logical Indeterminacy of a Free Choice; *Proceedings of the XIIth International Congress of Philosophy, Venice* (Sept. 1958).

5. (Revised version of 4): *Mind,* 69, 31-40 (1960).

6. The use of behavioural language to refer to mechanical processes; *British Journal for the Philosophy of Science,* 1962, XIII, 89-103.]

# CHAPTER 13

# The Mechanical Concept of Mind[1]

## MICHAEL SCRIVEN

Is there an essential difference between a man and a machine? To this question many answers have been suggested. One type of answer claims for the man some psychological quality such as intelligence, consciousness, or originality, whch is said to be necessarily lacking in the machine. Other examples are introspection, thought, freewill, humour, love, correlation of speech and senses. Throughout this paper the sole example of consciousness will be used. The argument follows very similar lines for the other terms. A machine is normally understood to be an artefact, a manufactured mechanical (and possibly electrical) contrivance. It will so be taken here. The purpose of this discussion will be to consider in detail the statement that machines are never conscious.

When it is said that it is impossible for a machine to be conscious, it is not always clear to what extent this is intended to be a logical objection, and to what extent it is empirical. It may be thought that some particular practical obstacle such as providing a machine with a means of communication, is insurmountable. But it must be remembered that such empirical obstacles may *conceivably* be surmounted: and an argument based on these differences alone is not logically demonstrative. This discussion will not consider *any* such practical differences to be essential differences: thus, the machines to be compared with man, will be capable of speech, gesture, perambulation, etc., and sensitive to light, sound, and other environmental conditions. They will be referred to as robots. A robot can do everything that a machine will ever do. The second question then

---

[1] Reprinted from *Mind,* 1953. The author's Postscript has been added to indicate the direction of his later thoughts on the issue of this article (editors' note).

arises; is there any essential difference between robots and human beings?

It may be thought that the original question has been overwhelmed by the considerable assumptions of the last paragraph. In fact this is so only if the question whether a machine can be conscious depends on its successful emulation of the behaviour of, say, a man, who, we should all agree, was conscious. For a robot, *ex hypothesi,* is capable of duplicating any human behaviour. If a man answers briskly when we whisper his name behind his chair (or criticises poetry, or declares himself to be in love), we have no doubt that he is conscious. But a machine might respond to the same sound frequencies with the same reply and we should not feel satisfied that it was conscious. The question we seek to answer with our everyday tests is whether a man is conscious or unconscious: whereas of machines we enquire whether they are capable of consciousness or not. We know that the question of consciousness is proper with a man: what concerns us in the case of a machine is not this question, but the question whether this question can sensibly be asked. It is thus not appropriate to demonstrate that a machine is capable of passing tests that would establish its consciousness were it a man, when we have not yet enquired whether a machine is essentially distinct from a man in *non-behavioural* respects, as far as they are relevant to the question of consciousness. The robot is simply a machine which is indistinguishable from man in behavioural respects. So the important question becomes: "Is a robot essentially distinct from a man?", and the replies to be considered are of the type "Men and not robots are conscious."

Is it blind prejudice which prevents us from extending the franchise of consciousness to robots? when robots can calculate more quickly, react more swiftly, see more clearly and remember more accurately than men. What is it that they lack when they can do everything? They do what humans do, but they cannot be what humans are: the electric pulse that activates them is not life. Like some spell-bound creature of the myths, they have every appearance of life yet they do not live. Years may pass and we are still deceived but if at last one cuts itself and fails to bleed, or in a mindless fury wrecks a building we would start back in horror, exclaiming "A robot! and all the while we thought it lived and breathed." It never felt nor suffered, thought nor dreamed, though never failed to give the signs. We can make machines to plough and harvest, to perform and imitate, but not to feel pleasure or self-pity. These things are possible only to conscious creatures, and no matter how ingenious the mechanism, how complex the behaviour of a machine, no matter whether it talks or plays chess. it's no more conscious than a clock. So we feel at first.

The sense of "conscious" in which it is contrasted with "incapable of being conscious" rather than with "unconscious" will be distinguished from the other by the use of a capital letter. In these terms the apparent paradox of sleeping creatures is resolved: for unconsciousness is quite different from Unconsciousness;[2] in fact unconsciousness (and consciousness) entails Consciousness. The question "Is it Conscious?" can be asked of anything. It is absurd to ask of a stone or a stop-watch "Is it conscious?" because it is absurd to talk of it being dead, asleep, drugged or stunned, i.e., unconscious. There are cases where it is very difficult to decide the question of Consciousness. Consider the living things of the world. Ferns and fruit-trees are not Conscious; nor algae, or the insect-eating plants. Protozoa and bacteria are not Conscious. But are jelly-fish Conscious, or earthworms? At what stage does the child in its development from Unconscious germ-plasm become Conscious? Here are cases where living things are not Conscious and cases where we are in doubt. But doubts arise only about living things. Machines are apparently not alive. There are even cases where it is difficult to decide the question of consciousness. For example, a man might have a completely anaesthetized cortex, his behaviour being controlled by an external operator employing radio waves to operate minute devices inserted at the efferent nerve-ends. Information from the afferent nerves is similarly relayed to the operator. This man is unconscious, a puppet, though outwardly conscious. But such difficulties arise only about Conscious beings.

It may be said that machines approach Consciousness along another path from the living things, that of behaviour. They are capable of greater complexity of behaviour than the simple creatures we have mentioned. Is complexity of behaviour (or degree of organisation) essentially connected with Consciousness: even behaviour as complex as a man's? This is our question once again, by now a paler figure than before.

We can sum up the problem very simply. Everyone knows what "conscious" means; everyone knows he is conscious when he is thinking or remembering, watching or reading. But there can be no inner tests of *other* people's mental conditions and we must judge them from without, *if we can judge them at all*. This is where the difficulties begin. First, though it may *in fact* be certain whether a man is conscious or unconscious, we cannot always be certain from watching him or testing his behaviour: he may be totally paralysed and so never move, yet still be conscious; or he may walk and talk under

2 Read as "capital Unconsciousness/Consciousness."

radio control with an anaesthetized brain, i.e., while really unconscious. So the outward signs (including speech) are not infallible
indications of consciousness. It is therefore quite certain that they are
not, even in men, whom we know may be conscious, the same thing
as consciousness. Second, there is the very different question of deciding whether something is Conscious, i.e., whether it is capable of
being conscious. To suggest that evidence of behaviour is sufficient
to prove the presence of Consciousness is like suggesting that the
response of a lift which starts coming up when we press the button
proves there is a man inside. In each case the evidence is appropriate
*only* if we have the other vital evidence (the inference-licence). By
itself it is worthless, as far from conclusive as a tinopener is from a
meal. Behaviour is not attached to Consciousness as thunder is to
lightning, nor as a sound to an echo, nor as clouds are to rain, but
only as pain is to torture. The one does not guarantee the other but
is guaranteed by it. An indefinitely long series of behavioural observations is not equivalent to the observation of consciousness, but there
are times when it is wrong to doubt it is a proof, e.g., a man driving
a car. A series of behavioural observations is not equivalent to the
observation of consciousness and *so* it is proper to doubt if it is ever
a proof of Consciousness. There is an essential connexion between
the capacity for complex behaviour and Consciousness; the one is a
necessary condition of the other. But it is not a sufficient condition;
and though we may decide which living things are Conscious from
their behaviour, we cannot decide if everything is Conscious from its
behaviour. Life is itself a necessary condition of Consciousness, and
though behaviour is a factor which sometimes decides the question
whether a certain system is alive, it is again not the only one. The
behaviour of an anti-aircraft gun-predictor system is more complex,
organised and adaptive than that of seaweed, but it is certainly not
alive. The seaweed is biochemically, not behaviourally more complex.
Robots, too, are machines; they are composed only of mechanical
and electrical parts, and cannot be alive. If it were announced that
scientists had discovered a way to create life, they would not be taken
seriously if they produced a complex machine as substantiation. It
is as if they announced that we can sometimes see objects below the
horizon, and proved this on the scientific definition used by astronomers or surveyors, according to which everything below the horizontal
line of sight is below the horizon, e.g. the ground at one's feet. The
fact that there may occur in machines as in living organisms the same
feature of directive organic unity is not enough to show that both live.
It is scarcely surprising that we can produce a mechanism which has
this comparatively simple property. It would be extremely surprising

if the production of such a mechanism was supposed to endow it with life. There are other tests which are relevant, and these it fails, simple though they are. Since it is nonsense to talk of a machine being dead, it is nonsense to talk of it being alive. Machines do not even belong to the *category* of things which can be dead or alive. It would, of course, be possible to employ organic materials in constructing the robot, but this would not alter the argument. Even if it proved prossible to create living cells and incorporate these, the result would not be a conscious machine, because a sufficient proportion to justify calling the thing itself (rather than parts of it) alive and hence possibly conscious would certainly be enough to prevent it being correctly called a machine. This is the last expedient and, like its predecessors, affords no escape from the conclusion that there can be no such thing as a conscious machine.

### SUMMARY

There appears to be a paradox associated with the concept of a conscious machine. On the one hand it does not seem that there is anything in the construction, constituents or behaviour of the human being which it is essentially impossible for science to duplicate and synthesise. On the other hand there seem to be some important and meaningful descriptions of human behaviour which can never be properly applied to machines. We feel puzzled that the basis for a description can be reproduced, yet the description cannot be re-applied.

This conflict once led people to deny the material composition of the body: in more recent times it has led people to deny that men have any attributes which must forever evade machines.

But only puzzles and problems have solutions: paradoxes have none, only sometimes resolutions. When we resolve a paradox, we do not decide in favour of one of the conflicting arguments and against the other; rather, we bring out the precise truth of each in order to show they do not conflict on the same ground. This is true of the familiar logical and pragmatic paradoxes as well as of those paradoxes at the root of philosophical problems such as the one considered in this discussion. Here we have come to see that the human being need have no transcendent element, yet that machines will never be conscious, because we have come to see that a reproduction of a man sufficiently exact to be conscious, is too exact to be still a machine.

### APPLICATIONS

It is necessary to discuss separately the application of analytical results such as those evolved here. The question to be decided is whether every possible machine is essentially distinct from a man. One particular answer considered suggests that a machine will never be conscious. The key words are "machine" and "conscious". Now it is entirely possible that the meaning of these words may change, hence that statements involving them may no longer stand in the same logical relation to other statements as they do now. This may occur for a variety of reasons: the most likely is that the forceful associations produced by them will lead to their employment in places where their strict meanings and less forceful associations render it inappropriate or incorrect. An example of this arises in connexion with the word "intelligent". One can well imagine a man whose work lies largely with one of the great electronic computers coming to apply this word to it. He often makes mistakes: it is faultless. His memory for figures is limited: it has an enormous storage capacity. He is intelligent, yet the machine is better at the job. At first as slang, then seriously, these machines will be called intelligent. A means for comparing the intelligence of different machines will perhaps be devised: connected with their speed and accuracy of working rather than mere capacity; perhaps also with their versatility and ease of programming. As better computers are produced, and they come to be used less for performing particular calculations than for solving complete problems, the notion of *consulting* a computer, rather than *using* one, will grow. In various other ways usage will reflect the increasing tendency to regard a computer as a specialist *par excellence*. Then one day a man may ask: "Can machines ever be really intelligent?" This is not one of the questions we have considered, though the words are the same. We have not given an answer for it, nor an indication of one: it is feasible to consider all possible machines, absurd to consider all possible meanings of the word "machine", or "intelligence".

Yet there are circumstances in which it is difficult to decide whether the descriptions employed or the statements made exhibit a change of meaning in their terms, or merely an unprecedented but not improper combination of terms. An example of an unprecedented combination which would involve no change of meaning is the description "blue grapefruit". An example of a change of meaning has just been discussed: it was suggested that the word "intelligent" had changed its meaning when it came to be applied to a computer. In the present meaning of the word it is not sensible to talk of a slide-rule or an abacus as intelligent, and the fact that they may be driven by a motor instead of being moved by our hands does nothing towards making them intelligent. An electronic computer is a complicated instrument which we operate for the same purposes as the slide-rule and abacus Unless operated by an intelligent being it is entirely useless: but even when it is operated by an intelligent being, it does not thereby become intelligent, only useful. It may be entirely similar in construction to a human brain; but the human brain is a physiological mechanism, no more intelligent than a muscle. Certainly the brain is an indispensable component of an intelligent being, unlike a muscle, and the relative intelligence of various creatures may be deducible from their brain structure. But it is the creature that is intelligent, not the brain: people have good brains or mediocre brains, but never intelligent brains: it is they who are intelligent. Now computers are not even as well placed in this competition as brains; for they are not indispensable to any-one's intelligence, any more than books are indispensable to memory. And one can no more say that a computer is intelligent than that a book remembers. This is the argument that shows "intelligent" to be an improper adjective for the noun "computer". It is also the argu-ment that shows there has been a change of meaning in one of these terms if the combination has a proper use. In the situation described above, there is a proper, though perhaps only a technical, use for this description. So there has been a change of meaning. Similarly, to con-sider a very simple example, we can say quite definitely that if there is ever a standard use of the description "childless parent", then the meaning of one of these terms has changed.

Now it was argued in the first part of this paper that the description "conscious machine" could have no proper use. In normal usage, it was suggested, the factors which contribute to the identification of machines are also factors which distinguish them from animate mat-ter and *a fortiori* from conscious beings. Conversely, the factors which lead us to use the adjective "conscious" include, explicitly or tacitly, the condition that the subject of description is not a mechanical contrivance. Should we be misled on this point, the subsequent dis-covery of inorganic composition and electric motivation would make us withdraw the adjective, in exactly the way we should withdraw the adjective "angry" from the description of an action by a man whom we later discover to have been acting. There is no difference between the behaviour of the robot and a conscious man, between that of the actor and an angry man. But the robot is not in fact conscious, just as the actor is not in fact angry. It follows from this that if we do use the description "conscious machine", one of these terms must have changed in meaning.

But there is a converse situation, in which we are not at first suffer-ing from inadequate information, but instead we are suddenly faced with the crime accomplished, the impossibility completed. Explorers land on another planet and on their return are accompanied by one of the inhabitants, a robot. He is a member of an extensive and cultured civilisation, a skilled and learned citizen, anthropoid in appearance, yet with some unusual powers. He spends many months on Earth, observing our social and economic structures with interest. It must be expected that in such circumstances many of the people that get to know him would talk of him in human terms. Suppose that someone suggested that this robot was an example of a conscious machine. It is not as simple to point out a fundamental incongruity in this description as it would be in any proposed application of the description "childless parent", or even of the description "intelligent computer".

But consider now how we should answer the persistent sceptic who refuses to believe that the robot is really a conscious machine. We might point out that the robot has been with us for some time and that we have got to know him as a friend and as a learned colleague. We would ask how this could be possible unless the robot was a conscious being, one genuinely capable of sympathy, of thought and of inner reflection. There is here no possibility that the sceptic can repeat the technique used to bring out the impossibility of an intelligent computer, for the robot is an autonomous creature, in no formal sense a mere instrument: and some autonomous beings can properly be called "conscious".

The sceptic first asks, Is it properly called a machine? True, he says, it is metallic and mechanical in appearance, both external and internal. Perhaps it is this alone that marks a machine, he says. But surely it is not enough for it to have this appearance. We must be certain that at every stage the behaviour of the components, and in large, of the robot itself is mechanical. For else it may be that the real origin of its movements, speech, and gestures is some non-mechanical influence—a soul perhaps, or an alien being. Moreover, he says, it will not even then suffice to understand the general nature of each connexion: to be certain that this robot is only a machine we must make sure that each part is quantitatively mechanical, that the measure of each response is exactly deducible from the measure of each stimulus together with the nature of the linkages. We must in fact, be able to see clearly that this is nothing more than a machine, that it has no 'will' of its own. Had we constructed it ourselves, of course, most people would have felt satisfied on this point. Suppose that we are successful in this analysis of the mechanism. Then it might be the case that we could easily predict every move of the robot. More probably, as with the big computers, although it would be possible *in principle* to predict every move, it would rarely be possible to do this as quickly as the machine acts. There is a sense in which one might say that the behaviour of human beings is in principle predictable, meaning that one believes them to be no exception to the materialist conception of nature, while not suggesting that on present knowledge we can predict their behaviour. In a slightly different sense one might say that the behaviour of a roulette wheel or the failure of an engine which suddenly breaks down is in principle predictable. When it is said here that we cannot be certain that the robot is a machine until we are certain that its behaviour is in principle predictable, however, it would follow that given time one could calculate the behaviour resulting from any given environmental stimuli. It does not follow that we can always say what the robot will do in a certain situation before he does it.

Now the relation between Consciousness and freewill is a rather complicated one. It is not easy to prove that the one is impossible without the other. But it is at least certain that we cannot prove that the robot is Conscious. For we now have a complete causal explanation of all its behaviour, and this explanation does not at any stage depend on its consciousness, and so its behaviour cannot be a proof of the possession of consciousness. Consciousness is not a property which can be detected in a machine by any physical examination, because it cannot be *identified* with any physical characteristics of a machine. Nor can it even be correlated with them, as the colour red can be correlated with certain wavelengths of light. The fundamental element in these correlations is the subjective impression and it is exactly this element whose presence in the robot is in question. For example, if we noticed increases in the robot's alpha-rhythm which nearly always correlated with the beginning of activity or speech, we might be tempted to say that this was the mark of consciousness. Equally well, however, it might be called a mark of mechanical preparation for speech or activity.

It is only philosophers who have doubted whether we can prove other people are conscious. They tend to do this partly because of the sources of error attendant on a diagnosis of certain mental states from other people's behaviour, which are absent from one's knowledge of these mental states in oneself. This is a philosophical and not a scientific doubt because there is (and could be) no correlation of the suggested difference with any scientifically observable differences. The doubt whether a robot can be conscious is not only philosophical but scientific because there are physical (not behavioural) differences between man and robot.

The case is in fact rather stronger that this, as the sceptic would point out. For there is a peculiar weakness about the claim that a robot may be conscious although its behaviour is entirely determined (whether or not it has freewill). Suppose the robot suggests that the question of consciousness is surely best known to itself, gives a good explanation of what the word means, and then claims to be conscious. Since we have exact knowledge of its mechanism, one might think that one could then determine whether it was lying and so finally decide the question of its consciousness. But to decide whether it is lying or not when it claims to be conscious one must first decide whether it is conscious or not, *i.e.* answer the original question. To decide if human beings are lying without knowing the truth ourselves we can use a lie-detector, but these depend on the effects of consciously uttering a falsehood and any comparable test on the robot would be impossible unless it could be decided whether it was ever conscious. A gramophone may produce lies but it does not lie; nor does it tell the truth. So the robot's testimony is of no value, because we cannot show that it is its own testimony. A robot, unlike a gramophone, has its own voice; but what it can say depends on how it is made and for what purpose. Again, we are troubled by doubts whether it is proper to speak of a machine when we cannot say whether or for what it was designed, whether it has ancestors and descendants or designers and mechanics.

In the first part of this paper, we worked on the basis of a fairly simple idea (an unanalysed concept) of machine and living organism. In this part, we have considered the case of a discovered robot with an unspecified background in an attempt to derive the minimum conditions for calling it a machine and Conscious. Having decided it is a machine on the minimum grounds, we find it still seems possible to *say* the robot is Conscious. But Consciousness has then become something entirely apart from the behaviour, a spectral Observer whose presence is without trace or influence. It is not true to say that consciousness is *necessary* to explain certain behaviour in machines, (e.g., the use of certain language); although one may feel that consciousness *goes with* certain behaviour by machines, it does not *follow from* it, as it does with men. Machines that seem to use the word "conscious" correctly, do so simply because they are programmed in a certain way: if there was any other explanation, they would not be merely machines.

The background of neglected characteristics here becomes important. If we find the robots on their native planet growing up like children, learning to think and speak, in some way becoming parents and dying, we might be convinced that the usual categories of "machine" and "living organism" need supplementation with a third, perhaps "android". It would then display a lack of understanding of the geography of the new concepts to ask if androids were really machines, but we might call them Conscious. If, instead, they emerge full-grown from automatic factories, the products of one factory being identical in general appearance, in their unchanging facial expression, their abilities and their vocabularies, we should perhaps judge them sufficiently well described as "machines". Perhaps, too, we might even here want to say they were Conscious, for men often tend to personify the machines with which they are familiar: but this would not constitute a good reason for believing they are really Conscious. If we did not have a causal explanation of their behaviour, if there were no valves and wheels inside them but only homogeneous plastic, or a cavity, the ascription of Consciousness could be readily understood as that age-old resource of ignorance, the anthropomorphising move. As it is, their behaviour is evidence of their construction, not their Consciousness. Now, it is true that our understanding of the robot mechanism does not make its behaviour more predictable, or less human (for we have assumed it behaves as a human): and so we are tempted to explain away the surprise and the humanity by saying it must be Conscious, as a human. Yet, though clocks are predictable, barographs and computers are not; and no one suggests they are Conscious. It is not the unpredictability but the apparent humanity of the robots that produces the reaction of saying they are Conscious. But they appear human simply because they were made to appear human. If there is some reason for doubting whether they were designed and made at all, as in the case of the androids, we count them Conscious but not machines. If there is no such reason, we count them machines, but to count them Conscious is to put the ghost of a ghost in the machine.

## POSTSCRIPT

Since writing this article I have devoted a good deal of thought to the same issue, some of which appears in "The Compleat Robot: A Prolegomena to Androidology" in S. Hook (ed.), *Dimensions of Mind,* New York University Press. In this later article I argue that, although the kind of performance that Turing* called for is not sufficient grounds for establishing consciousness in a robot, there *is* a test which would do this. It requires that three conditions be arranged: (a) The robot must be taught how to use mentalistic terminology in talking about people in the same way that ordinary humans use it of humans. He must be taught to use only behavioristic terminology in talking of himself and of other computers although not denying the possibility that mentalistic terminology might also be appropriate. The relationship between behavioristic and mentalistic terminology, in so far as it can be explained to an individual who is possibly "an

*Editors' note: see item 20 of the Selected Bibliography for Part IV.

outsider" is also explained, using definite descriptions, analogies, poetic imagery, etc. The robot is also given a name, and taught how to refer to itself by referring expressions of the usual kind. ("I", "my-self", etc.) (b) The robot is taught to distinguish truth from false-hood, in practice and abstractly. (c) The robot is then mechanically arranged so that it cannot produce a falsehood when it is asked for the truth. When these circumstances have been arranged, we now apply the test for consciousness, which is simply to ask the robot whether it is conscious or not. It will then be in a position from which it will be able to answer this question in the affirmative—if it is con-scious—with just as great understanding of what it is saying as a human being; while if it is not in possession of consciousness it will know that the behaviouristic description of its activities is all that is appropriate, and will reply negatively. With respect to all other performances and skills of which the human being is capable, it seems to me clear already that robots can be designed to do as well or bet-ter. With respect to *this* performance, I was at the time of writing the article not certain of the answer. On the answer there depends not only the question of matching a performance, but in my view also the crucial ontological question of the status of the robot as a person and thence the propriety of saying that it knows or believes or re-members, i.e., of using the human vocabulary for its performances. (If it is a person, of course it will have moral rights and hence po-litical rights.) I am, upon further deliberation, confident that robots can in principle be built that will pass this test too, because they are in fact conscious. Consciousness is, it now seems to me, automatically guaranteed by the capacity to categorise and discuss one's own re-actions, beliefs, etc.

# CHAPTER 14

# Minds, Machines and Gödel

JOHN LUCAS

Gödel's theorem seems to me to prove that Mechanism is false, that is, that minds cannot be explained as machines. So also has it seemed to many other people: almost every mathematical logician I have put the matter to has confessed to similar thoughts, but has felt reluctant to commit himself definitely until he could see the whole argument set out, with all objections fully stated and properly met.[1] This I attempt to do.

Gödel's theorem states that in any consistent system which is strong enough to produce simple arithmetic there are formulae which cannot be proved-in-the-system, but which we can see to be true. Essentially, we consider the formula which says, in effect, "This formula is unprovable-in-the-system". If this formula were provable-in-the-system, we should have a contradiction: for if it were provable-in-the-system, then it would not be unprovable-in-the-system, so that "This formula is unprovable-in-the-system" would be false: equally, if it were provable-in-the-system, then it would not be false, but would be true, since in any consistent system nothing false can be proved-in-the-system, but only truths. So the formula "This formula is unprovable-in-the-system" is not provable-in-the-system, but unprovable-in-the-system. Further, if the formula "This formula is unprovable-in-the-system" is unprovable-in-the-system, then it is true that that

[1] See A. M. Turing, "Computing Machinery and Intelligence," *Mind* (1950), pp. 433-60, reprinted in *The World of Mathematics,* edited by James R. Newmann, pp. 2099-123; and K. R. Popper, "Indeterminism in Quantum Physics and Classical Physics," *British Journal for Philosophy of Science,* I (1951), 179-88. The question is touched upon by Paul Rosenbloom; *Elements of Mathematical Logic,* pp. 207-8; Ernest Nagel and James R. Newmann, *Gödel's Proof,* pp. 100-2; and by Hartley Rogers, *Theory of Recursive Functions and Effective Computability* (mimeographed), 1957, Vol. I, pp. 152 ff.

formula is unprovable-in-the-system, that is, "This formula is un-provable-in-the-system" is true.

The foregoing argument is very fiddling, and difficult to grasp fully: it is helpful to put the argument the other way round, consider the possibility that "This formula is unprovable-in-the-system" might be false, show that that is impossible, and thus that the formula is true; whence it follows that it is unprovable. Even so, the argument remains persistently unconvincing: we feel that there must be a catch in it somewhere. The whole labour of Gödel's theorem is to show that there is no catch anywhere, and that the result can be established by the most rigorous deduction; it holds for all formal systems which are (i) consistent, (ii) adequate for simple arithmetic —i.e., contain the natural numbers and the operations of addition and multiplication—and it shows that they are incomplete—i.e., contain unprovable, though perfectly meaningful, formulae, some of which, moreover, we, standing outside the system, can see to be true.

Gödel's theorem must apply to cybernetical machines, because it is of the essence of being a machine, that it should be a concrete instantiation of a formal system. It follows that given any machine which is consistent and capable of doing simple arithmetic, there is a formula which it is incapable of producing as being true—i.e., the formula is unprovable-in-the-system—but which we can see to be true. It follows that no machine can be a complete or adequate model of the mind, that minds are essentially different from machines.

We understand by a cybernetical machine an apparatus which performs a set of operations according to a definite set of rules. Normally we "programme" a machine: that is, we give it a set of instructions about what it is to do in each eventuality; and we feed in the initial "information" on which the machine is to perform its calculations. When we consider the possibility that the mind might be a cybernetical mechanism we have such a model in view; we suppose that the brain is composed of complicated neural circuits, and that the information fed in by the senses is "processed" and acted upon or stored for future use. If it is such a mechanism, then given the way in which it is programmed—the way in which it is "wired up"— and the information which has been fed into it, the response—the "output"—is determined, and could, granted sufficient time, be calculated. Our idea of a machine is just this, that its behaviour is completely determined by the way it is made and the incoming "stimuli": there is no possibility of its acting on its own: given a certain form of construction and a certain input of information, then it must act in a certain specific way. We, however, shall be concerned not with what a machine *must* do, but with what it *can* do. That is, instead of considering the whole set of rules which together determine exactly what a machine will do in given circumstances, we shall consider only an outline of those rules, which will delimit the possible responses of the machine, but not completely. The complete rules will determine the operations completely at every stage; at every stage there will be a definite instruction, e.g., "If the number is prime and greater than two add one and divide by two: if it is not prime, divide by its smallest factor": we, however, will consider the possibility of there being alternative instructions, e.g., "In a fraction you may divide top and bottom by *any* number which is a factor of both numerator and denominator". In thus relaxing the specification of our model, so that it is no longer completely determinist, though still entirely mechanistic, we shall be able to take into account a feature often proposed for mechanical models of the mind, namely that they should contain a randomizing device. One could build a machine where the choice between a number of alternatives was settled by, say, the number of radium atoms to have disintegrated in a given container in the past half-minute. It is *prima facie* plausible that our brains should be liable to random effects: a cosmic ray might well be enough to trigger off a neural impulse. But clearly in a machine a randomizing device could not be introduced to choose any alternative whatsoever: it can only be permitted to choose between a number of allowable alternatives. It is all right to add *any* number chosen at random to both sides of an equation, but not to add one number to one side and another to the other. It is all right to choose to prove one theorem of Euclid rather than another, or to use one method rather than another, but not to "prove" something which is not true, or to use a "method of proof" which is not valid. Any randomizing devices must allow choices only between those operations which will not lead to inconsistency: which is exactly what the relaxed specification of our model specifies Indeed, one might put it this way: instead of considering what a completely determined machine *must* do, we shall consider what a machine might be able to do if it had a randomizing device that acted whenever there were two or more operations possible, none of which could lead to inconsistency.

If such a machine were built to produce theorems about arithmetic (in many ways the simplest part of mathematics), it would have only a finite number of components, and so there would be only a finite number of types of operation it could do, and only a finite number of initial assumptions it could operate on. Indeed, we can go further, and say that there would only be a *definite* number of types of operation, and of initial assumptions, that could be built into it. Machines are definite: anything which was indefinite or infinite we should not count as a machine. Note that we say number of *types* of operation, not number of operations. Given sufficient time, and provided that it did not wear out, a machine could go on repeating an operation indefinitely: it is merely that there can be only a definite number of different *sorts* of operation it can perform.

If there are only a definite number of types of operation and initial assumptions built into the system, we can represent them all by suitable symbols written down on paper. We can parallel the operation by rules ("rules of inference" or "axiom schemata") allowing us to go from one or more formulae (or even from no formula at all) to another formula, and we can parallel the initial assumptions (if any) by a set of initial formulae ("primitive propositions", "postulates" or "axioms"). Once we have represented these on paper, we can represent every single operation: all we need do is to give formulae representing the situation before and after the operation, and note which rule is being invoked. We can thus represent on paper any possible sequence of operations the machine might perform. However long the machine went on operating, we could, give enough time, paper and patience, write down an analogue of the machine's operations. This analogue would in fact be a formal proof: every operation of the machine is represented by the application of one of the rules: and the conditions which determine for the machine whether an operation can be performed in a certain situation, become, in our representation, conditions which settle whether a rule can be applied to a certain formula, i.e., formal conditions of applicability. Thus, construing our rules as rules of inference, we shall have a proof-sequence of formulae, each one being written down in virtue of some formal rule of inference having been applied to some previous formula or formulae (except, of course, for the initial formulae, which are given because they represent initial assumptions built into the system). The conclusions it is possible for the machine to produce as being true will therefore correspond to the theorems that can be proved in the corresponding formal system. We now construct a Gödelian formula in this formal system. This formula cannot be *proved-in-the-system*. Therefore the machine cannot produce the corresponding formula as being true. But *we* can see that the Gödelian formula is true: any rational being could follow Gödel's argument, and convince himself that the Gödelian formula, although unprovable-in-the-system, was nonetheless—in fact, for that very reason—true. Now any mechanical model of the mind must include a mechanism which can enunciate truths of arithmetic, because this is something which minds can do: in fact, it is easy to produce mechanical models which will in many respects produce truths of arithmetic far better than human beings can. But in this one respect they cannot do so well: in that for every machine there is a truth which it cannot produce as being true, but which a mind can. This shows that a machine cannot be a complete and adequate model of the mind. It cannot do *everything* that a mind can do, since however much it can do, there is always something which it cannot do, and a mind can. This is not to say that we cannot build a machine to simulate *any* desired piece of mind-like behaviour: it is only that we cannot build a machine to simulate *every* piece of mind-like behaviour. We can (or shall be able to one day) build machines capable of reproducing bits of mind-like behaviour, and indeed of outdoing the performances of human minds: but however good the machine is, and however much better it can do in nearly all respects than a human mind can, it always has this one weakness, this one thing which it cannot do, whereas a mind can. The Gödelian formula is the Achilles' heel of the cybernetical machine. And therefore we cannot hope ever to produce a machine that will be able to do all that a mind can do: we can never not even in principle, have a mechanical model of the mind.

This conclusion will be highly suspect to some people. They will object first that we cannot have it both that a machine *can* simulate *any* piece of mind-like behaviour, and that it *cannot* simulate *every* piece. To some it is a contradiction: to them it is enough to point out that there is no contradiction between the fact that for any natural number there can be produced a greater number, and the fact that a number cannot be produced greater than every number. We can use the same analogy also against those who, finding a formula their first machine cannot produce as being true, concede that that machine is indeed inadequate, but thereupon seek to construct a second, more adequate, machine, in which the formula *can* be produced as being true. This they can indeed do: but then the second machine will have a Gödelian formula all of its own, constructed by applying Gödel's procedure to the formal system which represents its (the second machine's) own, enlarged, scheme of operations. And this formula the second machine will not be able to produce as being true, while a mind will be able to see that it is true. And if now a third machine is constructed, able to do what the second machine was unable to do, exactly the same will happen: there will be yet a third formula, the Gödelian formula for the formal system corresponding to the third machine's scheme of operations, which the third machine is unable to produce as being true, while a mind will still be able to see that it is true. And so it will go on. However complicated a machine we construct, it will, if it is a machine, correspond to a formal system, which in turn will be liable to the Gödel procedure for finding a formula unprovable-in-that-system. This formula the machine will be unable to produce as being true, although a mind can see that it is true. And so the machine will still not be an adequate model of the mind. We are trying to produce a model of the mind which is mechanical—which is essentially "dead"—but the mind, being in fact "alive", can always go one better than any formal, ossified, dead, system can. Thanks to Gödel's theorem, the mind always has the last word.

A second objection will now be made. The procedure whereby the Gödelian formula is constructed is a standard procedure—only so could we be sure that a Gödelian formula can be constructed for every formal system. But if it is a standard procedure, then a machine should be able to be programmed to carry it out too. We could construct a machine with the usual operations, and in addition an operation of going through the Gödel procedure, and then producing the conclusion of that procedure as being true; and then repeating the procedure, and so on, as often as required. This would correspond to having a system with an additional rule of inference which allowed one to add, as a theorem, the Gödelian formula of the rest of the formal system, and then the Gödelian formula of this new, strengthened formal system, and so on. It would be tantamount to adding to the original formal system an infinite sequence of axioms, each the Gödelian formula of the system hitherto obtained. Yet even so, the matter is not settled: for the machine with a Gödelizing operator, as we might call it, is a *different* machine from the machines without such an operator; and, although the machine with the operator would be able to do those things in which the machines without the operator were outclassed by a mind, yet we might expect a mind, faced with a machine that possessed a Gödelizing operator, to take this into account, and out-Gödel the new machine, Gödelizing operator and all. This has, in fact, proved to be the case. Even if we adjoin to a formal system the infinite set of axioms consisting of the successive Gödelian formulae, the resulting system is still incomplete, and contains a formula which cannot be proved-in-the-system, although a rational being can, standing outside the system, see that it is true.[2] We had expected this, for even if an infinite set of axioms were added, they would have to be specified by some finite rule or specification, and this further rule or specification could then be taken into account by a mind considering the enlarged formal system. In a sense, just because the mind has the last word, it can always pick a hole in any formal system presented to it as a model of its own workings. The

[2] Gödel's original proof applies; v. § 1 init. § 6 init. of his Lectures at the Institute of Advanced Study, Princeton, N.J., U.S.A., 1934.

mechanical model must be, in some sense, finite and definite: and then the mind can always go one better.

This is the answer to one objection put forward by Turing.[3] He argues that the limitation to the powers of a machine do not amount to anything much. Although each individual machine is incapable of getting the right answer to some questions, after all each individual human being is fallible also: and in any case "our superiority can only be felt on such an occasion in relation to the one machine over which we have scored our petty triumph. There would be no question of triumphing simultaneously over *all* machines." But this is not the point. We are not discussing whether machines or minds are superior, but whether they are the same. In some respect machines are undoubtedly superior to human minds; and the question on which they are stumped is admittedly, a rather niggling, even trivial, question. But it is enough, enough to show that the machine is *not the same* as a mind. True, the machine can do many things that a human mind cannot do: but if there is of necessity something that the machine cannot do, though the mind can, then, however trivial the matter is, we cannot equate the two, and cannot hope ever to have a mechanical model that will adequately represent the mind. Nor does it signify that it is only an individual machine we have triumphed over: for the triumph is not over only *an* individual machine, but over *any* individual that anybody cares to specify—in Latin *quivis* or *quilibet,* not *quidam*—and a mechanical model of a mind must be an individual machine. Although it is true that any particular "triumph" of a mind over a machine could be "trumped" by another machine able to produce the answer the first machine could not produce, so that "there is no question of triumphing simultaneously over all machines", yet this is irrelevant. What is at issue is not the unequal contest between one mind and all machines, but whether there could be any, single, machine that could do all a mind can do. For the mechanist thesis to hold water, it must be possible, in principle, to produce a model, a single model, which can do everything the mind can do. It is like a game.[4] The mechanist has first turn. He produces *a—any,* but only a *definite one*—mechanical model of the mind. I point to something that it cannot do, but the mind can. The mechanist is free to modify his example, but each time he does so, I am entitled to look for defects in the revised model. If the mechanist can devise a model that I cannot find fault with, his

3 *Mind,* 1950, pp. 445-5; Newman, p. 2110.
4 For a similar type of argument, see J. R. Lucas: "The Lesbian Rule"; PHILOSOPHY (July 1955) pp. 202-6; and "On Not Worshipping Facts"; *The Philosophical Quarterly* (April 1958), p. 144.

thesis is established: if he cannot, then it is not proven: and since—as it turns out—he necessarily cannot, it is refuted. To succeed, he must be able to produce some definite mechanical model of the mind —any one he likes, but one he can specify, and will stick to. But since he cannot, in principle cannot, produce any mechanical model that is adequate, even though the point of failure is a minor one, he is bound to fail, and mechanism must be false.

Deeper objections can still be made. Gödel's theorem applies to deductive systems, and human beings are not confined to making only deductive inferences. Gödel's theorem applies only to consistent systems, and one may have doubts about how far it is permissible to assume that human beings are consistent. Gödel's theorem applies only to formal systems, and there is no *a priori* bound to human ingenuity which rules out the possibility of our contriving some replica of humanity which was not representable by a formal system.

Human beings are not confined to making deductive inferences, and it has been urged by C. G. Hempel[5] and Hartley Rogers[6] that a fair model of the mind would have to allow for the possibility of making non-deductive inferences, and these might provide a way of escaping the Gödel result. Hartley Rogers makes the specific suggestion that the machine should be programmed to entertain various propositions which had not been proved or disproved, and on occasion to add them to its list of axioms. Fermat's last theorem or Goldbach's conjecture might thus be added. If subsequently their inclusion was found to lead to a contradiction, they would be dropped again, and indeed in those circumstances their negations would be added to the list of theorems. In this sort of way a machine might well be constructed which was able to produce as true certain formulae which could not be proved from its axioms according to its rules of inference. And therefore the method of demonstrating the mind's superiority over the machine might no longer work.

The construction of such a machine, however, presents difficulties. It cannot accept all unprovable formulae, and add them to its axioms, or it will find itself accepting both the Gödelian formula and its negation, and so be inconsistent. Nor would it do if it accepted the first of each pair of undecidable formulae, and, having added that to its axioms, would no longer regard its negation as undecidable, and so would never accept it too: for it might happen on the wrong member of the pair: it might accept the negation of the Gödelian formula rather than the Gödelian formula itself. And the system constituted

5 In private conversation.
6 *Theory of Recursive Functions and Effective Computability*, 1957, Vol. I, pp. 152 ff.

by a normal set of axioms with the negation of the Gödelian formula adjoined, although not inconsistent, is an unsound system, not admitting of the natural interpretation. It is something like non-Desarguian geometries in two dimensions: not actually inconsistent, but rather wrong, sufficiently much so to disqualify it from serious consideration. A machine which was liable to infelicities of that kind would be no model for the human mind.

It becomes clear that rather careful criteria of selection of unprovable formulae will be needed. Hartley Rogers suggests some possible ones. But once we have rules generating new axioms, even if the axioms generated are only provisionally accepted, and are liable to be dropped again if they are found to lead to inconsistency, then we can set about doing a Gödel on this system, as on any other. We are in the same case as when we had a rule generating the infinite set of Gödelian formulae as axioms. In short, however a machine is designed, it must proceed either at random or according to definite rules. In so far as its procedure is random, we cannot outsmart it: but its performance is not going to be a convincing parody of intelligent behaviour: in so far as its procedure is in accordance with definite rules, the Gödel method can be used to produce a formula which the machine, according to those rules, cannot assert as true, although we, standing outside the system, can see it to be true.[7]

Gödel's theorem applies only to consistent systems. All that we can prove *formally* is that *if* the system is consistent, then the Gödelian formula is unprovable-in-the-system. To be able to say categorically that the Gödelian formula is unprovable-in-the-system, and therefore true, we must not only be dealing with a consistent system, but be able to say that it is consistent. And, as Gödel showed in his second theorem—a corollary of his first—it is impossible to prove in a consistent system that that system is consistent. Thus in order to fault the machine by producing a formula of which we can say both that it is true and that the machine cannot produce it as true, we have to be able to say that the machine (or, rather, its corresponding formal system) is consistent; and there is no absolute proof of this. All we can do is to examine the machine and see if it appears consistent. There always remains the possibility of some inconsistency not yet detected. At best we can say that the machine is consistent, provided we are. But by what right can we do this? Gödel's second

---

[7] Gödel's original proof applies if the rule is such as to generate a primitive recursive class of additional formulae; v § 1 init. and § 6 init. of his Lectures at the Institute of Advanced Study, Princeton, N.J., U.S.A., 1934. It is in fact sufficient that the class be recursively enumerable. See Barkley Rosser: "Extensions of some theorems of Gödel and Church," *Journal of Symbolic Logic,* I (1936), 87-91.

theorem seems to show that a man cannot assert his own consistency, and so Hartley Rogers[8] argues that we cannot really use Gödel's first theorem to counter the mechanist thesis unless we can say that "there are distinctive attributes which enable a human being to transcend this last limitation and assert his own consistency while still remaining consistent".

A man's untutored reaction if his consistency is questioned is to affirm it vehemently: but this, in view of Gödel's second theorem, is taken by some philosophers as evidence of his actual inconsistency. Professor Putnam[9] has suggested that human beings are machines, but inconsistent machines. If a machine were wired to correspond to an inconsistent system, then there would be no well-formed formula which it could not produce as true; and so in no way could it be proved to be inferior to a human being. Nor could we make its inconsistency a reproach to it—are not men inconsistent too? Certainly women are, and politicians; and even male non-politicians contradict themselves sometimes, and a single inconsistency is enough to make a system inconsistent.

The fact that we are all sometimes inconsistent cannot be gainsaid, but from this it does not follow that we are tantamount to inconsistent systems. Our inconsistencies are mistakes rather than set policies. They correspond to the occasional malfunctioning of a machine, not its normal scheme of operations. Witness to this that we eschew inconsistencies when we recognize them for what they are. If we really were inconsistent machines, we should remain content with our inconsistencies, and would happily affirm both halves of a contradiction. Moreover, we would be prepared to say absolutely anything—which we are not. It is easily shown[10] that in an inconsistent formal system everything is provable, and the requirement of consistency turns out to be just that not everything can be proved in it—it is not the case that "anything goes." This surely is a characteristic of the mental operations of human beings: they are selective: they do discriminate between favoured—true—and unfavoured—false—statements: when a person is prepared to say anything, and is prepared to contradict himself without any qualm or repugnance, then he is adjudged to have "lost his mind". Human beings, although not perfectly consistent, are not so much inconsistent as fallible.

A fallible but self-correcting machine would still be subject to Gödel's results. Only a fundamentally inconsistent machine would

8 *Op. cit.*, p. 154.
9 University of Princeton, N.J., U.S.A. in private conversation.
10 See, e.g., Alonzo Church: *Introduction to Mathematical Logic, Princeton*, Vol. I, § 17, p. 108.

escape. Could we have a fundamentally inconsistent, but at the same time self-correcting machine, which both would be free of Gödel's results and yet would not be trivial and entirely unlike a human being? A machine with a rather *recherché* inconsistency wired into it, so that for all normal purposes it was consistent, but when presented with the Gödelian sentence was able to prove it?

There are all sorts of ways in which undesirable proofs might be obviated. We might have a rule that whenever we have proved *p* and not-*p*, we examine their proofs and reject the longer. Or we might arrange the axioms and rules of inference in a certain order, and when a proof leading to an inconsistency is proffered, see what axioms and rules are required for it, and reject that axiom or rule which comes last in the ordering. In some such way as this we could have an inconsistent system, with a stop-rule, so that the inconsistency was never allowed to come out in the form of an inconsistent formula.

The suggestion at first sight seems attractive: yet there is something deeply wrong. Even though we might preserve the façade of consistency by having a rule that whenever two inconsistent formulae appear we were to reject the one with the longer proof, yet such a rule would be repugnant in our logical sense. Even the less arbitrary suggestions are too arbitrary. No longer does the system operate with certain definite rules of inference on certain definite formulae. Instead, the rules apply, the axioms are true, provided . . . we do not happen to find it inconvenient. We no longer know where we stand. One application of the rule of Modus Ponens may be accepted while another is rejected: on one occasion an axiom may be true, or another apparently false. The system will have ceased to be a formal logical system, and the machine will barely qualify for the title of a model for the mind. For it will be far from resembling the mind in its operations: the mind does indeed try out dubious axioms and rules of inference; but if they are found to lead to contradiction, they are rejected altogether. We try out axioms and rules of inference provisionally—true: but we do not keep them, once they are found to lead to contradictions. We may seek to replace them with others, we may feel that our formalization is at fault, and that though some axiom or rule of inference of this sort is required, we have not been able to formulate it quite correctly: but we do not retain the faulty formulations without modification, merely with the proviso that when the argument leads to a contradiction we refuse to follow it. To do this would be utterly irrational. We should be in the position that on some occasions when supplied with the premisses of a Modus Ponens, say, we applied the rule and allowed the conclusion, and on other occasions we refused to apply the rule, and disallowed the conclusion. A person, or a machine, which did this without being able to give a good reason for so doing, would be accounted arbitrary and irrational. It is part of the concept of "arguments" or "reasons" that they are in some sense general and universal: that if Modus Ponens is a valid method of arguing when I am establishing a desired conclusion, it is a valid method also when you, my opponent, are establishing a conclusion I do not want to accept. We cannot pick and choose the times when a form of argument is to be valid; not if we are to be reasonable. It is of course true, that with our informal arguments, which are not fully formalized, we do distinguish between arguments which are at first sight similar, adding further reasons why they are nonetheless not really similar: and it might be maintained that a machine might likewise be entitled to distinguish between arguments at first sight similar, if it had good reason for doing so. And it might further be maintained that the machine had good reason for rejecting those patterns of argument it did reject, indeed the best of reasons, namely the avoidance of contradiction. But that, if it is a reason at all, is too good a reason. We do not lay it to a man's credit that he avoids contradiction merely by refusing to accept those arguments which would lead him to it, for no other reason than that otherwise he would be led to it. Special pleading rather than sound argument is the name for that type of reasoning. No credit accrues to a man who, clever enough to see a few moves of argument ahead, avoids being brought to acknowledge his own inconsistency, by stonewalling as soon as he sees where the argument will end. Rather, we account him inconsistent too, not, in his case, because he affirmed and denied the same proposition, but because he used and refused to use the same rule of inference. A stop-rule on actually enunciating an inconsistency is not enough to save an inconsistent machine from being called inconsistent.

The possibility yet remains that we are inconsistent, and there is no stop-rule, but the inconsistency is so *recherché* that it has never turned up. After all, *naïve* set-theory, which was deeply embedded in common-sense ways of thinking did turn out to be inconsistent. Can we be sure that a similar fate is not in store for simple arithmetic too? In a sense we cannot, in spite of our great feeling of certitude that our system of whole numbers which can be added and multiplied together is never going to prove inconsistent. It is just conceivable we might find we had formalized it incorrectly. If we had, we should try and formulate anew our intuitive concept of number, as we have our intuitive concept of a set. If we did this, we should of course recast our system: our present axioms and rules of inference would be utterly rejected: there would be no question of our using and not using them in an "inconsistent" fashion. We should, once we had recast the system, be in the same position as we are now, possessed of a system believed to be consistent, but not provably so. But then could there not be some other inconsistency? It is indeed a possibility. But again no inconsistency once detected will be tolerated. We are determined not to be inconsistent, and are resolved to root out inconsistency, should any appear. Thus, although we can never be completely certain or completely free of the risk of having to think out our mathematics again, the ultimate position must be one of two: either we have a system of simple arithmetic which to the best of our knowledge and belief is consistent: or there is no such system possible. In the former case we are in the same position as at present: in the latter, if we find that no system containing simple arithmetic can be free of contradictions, we shall have to abandon not merely the whole of mathematics and the mathematical sciences, but the whole of thought.

It may still be maintained that although a man must in this sense assume, he cannot properly affirm, his own consistency without thereby belying his words. We may be consistent; indeed we have every reason to hope that we are: but a necessary modesty forbids us from saying so. Yet this is not quite what Gödel's second theorem states. Gödel has shown that in a consistent system a formula stating the consistency of the system cannot be proved *in that system*. It follows that a machine, if consistent, cannot produce as true an assertion of its own consistency: hence also that a mind, *if it were really a machine,* could not reach the conclusion that it was a consistent one. For a mind which is not a machine no such conclusion follows. All that Gödel has proved is that a mind cannot produce a formal proof of the consistency of a formal system inside the system itself: but there is no objection to going outside the system and no objection to producing informal arguments for the consistency either of a formal system or of something less formal and less systematized. Such informal arguments will not be able to be completely formalized: but then the whole tenor of Gödel's results is that we ought not to ask, and cannot obtain, complete formalization. And although it would have been nice if we could have obtained them, since completely formalized arguments are more coercive than informal ones, yet since we cannot have all our arguments cast into that form, we must not hold it against informal arguments that they are informal or regard them all as utterly worthless. It therefore seems to me both proper and reasonable for a mind to assert its own consistency: proper, because although machines, as we might have expected, are unable to reflect fully on their own performance and powers, yet to be able to be self-conscious in this way is just what we expect of minds: and reasonable, for the reasons given. Not only can we fairly say simply that we *know* we are consistent, apart from our mistakes, but we must in any case *assume* that we are, if thought is to be possible at all; moreover we are selective, we will not, as inconsistent machines would, say anything and everything whatsover: and finally we can, in a sense, *decide* to be consistent, in the sense that we can resolve not to tolerate inconsistencies in our thinking and speaking, and to eliminate them, if ever they should appear, by withdrawing and cancelling one limb of the contradiction.

We can see how we might almost have expected Gödel's theorem to distinguish self-conscious beings from inanimate objects. The essence of the Gödelian formula is that it is self-referring. It says that "This formula is unprovable-in-this-system". When carried over to a machine, the formula is specified in terms which depend on the particular machine in question. The machine is being asked a question about its own processes. We are asking it to be self-conscious, and say what things it can and cannot do. Such questions notoriously lead to paradox. At one's first and simplest attempts to philosophize, one becomes entangled in questions of whether when one knows something one knows that one knows it, and what, when one is thinking of oneself, is being thought about, and what is doing the thinking. After one has been puzzled and bruised by this problem for a long time, one learns not to press these questions: the concept of a conscious being is, implicitly, realized to be different from that of an unconscious object. In saying that a conscious being knows something, we are saying not only that he knows it, but that he knows that he knows it, and that he knows that he knows that he knows it, and so on, as long as we care to pose the question: there is, we recognize, an infinity here, but it is not an infinite regress in the bad sense, for it is the questions that peter out, as being pointless, rather than the answers. The questions are felt to be pointless because the concept contains within itself the idea of being able to go on answering such questions indefinitely. Although conscious beings have the power of going on, we do not wish to exhibit this simply as a succession of tasks they are able to perform, nor do we see the mind as an infinite sequence of selves and super-selves and super-super-selves. Rather, we insist that a conscious being is a unity, and though we talk about parts of the mind, we do so only as a metaphor, and will not allow it to be taken literally.

The paradoxes of consciousness arise because a conscious being can be aware of itself, as well as of other things, and yet cannot really be construed as being divisible into parts. It means that a conscious being can deal with Gödelian questions in a way in which a machine cannot, because a conscious being can both consider itself and its performance and yet not be other than that which did the performance. A machine can be made in a manner of speaking to "consider" its own performance, but it cannot take this "into account" without thereby becoming a different machine, namely the old machine with a "new part" added. But it is inherent in our idea of a conscious mind that it can reflect upon itself and criticize its own performances, and no extra part is required to do this: it is already complete, and has no Achilles' heel.

The thesis thus begins to become more a matter of conceptual analysis than mathematical discovery. This is borne out by considering another argument put forward by Turing.[11] So far, we have constructed only fairly simple and predictable artefacts. When we increase the complexity of our machines there may, perhaps, be surprises in store for us. He draws a parallel with a fission pile. Below a certain "critical" size, nothing much happens: but above the critical size, the sparks begin to fly. So too, perhaps, with brains and machines. Most brains and all machines are, at present, "subcritical"—they react to incoming stimuli in a stodgy and uninteresting way, have no ideas of their own, can produce only stock responses —but a few brains at present, and possibly some machines in the future, are super-critical, and scintillate on their own account. Turing is suggesting that it is only a matter of complexity, and that above a certain level of complexity a qualitative difference appears, so that "super-critical" machines will be quite unlike the simple ones hitherto envisaged.

This may be so. Complexity often does introduce qualitative differences. Although it sounds implausible, it might turn out that above a certain level of complexity, a machine ceased to be predictable, even in principle, and started doing things on its own account, or, to use a very revealing phrase, it might begin to have a mind of its own. It might begin to have a mind of its own. It would begin to have a mind of its own when it was no longer entirely predictable and entirely docile, but was capable of doing things which we recognized as intelligent, and not just mistakes or random shots, but which we had not programmed into it. But then it would cease to be a machine, within the meaning of the act. What is at stake in the mechanist debate is not how minds are, or might be, brought into being, but how they operate. It is essential for the mechanist thesis that the mechanical model of the mind shall operate according

11 *Mind*, 1950, p. 454; Newman, pp. 2117-18.

to "mechanical principles", that is, that we can understand the operation of the whole in terms of the operations of its parts, and the operation of each part either shall be determined by its initial state and the construction of the machine, or shall be a random choice between a determinate number of determinate operations. If the mechanist produces a machine which is so complicated that this ceases to hold good of it, then it is no longer a machine for the purposes of our discussion, no matter how it was constructed. We should say, rather, that he had created a mind, in the same sort of sense as we procreate people at present. There would then be two ways of bringing new minds into the world, the traditional way, by begetting children born of women, and a new way by constructing very, very complicated systems of, say, valves and relays. When talking of the second way, we should take care to stress that although what was created looked like a machine, it was not one really, because it was not just the total of its parts. One could not tell what it was going to do merely by knowing the way in which it was built up and the initial state of its parts: one could not even tell the limits of what it could do, for even when presented with a Gödel-type question, it got the answer right. In fact we should say briefly that any system which was not floored by the Gödel question was *eo ipso* not a Turing machine, i.e., not a machine within the meaning of the act.

If the proof of the falsity of mechanism is valid, it is of the greatest consequence for the whole of philosophy. Since the time of Newton, the bogey of mechanist determinism has obsessed philosophers. If we were to be scientific, it seemed that we must look on human beings as determined automata, and not as autonomous moral agents; if we were to be moral, it seemed that we must deny science its due, set an arbitrary limit to its progress in understanding human neurophysiology, and take refuge in obscurantist mysticism. Not even Kant could resolve the tension between the two standpoints. But now, though many arguments against human freedom still remain, the argument from mechanism, perhaps the most compelling argument of them all, has lost its power. No longer on this count will it be incumbent on the natural philosopher to deny freedom in the name of science: no longer will the moralist feel the urge to abolish knowledge to make room for faith. We can even begin to see how there could be room for morality, without its being necessary to abolish or even to circumscribe the province of science. Our argument has set no limits to scientific enquiry: it will still be possible to investigate the working of the brain. It will still be possible to produce mechanical models of the mind. Only, now we can see that no mechanical model will be completely adequate, nor any explanations in purely mechanist terms. We can produce models and explanations, and they will be illuminating: but, however far they go, there will always remain more to be said. There is no arbitrary bound to scientific enquiry: but no scientific enquiry can ever exhaust the infinite variety of the human mind.

# Selected Bibliography for Part IV

1. Ashby, W. R., "What is an Intelligent Machine?," *Proceedings of the Western Joint Computer Conference*, Vol. 19 (1961), pp. 275-280.
2. Boring, E. G., "Mind and Mechanism," *American Journal of Psychology*, Vol. 59 (April 1946), pp. 173-192.
3. Bunge, Mario, "Do Computers Think?," *The British Journal for the Philosophy of Science*, Vol. 7 (1956-57), pp. 139-148, 212-219.
4. Chappell, V. C., (ed.), *The Philosophy of Mind*. Englewood Cliffs: Prentice-Hall, Inc., 1962.
5. Feigl, H., Scriven, M., and Maxwell, G., (eds.), *Minnesota Studies in the Philosophy of Science*, Vol. II, *Concepts, Theories and the Mind-Body Problem*. Minneapolis: University of Minnesota Press, 1958.
6. George, F. H., "Could Machines Be Made to Think?," *Philosophy*, Vol. 31 (1956), pp. 244-252.
7. Hook, S. (ed.), *Dimensions of Mind*. New York: New York University Press, 1960.
8. Kapp, R. O., "Living and Lifeless Machines," *The British Journal for the Philosophy of Science*, Vol. 5 (1954), pp. 91-103.
9. Kattsoff, L. O., "Brains, Thinking and Machines," *Methodos*, Vol. 6 (1954), pp. 279-286.
10. Kemeny, J. G., "Man Viewed as a Machine," *Scientific American*, Vol. 192, (April 1955), pp. 58-67.
11. Lacey, A. R., "Men and Robots," *The Philosophical Quarterly*, Vol. 10 (January 1960), pp. 61-72.
12. MacKay, D. M., "Mentality in Machines," *Aristotelian Society Supplementary Volume 26* (1952), pp. 61-86.
13. Miles, T. R., "On the Difference Between Men and Machines," *The British Journal for the Philosophy of Science*, Vol. 7 (1956-57), pp. 277-292.
14. Minsky, M., "Steps Toward Artificial Intelligence," *Proceedings of the Institute of Radio Engineers*, Vol. 49 (1961), pp. 8-30. Reprinted in *Computers and Thought*, Feldman and Feigenbaum (eds.).
15. Newell, A., and Simon, H. A., "Computer Simulation of Human Thinking," *Science*, 134:3495 (December 22, 1961), pp. 2011-2017.
16. Pinsky, L., "Do Machines Think about Machines Thinking?," *Mind*, Vol. 60 (1951), pp. 397-398.
17. Spilsbury, R. J., "Mentality in Machines," *Aristotelian Society Supplementary Volume 26* (1952), pp. 27-60.
18. Szasz, T. S., "Men and Machines," *The British Journal for the Philosophy of Science*, Vol. 8 (1957-58), pp. 310-317.
19. Taube, M., *Computers and Common Sense: The Myth of Thinking Machines*. New York: Columbia University Press, 1961.
20. Turing, A. M., "Computing Machinery and Intelligence," *Mind*, Vol. 59 (1950), pp. 433-460.
21. Wiener, N., *Cybernetics*. Cambridge: Technology Press, 2nd edition, 1961.
22. Wisdom, J. O., "Mentality in Machines," *Aristotelian Society Supplementary Volume 26* (1952), pp. 1-26.

# Biographical Notes

Frederick J. Crosson, born April 27, 1926, Belmar, New Jersey, A.B., 1949, M.A., 1950, Catholic University of America, Ph.D. 1957, University of Notre Dame. Studied also at Laval University and the University of Paris. Instructor, Assistant Professor, Associate Professor at the University of Notre Dame. Belgian American Foundation Fellow, 1957-58, at the University of Louvain. Author of *Phenomenology* (Prentice-Hall, forthcoming), co-editor of *The Modeling of Mind*, translator of Lorenzen's *Formal Logic*. Author of articles in several professional journals.

Aron Gurwitsch, born January 17, 1901, Wilna, Lithuania. Ph.D., 1929, Göttingen. Lecturer in philosophy, 1933-40, Sorbonne; University lecturer, 1940-42, Johns Hopkins University; Instructor in physics, 1943-46, Harvard University; Lecturer in mathematics, 1947-48, Wheaton College; Assistant Professor, 1948-51, Associate Professor, Brandeis University; Professor, New School for Social Research. Author of *Théorie du Champ de la Conscience*, and of several articles, some of which are to be reprinted in a forthcoming collection *Studies in Phenomenology and Psychology*, Northwestern University Press.

Lejaren A. Hiller, Jr., born February 23, 1924, New York, N. Y. A.B., 1944, M.A., 1946, Ph.D., 1947, Princeton University; M.Mus., 1958, University of Illinois. Assistant in Chemistry, 1944-45, Research Fellow, 1945-47, Princeton University; Research Chemist, 1947-52, Textile Fibers Division, E. I. Du Pont de Nemours, Inc., Waynesboro, Virginia; Research Associate, 1952-55, Assistant Professor of Chemistry, 1955-58, Department of Chemistry and Chemical Engineering, University of Illinois; Assistant Professor of Music, 1958-61; Associate Professor of Music, 1961-, School of Music, University of Illinois. Author of *Experimental Music* (with Leonard M. Isaacson), 1959; *Principles of Chemistry* (with Rolfe H. Herber), 1960. Author of about thirty articles on scientific and musical topics. Composer of about thirty-five music scores of all types, both experimental (electronic, computational, etc.) and more conventional (instrumental, symphonic, and for theater, films, dance, etc.).

Leonard M. Isaacson, born December 15, 1925, Chicago, Illinois. B.S., Roosevelt University, 1949; Ph.D., University of Illinois, 1956. Computer analyst,

Standard Oil Company of California, 1957-. Author of *Experimental Music* (with Lejaren A. Hiller), 1959.

*John R. Lucas,* born June 18, 1929. B.A., 1951, M.A., 1954, Oxford. John Locke Scholarship, University of Oxford, 1952; Junior Research Fellow, Merton College, Oxford, 1953-56; Fellow of Corpus Christi College, Cambridge, 1956-59; Jane Eliza Procter Visiting Fellow, Princeton University, 1957-58; Leverhulme Fellow in the Philosophy of Science, Leeds University, 1959-60; Fellow and Tutor of Merton College, Oxford, 1960-.

*Donald M. MacKay,* born August 9, 1922, Lybster, Scotland. B.Sc., 1943, St. Andrews University; Ph.D., 1951, London University. Radar Research (Admiralty) 1943-46; Lecturer and Reader in Physics, King's College London, 1946-60; Research Professor of Communication, University of Keele, 1960-. Rockefeller Fellow, U.S.A., 1951. Author (with M. E. Fisher) of *Analogue Computing at Ultra-High Speed* (Chapman and Hall and Wiley, 1962), *The Science of Communication—A Bridge between Disciplines* (Inaugural Lecture, University of Keele, 1961); and chapters in several professional journals and collected works.

*Allen Newell,* born March 19, 1927, San Francisco, California. B.S. Stanford University, 1949; graduate study Princeton University, 1949-50; Ph.D. Carnegie Institute of Technology, 1957. Research Scientist, the RAND Corporation, 1950-61; Institute Professor of Systems and Communication Sciences, Carnegie Institute of Technology, 1960-; Consultant, the Rand Corporation, 1961-. Author (variously with J. C. Shaw and H. A. Simon) of several articles and chapters in professional and technical journals and collections.

*Michael Polanyi,* born March 12, 1891, Budapest, Hungary. Educated at Karlsruhe, Budapest. Privatdozent Technische Hochschule, Berlin, 1928; Member Kaiser Wilhelm Institute für Physikalische Chemie, 1923-33; Professor of Physical Chemistry, Victoria University, 1933; Lecturer, University of Durham, 1945; Lecturer, Manchester University, 1946; Visiting Professor, University of Chicago, 1954; Lindsay Memorial Lecturer, Keele, 1958; Eddington Lecturer, Cambridge, 1960; Senior Research Fellow, Oxford, 1959-61; Distinguished Research Fellow, University of Virginia, 1961; McEnnemy Lecturer, Berkeley, 1961; Terry Lecturer, Yale, 1962. F.R.S., 1944; Hon. D.Sc., Princeton (1946), Leeds (1947); Hon. Ll.D., Aberdeen (1959). Author of several books and many articles in the fields of science, philosophy, and economics.

*Anatol Rapoport,* born May 22, 1911, Lozovaya, Russia; American citizen since 1928. S.B., 1938, University of Chicago; graduate study, University of Chicago 1938-41; Ph.D., 1941, University of Chicago (Mathematics). Lt., then Captain U.S. Army Air Forces, 1942-46. Instructor, Mathematics, Illinois Institute of Technology, 1946-47; Research associate, then assistant professor, Committee on Mathematical Biology, University of Chicago, 1947-54; Fellow, Center for Advanced Study in Behavioral Sciences, 1954-55; Associate Professor, then professor of mathematical biology, Mental Health Research Institute, University of Michigan, 1955. Author of *Science and the Goals of Man* (Harper and Bros., 1950), *Operational Philosophy* (Harper and Bros., 1953), *Fights, Games, and Debates* (University of Michigan Press, 1960), and several articles on mathematical models, general semantics, and other topics.

*Gilbert Ryle,* born August 19, 1900, Brighton, England. M.A. of Oxford University. Educated at Brighton College and The Queen's College, Oxford. Student and Tutor at Christ Church, Oxford, 1924-1945. Waynfleete Professor of Metaphysical Philosophy in the University of Oxford, 1945-. Editor of *Mind*, 1947-. Author of *The Concept of Mind*, 1949, and *Dilemmas*, 1959.

*Kenneth M. Sayre*, born August 13, 1928, Scottsbluff, Nebraska. A.B., 1952, Grinnell College; M.A., 1954, and Ph.D., 1958, Harvard University. Teaching Fellow, Harvard University, 1954; Member of Staff of Lincoln Laboratory, Massachusetts Institute of Technology, 1956-58; Research Scientist, Sylvania Electric Products, Inc., 1959; Consultant, Lincoln Laboratory, 1960-61; Instructor, then Assistant Professor, University of Notre Dame, 1958-; Director of research group under National Science Foundation, 1962-. Co-editor of *The Modeling of Mind*, author of several articles and studies in the fields of philosophy of science, theory of knowledge, systems analysis, and human factors.

*Michael John Scriven*, born March 28, 1928, Beaulieu, England. B.A. (Honors School of Mathematics) Melbourne University, Australia, 1948; M.A., Melbourne, 1950; D. Phil., Oxford University, 1956. Instructor, Department of Philosophy, and Research Associate, Minnesota Center for Philosophy of Science, University of Minnesota, 1952-56; Assistant Professor, Department of Philosophy, Swarthmore College, 1956-60; Professor, Department of History and Logic of Science, Indiana University, 1960-. Fellow, Center for Advanced study in the Behavioral Sciences, 1962; Research supported by Nuffield Foundation, National Science Foundation, Carnegie Foundation, etc.; Consultant, Rand Corporation, 1963; Co-editor and contributor to *Minnesota Studies in the Philosophy of Science*, Vols. I and II (with Herbert Feigl). Co-author of *Psychology* (Allyn and Bacon, 1961).

*Norman Stuart Sutherland*, born 1927, London, England. B.A., 1949, D. Phil., 1957, Oxford University. Fellow of Magadalen College, Oxford, 1954-58. Lecturer in Experimental Psychology, Oxford University, 1959-63. Professor of Experimental and Comparative Psychology, Massachusetts Institute of Technology, 1963-. Author of *Shape Discrimination by Animals* (1961).

*Hao Wang*, born May 20, 1921, Tsinan, China. B.S., 1943, National Southwestern Associated University; Ph.D., 1948, Harvard University. Junior Fellow, Society of Fellows, Harvard University, 1948-51; Assistant Professor of Philosophy, Harvard University, 1951-56; John Locke Lecturer in Philosophy, Oxford University, 1955; Reader in the Philosophy of Mathematics, Oxford University, 1956-61; Gordon Mc Kay Professor of Mathematical Logic and Applied Mathematics, Harvard University, 1961-; Fellow, American Academy of Arts and Sciences; Author of *A Survey of Mathematical Logic* (1962).

*Ludwig Wittgenstein*, born April 26, 1889. Studied engineering at Manchester prior to 1911; studied at Cambridge around 1911. In military service 1914-19; P.O.W. in Italy at Armistice. Trained subsequently as elementary school teacher, and taught 1922-26. Succeeded Moore at Cambridge, 1938. Worked as dispensary porter, London, 1943-44. Chair in philosophy, Cambridge, 1944-47. Traveled Ireland, U.S.A., Vienna, Oxford, 1949-51. Died at his doctor's house in Cambridge, April 29, 1951. Author of *Tractatus Logico-Philosophicus* (1922), *Philosophical Investigations* (1953), *Remarks on the Foundations of Mathematics* (1956), *The Blue and Brown Books* (1958), *Notebooks 1914-16* (1961).